Dystopia and Education

Insights Into Theory, Praxis, and Policy in an Age of Utopia-Gone-Wrong

A Volume in
Studies in the Philosophy of Education

Series Editor:
John E. Petrovic,
The University of Alabama

Studies in the Philosophy of Education

John E. Petrovic, Series Editor

Dystopia and Education: Insights Into Theory, Praxis, and Policy in an Age of Utopia-Gone-Wrong (2013)
edited by Jessica A. Heybach and Eric C. Sheffield

Dystopia and Education

Insights Into Theory, Praxis, and Policy in an Age of Utopia-Gone-Wrong

Edited by

Jessica A. Heybach
Aurora University

and

Eric C. Sheffield
Missouri State University

Information Age Publishing, Inc.
Charlotte, North Carolina • www.infoagepub.com

Library of Congress Cataloging-in-Publication Data

CIP data for this book can be found on the Library of Congress website http://www.loc.gov/index.html

ISBNs: Paperback: 978-1-62396-283-8
Hardcover: 978-1-62396-284-5
eBook: 978-1-62396-285-2

Printed in the United States of America

To Those Who Question and Resist....

Praise for *Dystopia & Education: Insights Into Theory, Praxis, and Policy in an Age of Utopia-Gone-Wrong*

A fascinating and highly readable collection that reminds us of the power of the stories we have imbibed from childhood on that both demonize and glorify, and also can make us think more deeply.

—**Deborah Meier,** senior scholar, New York University Steinhardt School, and board member of the Coalition of Essential Schools, FairTest, SOS, Dissent, and The Nation

While utopias present an imagined future to provide direction, dystopias depict an exaggerated present to provide grounding. *Dystopia & Education* offers 16 different visions of our dystopic moment, helping us, among other things, to disperse the mist of the fog machine called school reform. Some of these essays you will find dead on, some you will find wildly miss the mark. But even your best friend is likely to think differently about which is which. Sixteen great reads that will stimulate dozens of excellent conversations about our present world, education, and hope.

—**Richard Quantz,** Professor, Social Foundations of Education, Miami University

More praise on back cover

CONTENTS

FOREWORD

Dystopia and Education

William Ayers

Imagination lights the slow fuse of possibility.
—Emily Dickinson (1960, p. 657)

Reflection, fantasy, theory, nightmares and dreams—all of this has animated human beings throughout the ages, demobilizing and challenging the given world, inviting us to leap into the unknown, to jump off the edge, to change our lives, to escape at times, and to move forward positively at other times. ***Dystopia and Education*** invites us to reanimate our minds once again, and to get busy in a project of creative repair.

Where would we be without the capacity to imagine a better world? Utopians have spawned the weirdest cults imaginable, and, on the other hand, have collected together the most thoughtful and righteous people to create powerful and positive social movements, plot revolutions, and build a wildly diverse range of intentional communities—spiritual, Christian, Buddhist, socialist, technological, environmental, economic—with names like New Harmony, Fruitlands, Total Loss, and Walden Two. I leapt into the commune movement myself in the 1960s—Free Land/Free Love!

Dystopia and Education:
Insights Into Theory, Praxis, and Policy in an Age of Utopia-Gone-Wrong, pp. xi–xvi

The Personal is Political!—and have lived in intentional communities off and on from 1968 to the present. What fun! And, yes, yes, yes—how very weird!

The Garden of Eden, nirvana, heaven—utopias of innocent joy and pure delight, free of worry or pain or suffering or conflict or struggle or death, free, in fact, of the core elements of the human condition—stand side by side with images of agony, torment, unending misery, and the nightmare of hell.

In many ways the most instructive, useful, and even prescient images are not those of the sunny utopians—Thomas More, Saint-Simon, Robert Owen, Edward Bellamy, heaven on earth—but the cautionary tales of their darker dystopian cousins, *Fahrenheit 451* (Bradbury, 1953/1987), *The Handmaid's Tale* (Atwood, 1998), *Blindness* (Saramago, 1998). The contrasting visions of terrifying totalitarianism conjured up in the whirlwind of the 20th century by George Orwell (1949/1977) in *1984* and Aldous Huxley (1932/1998) in *Brave New World*, stand as chilling indictments of the world we already inhabit, as well as horrifying projections of the ready road to perdition.

Orwell (1940), who had been a student of Huxley's at Eton, thought *Brave New World* "a brilliant caricature of the present (he meant 1930 Europe)," "the hedonistic principle ... pushed to its utmost, the whole world ... turned into a Riviera hotel," but felt it inadequate and unhelpful as a lamp to the future: "No society of that kind would last ... because a ruling class that thought principally of a 'good time' would soon lose its vitality. A ruling class has got to have a strict morality, a quasi-religious belief in itself, a *mystique*" (as cited in Orwell & Angus, 1968, p. 31). Several years later, Orwell sent Huxley an advanced copy of *1984*, and Huxley (1949/1977) wrote back to his former student that it was a fine and important book, but that it was more likely that the authoritarian rulers of the future would find that "infant-conditioning and narco-hypnosis are more efficient ... than clubs and prisons, and that the lust for power can be just as completely satisfied by suggesting people into loving their servitude as by flogging and kicking them into obedience" (as cited in Smith, 1969, p. 605). Huxley felt that the brutal nightmare would surely evolve into a softer, gentler form of authoritarianism—the people anesthetized with drugs and easy pleasures—and that the change would be "brought about as a result of a felt need for increased efficiency" (as cited in Smith, 1969, p. 605). They each conceived a nightmare, and they each fabricated a horror out of the actual materials at hand—society as such.

The crucial differences in their dystopian visions reveal, as well, an alarming likeness of results: Orwell imagined a world where free thought and speech were suppressed, and books were banned; Huxley saw a world where people could say or read whatever they wanted, but no one had anything to say or any desire to read—too busy being free to have the most wonderful time. In each case, Margaret Thatcher's deathless version of reality is made manifest: there is no alternative.

In Ray Bradbury's (1953/1987) *Fahrenheit 451* the fire department is charged with burning books, and the most remarkable explanation of why they do the work they do comes from the fire chief, Captain Beatty, who points out that the people themselves demanded that the books be burned, because books with their "great welter of nouns and verbs and adjectives" make a simple world much too complicated to enjoy (p. 107). Complexity and contradiction, recognition of diversity, mutuality and compromise and dialogue—all the basics of life as it is actually lived—these are the enemies of every form of fundamentalism on earth. Totalitarians have nothing to learn since all the answers are ready-made and at-hand, and nothing to lose since the goal is one-dimensional and rather simple: my way or no way, and, therefore, a vicious fight to the finish with the infidels.

Orwell and Huxley portray war, the threat of war, and manufactured fear as essential to the authoritarian project: liberty is always (and rather easily) sacrificed in crisis. Orwell's (1949/1977) war without end created a corresponding steady stream of fabricated fear, everyone in line and cowering; Huxley's (1932/1998) vision includes a population always reminded of the Nine Years War that preceded the new world order, everyone besotted and smashed with mindless pleasure. Orwell warned of a police state and a massive secret security apparatus with eyes and ears everywhere; Huxley's population was so diverted by scandal and idle gossip that it had no use for evidence or reason.

Both visions also illuminate the importance of collective amnesia—the forced or clever erasure of memory, history, and culture—as central to autocratic rule: freedom can only breathe in the presence of independent thought. "History is bunk" is one of the "beautiful and inspired" founding slogans of The World State Huxley (1932/1998) imagined (p. 34); newspeak, the language of Oceania—a language that allows for doublethink so crucial to the party's hold on power in Orwell's (1949/1977) nightmare. In one amnesia is achieved through the wide distribution of *soma* and attending the "feelies," and we are seduced to submit; in the other we are beaten into submission and laid low through the "thought police" and "Room 101," intimidated and tortured. The results are the same: compliance, conformity, political paralysis, and complete obedience.

What is most disturbing is how deftly each author draws upon the familiar, every day, common-place aspects of society as it is, and then gins them up and weaves them into a nightmare of gigantic proportions. "The debate," as Chris Hedges (2010) wrote, "between those who watched our descent towards corporate totalitarianism," was always which one got it right: Orwell who highlighted the traditional jackboots, clubs, bombs, and bullies, "a repressive surveillance and security state that used crude and violent forms of control," or Huxley, who emphasized the allure of drugs and sex and materialism, as well as the early and near-total conditioning of the young, everyone "entranced by entertainment and spectacle, captivated by technology and seduced by profligate consumption to embrace our own oppression?" Hedges concluded that they were both right; Huxley described "The World State," Orwell "Oceania," but they are in fact two sides of a coin: "Huxley saw the first stage of our enslavement," Hedges notes. "Orwell saw the second" (para. 1).

It is not at all difficult to draw straight lines connecting the dystopian visions conjured up by Huxley and Orwell to the actual world we inhabit, right here, right now. ***Dystopia and Education*** can help educators' further heed and pursue the deepest questions:

- How did we get here, and where do we want to go?
- What is our map of the known world, and how might things be otherwise?
- What is our responsibility as world citizens to one another and to future generations?
- What kind of society do we want to inhabit?
- Who do we want to be as people?
- What can we become?
- What positive and humanizing aspects of work and labor do we embrace?
- What gives meaning to our lives?
- What time is it on the clock of the world?

Diving into the wreckage and swimming as hard as we are able toward a distant and indistinct shore, overcoming difficulties and reimagining life's possibilities along the way—this is the spirit we might bring to these questions.

That is often easier to say than to do. When we feel ourselves shackled, bound, and gagged or when we are badly beaten down, struggling just to survive, living with dust in our mouths, the horizons of our hope can become lowered, sometimes fatally, and asking questions like these can seem idle and silly. What kind of world do we want to inhabit? When no alternatives are apparent or available, action becomes pointless. We all live in our time and place, immersed in what is; imagining a social scene different from what's immediately before us requires a combination of "somethings": seeds, surely; desire, yes; necessity and desperation at times; and, at other times a willingness to dance out on a limb without a safety net—no guarantees.

Imagination, then, is more a process than a product, more "stance" than "thing," and engaging the imagination involves the dynamic work of mapping the world as such, and leaning toward a world that might be but is not yet. Most of us most of the time accept our lot-in-life as inevitable—for decades, generations, even centuries; when a revolution is in reach, when a lovelier life heaves into view, or when a possible world becomes somehow visible, the status quo becomes suddenly unendurable. We then reject the fixed and the stable, and begin to look at the world as if it could be otherwise, and we begin the important work of reweaving our shared world.

Cultivating imagination, and creating the conditions where more of us more of the time can wonder about our ability to create something else, to collectively conceive humane alternatives, calls for a politics that is process-oriented, more skeptical than certain, improvisational before formal, open to shifts and changes in a dynamic world. Nourishing the radical imagination means going to the source or foundation of things—the first meaning of "radical" is at the root—searching for causes and connections while struggling in the here and now for relatively more peace and equality, comparatively more joy and justice, pound for pound more participatory democracy, an expanded field of hope.

Choice and confidence is a necessary politics. I don't want to minimize the horror, but neither am I stuck in its thrall. Hope is an antidote to cynicism and despair; it is the capacity to notice or invent alternatives; it is nourishing the sense that standing directly against the world *as such* is a world that *could* be, or *should* be. Whatever *is* the case stands side-by-side with what *could* be or *should* be the case. Without that vital sense of possible worlds, doors close, curtains drop, and we become stranded: we cannot adequately oppose injustice; we cannot act freely; we cannot inhabit the most vigorous moral spaces. We are never freer, all of us and each of us, than when we refuse the situation before us as settled and certain and determined—the absolute end of the matter, like the preposterous end-of-history doctrine promoted by the over-privileged everywhere—and break the chains that entangle us.

Dystopia and Education show us what is the case; suggests what might be the case; and in that, provides a hopeful antidote to cynicism and despair.

REFERENCES

Atwood, M. (1998). *The handmaid's tale*. New York, NY: Anchor Books.

Bradbury, R. (1987). *Fahrenheit 451*. New York, NY: Ballentine. (Original work published 1953)

Dickinson, E. (1960). The gleam of a heroic act. In T. H. Johnson (Ed.), *The complete poems* (p. 65). Boston, MA: Little Brown.

Hedges, C. (2010). *2011: A brave new dystopia*. Retrieved from http://archive.truthout.org/2011-a-brave-new-dystopia66307.

Huxley, A. (1998). *Brave new world*. New York, NY: HarperCollins. (Original work published 1932)

Orwell, G. (1977). *1984*. NY: Penguin. (Original work published 1949)

Orwell, S., & Angus, I. (1968). *The collected essays, journalism and letters of George Orwell: My country right or left 1940-1943*. New York, NY: Harcourt, Bruce & World, Inc.

Saramago, J. (1998). *Blindness*. Boston, MA: Houghton Mifflin Harcourt.

Smith, G. (Ed.). (1969). *Letters of Aldous Huxley*. New York, NY: Harper & Row.

PREFACE

Dystopia and Education?

Jessica A. Heybach and Eric C. Sheffield

dys·to·pi·a dĭstōpēə

An imaginary place or state in which the condition of life is extremely bad, as from deprivation, oppression, or terror.

—Free Online Dictionary

In principle, dystopian texts express world views that postulate end-of-utopia, utopia-gone-wrong and even anti-utopia, and entail responses to and a critique of utopia.

—Elfriede Dreyer and Jacob Lebeko (2009)

The above definitions of dystopia might strike our readers—parents, teachers, professors, policymakers and the like—as fear-mongering overstatements if the object of critique is our nation's schools. Has the one institution meant to nurture our children toward successful democratic adulthood *really* been transformed into a space overrun with systemic

Dystopia and Education:
Insights Into Theory, Praxis, and Policy in an Age of Utopia-Gone-Wrong, pp. xvii–xxvi

deprivation, terror, and oppression? Has it become so bad that Orwellian-like narratives can be used to illuminate contemporary educational theory, praxis, and policy in meaningful ways? These are certainly questions we pondered as we considered this project—questions we ultimately answered with a qualified "yes, it seems so."

We say *qualified* because clearly American schools have not become spaces where actual physical and emotional torture, deprivation, and oppression, such as that seen in the quintessential dystopian text *1984*. Orwell (1949/2001) overtly utilized terror to destroy individual self-hood, and replaced it with an institutionalized self stripped of all agency. To date, we know of no school that has an Orwellian "Ministry of Love." On the other hand, education is a powerful tool (think Hitler's Germany and Stalin's Soviet Union), and dystopian themes and practices constitute the slipperiest of slopes. It might just be that today we are engaged in the *covert* institutional destruction of self, rather than the *overt* version found in *1984*, which is most difficult to locate and fight. The authors in this collection seem to believe so as they consistently point to the dystopian reality and potential that exists in contemporary schooling practices.

DYSTOPIA: A BRIEF HISTORY

The dystopian themes and individual artistic renderings of dystopia taken up in this collection are, historically speaking, relative newcomers to the human endeavor. However, their precursor—the antonymic source of dystopia—utopia, certainly is not. We hope that most of our readers are at least somewhat familiar with the first and best known western utopian creation: the perfect city of Plato's *Republic* where citizens were fit "naturally" into a utopian classist scheme and were ruled by a benevolent philosopher king. As Alfred North Whitehead (1979) famously stated, "all of Western philosophy consists of footnotes to Plato"; we find this sentiment aptly true in the case of theorizing dystopia (p. 39). In Plato's imagined perfect city, the notion of dystopia—as a hard and difficult place—is conceptually conceived as well.

Plato's vision of the utopian city allowed the more creative among us to imagine its opposite: the dehumanizing, horrifying city and the psychic torment such cities and their institutions visit on us. John Stuart Mill was kind enough to coin the word we use to denote such cities and their tormentors: "dys-topian(s)." In a speech delivered to the English House of Commons in 1868 in which Mill argued against capital punishment, he suggests, "they ought rather to be called dys-topians, or cacotopians. What is commonly called Utopian is something too good to be practicable; but what they appear to favor is too bad to be practicable" (para. 11). Not long after the coining of the term, dystopian literature and art began appearing en masse, and as the postmodern era dawned, the genre proliferated and continues to grow in popularity today. Numerous of the historically essential dystopian texts as well as more contemporary dystopian art, film, and video games are utilized in this volume to construct dystopian lenses through which educational theory, policy, and practice are, we believe, successfully examined and critiqued.

THE CONTEMPORARY EDUCATIONAL CONTEXT

The impetus for this book was a panel discussion that took up the issue of dystopian insights for contemporary education 3 years ago at the annual meeting of The American Educational Studies Association. Following that panel presentation (and further discussion over dinner and drinks), the panel members were increasingly convinced that contemporary educational policy as manifested most vehemently in No Child Left Behind (NCLB) and Race to the Top (RTT) is the epitome of utopian educational theory, praxis, and policy. Maybe Mill (1868) said it best: the expectations contained in these policies and others are "too good to be practicable;" the authors in this volume provide the constant reminder that something too good to be practicable, often turns into something "too bad to be practicable."

The classic characteristics of the utopia-turned-dystopia narrative (as our authors will argue) provide, we believe, some important insights into our claim that the contemporary educational context is rife with dystopian themes: an unattainable utopian vision; globally/nationally directed mandates to achieve the unattainable; macro- and microsurveillance to ensure its implementation; oppression through technical control; dehumanizing policy mandates; the restriction of human agency; devaluing human emotion; limitations on human creativity; positivistic measuring and describing; punitive consequences for those who stray—individually and institutionally; limitations of what constitutes knowledge; destruction of self for the good of the unattainable goal; less than ethical behavior enacted to meet the goal; the commodification of human experience; and, as our authors here contend, there are certainly others.

Evidence, both anecdotal and technical, that such dystopian themes are playing out in the contemporary educational context is growing. We leave the specifics of that evidence to our authors. We will note, however, that numerous educational scholars of merit have seen the troubles lying ahead as well; in fact, we write in the midst of what might very well be the largest political movement for and by educators in our nation's history. That movement is being spearheaded by some of our best-known educational activist-scholars: Jonathan Kozol, Pedro Noguerra, Diane Ravitch—having made a 180 degree turn in her thinking—and most recently through collective action as that seen in the 2012 Chicago teacher's union strike, and recent events in Wisconsin where the issue of labor rights came into sharp focus. All of these acts of resistance are in protest to what we believe is an increasingly dystopian schooling context.

LEARNING TO SEE DYSTOPIA

Dreyer and Lebeko (2009) opened a South African art exhibit titled *Dystopia* with the following passage:

> In the dystopian genre the imagination is tweaked as a critical instrument set on deconstructing existing or potential ills, injustices and hypocrisies in society, mainly brought on by a utopian ideological blueprint of globalization that has created diasporic cultures and nomadic identities; about unjust utopian political ideas that create social restriction, impaired mobility, repression or oppression; or about post-utopian space and loss of religious belief and direction. It might recount post-human conditions as a result of the dominating influence of the technological utopianism, evident in dysfunctional cyber relationships and telematic influences leading to rampant violence, threat to self, insensitivity and indifference to critical socio-cultural problems. (Introduction, para. 3)

If Dryer and Lebeko are correct, and the "imagination is tweaked as a critical instrument" in dystopia, then this text serves a vital role for those committed to the critical study of education and schooling in America. Although the imagination has often been constructed in a lilting manner to escape difficult social realities rather than as the means to confront them, a truly viable social imagination demands that our individual imaginations be disturbed and provoked. Maxine Greene (2000) described the social imagination as, "the capacity to invent visions of what should be and what might be in our deficient society, on the streets we live in, in our schools" (p. 5). Yet, in the postmodern world, individual imagination has been corrupted—bought and sold—exploited for unremitting profit. One powerful way to recover individual imagination, and thereby our social imagination, is through an exaggerated, dystopian rendering of the world—a rendering of the world that makes visible that which is normally submerged—a point consistently made by the authors in this collection.

In the midst of reading chapters for this project, we attended the 2012 NATO protest in Chicago and the cover of this book is adorned with photos we took that day. To our surprise, all the themes of this book became three-dimensional and animated by the others we met who had taken to the streets to kick and scream—to question the world, asking why we could not imagine it differently. As we marched through the Chicago loop on an oppressively sweltering hot summer afternoon, the scene was part theater and part serious political action. Spectators were certainly treated to a philosophical cacophony of agendas and ideas—where else could one see a Max Horkheimer quote on a sign alongside veterans throwing back their medals, teachers fighting for union rights, activists demanding the end of torture, and citizens insisting our food supply not be treated with destructive chemicals? It was a spectacle—par excellence—the type of spectacle that has always been needed to interrogate our assumptions and presuppositions about the impact of human actions.

Alongside the deeply pedagogical signage was the police presence: batons in hand, pockets bursting with zip ties as makeshift handcuffs, stern faces, and a demeanor that startled us (as we are from the generation(s) that missed the 1960s). We were also offered ear plugs at various junctures along the march route just in case the authorities in Chicago decided to use their newly purchased long-range acoustic device—sound seems to have become the next frontier of social control and fear manufacturing ("Chicago Police," 2012; "Protest Spur Sales," 2012). As we exited the march, we were met by a fleet of police officers in full black-padded riot suits—some waiting on buses to be deployed, others herding demonstrators toward the only available route of escape. One of them smiled at us as we took his picture—a bizarre moment when the traditional demonization of "cop" and "anarchist" were complicated in an exaggerated dystopian moment. That moment reminded us, as we hope this book reminds our readers, that we only see what it is we believe to be

Figure 1. Photos taken by the editors at the 2012 NATO protest in Chicago.

the case, and until what we believe to be the case is subjected to exaggeration, metaphor, and dystopia we believe very little will change.

On another occasion as we worked on this project, we found ourselves at a student art show sitting alongside elementary and middle school students making thaumatropes. In Victorian times, thaumatropes were invented as a sort of optical toy which only work because of the persistence of vision our eyes provide and the way our minds, somewhat covertly, organize the images for us. A thaumatrope consists of a small disc with strings that can be twisted to move the disc back and forth; there are different images on each side that become one as the disc is quickly flipped back and forth. We were struck by the idea that the utopia/dystopia binary might best be seen as a thaumatrope of sorts—different sides of the same coin—and that when one or the other side of a thaumatrope is severely privileged over the other, our vision and organization of it can become seriously skewed. We believe the utopian, often blindly optimistic, side of our contemporary education thaumatrope has been severely privileged of late. And in the favoring of our optimistic tendencies, we have failed to see the consequences of our best laid plans for schools—even though those consequences are right before our very eyes. We hope this collection can aid us all in seeing the consequences grand utopian ideas have wrought—consequences we have not yet fully comprehended.

STRUCTURE

The structure of the book is simple: it is divided into sections (theory, praxis, policy) and within each section you will find an introduction and chapters generally fitting of that theme. This organization is done with ease of use in mind rather than suggesting that these themes are mutually exclusive—certainly theory bleeds into praxis; praxis into policy; policy into theory; and so on. We hope the structure lends itself to reorganizing the readings based on the audience it serves and the needs they have. We certainly do not suggest it be read from front to back in order, though it might be.

Section I is organized around dystopian educational theory and includes five chapters. Chapter 1, written by Kerry Freedman, takes up what she calls an "aesthetic of horror" that is, Freedman claims, indicative of contemporary educational spaces. In Chapter 2, Kip Kline examines the insights the film *Fight Club* (Linson, Chaffin, & Bell, 1999) provides for understanding the development of self via Hegel's (1807/1977) slave/master relationship. Kline argues that "self" emerges in the self/institution tension in contemporary schools. Chapter 3, a Foucauldian analysis of Michael Young's (1961) satire "The Rise of Meritocracy," by Benjamin

Baez, challenges an often taken for granted concept: Deweyan Democracy. In the fourth chapter, F. Tony Carusi discusses Eugene Ionesco's (1960) dystopian play, *Rhinoceros*. From his analysis of the play, Carusi develops a theoretical framework for examining educational policy and practice based on two literary tropes: synecdoche and irony. This first section on dystopian theory closes with Andrew N. McKnight's chapter that consists of an analysis of Don DeLillo's 1985 novel, *White Noise*. Utilizing the work of Erich Fromm (1981), McKnight describes the dystopian consumerism and commoditization he sees in contemporary schooling.

The second section of the book is generally oriented toward praxis. In the first chapter of Section Two, Eric C. Sheffield posits and describes what he calls an "aesthetic-in-two-parts," one utilized in Anthony Burgess's (1962/1986) classic coming of age story, *A Clockwork Orange*, and one seen increasingly, Sheffield claims, in P-12 educational practice. In Chapter 7, Eric D. Smith and Philip E. Kovacs argue that Lois Lowry's (1993) *The Giver* provides promising avenues for deconstructing educational "givens" found in 21st century U.S. public schools. From this deconstruction, they provide practical suggestions for teaching in contemporary school contexts. Chapter 8 takes us back to where we started: Steven P. Jones provides the reader a comparative study of Plato's (1968) *Republic* and Aldous Huxley's (1932/1998) classic dystopian novel, *Brave New World*, intimating that Huxley engages his readers in a "turning inside out" of platonic educational ideals. Chapter 9 is the story of teaching the most recent, most popular, adolescent dystopian novel, *The Hunger Games* (Collins, 2008). Becky L. Noel Smith describes the reactions a group of "low-performing" readers had to Susan Collins' very popular novel series. We close the second section with reflection on video games. Regular video game player, Stefan Sheffield, explains the educational insights he has garnered in playing *Bioschock* (Levine, 2008), a game set in the dystopian society known as Rapture—a society based on the philosophy of Ayn Rand—and other video games, concluding that such games should be considered for use in classroom instruction.

We close the book with several chapters on dystopia and educational policy. In Chapter 11, John E. Petrovic explores the ramifications that Kurt Vonnegut's (1968) classic dystopian short story *Harrison Bergeron* has had, and might have, for educational policy, particularly in light of two recent court cases and conservative interpretations of the story. Bradley Rowe and Taylor Klassman follow up Petrovic by taking us back in time to one of the original dystopian novels. In their reading of Mary Shelley's (1831/2001) classic gothic piece, *Frankenstein*, they see the means to critique education "in the age of Obama" as increasingly narrow, technical, and oriented toward job training. In Chapter 13, Dennis Attick tackles the quintessential Western dystopian novel, *1984* (Orwell, 1949/2001), with attention to surveillance, control, and fear. Attick concludes that these dystopian themes are frighteningly reflective of current school policy. Joshua Garrison and Leslie Grey follow up Attick with another contemporary dystopian novel series—that of teenage author Isamu Fukui. Utilizing the work of French theorist Michel Foucault, Garrison, and Grey argue that Fukui's (2008, 2009) *Truancy* novels speak to a valuable student resistance to dystopian educational policy that might be undertaken by students toiling in public schools. In Chapter 15, Alison Happel and Becky Atkinson argue that the handmaids in Margaret Atwood's (1986) *The Handmaid's Tale* can be used to understand the dystopian loss of particularly feminist teacher autonomy that has resulted from No Child Left Behind/Race to the Top federal mandates. Finally, and to end the book, we come full circle—back to dystopian horror. Our concluding chapter penned by father/son authors Richard and Nicholas McDonald revel in a dialogue about classic horror films suggesting that these films provide important insights into understanding "the other" in our postmodern, dystopian educational context.

INSIGHTS INTO DEMOCRATIC EDUCATION

On the eve of the most utopian-turned-dystopian public school reform expectation in American history—No Child Left Behind's 2014 requirement of universal proficiency in math and reading—we offer readers this collection as a means to reflect on where we seem to be going educationally speaking. In so doing, we hope to shine a critical light on the current state of education, and the social forces that have conspired to create such a system. We think there is great value in utilizing a vehement dystopian lens to crack open a covert and creeping dystopian evolution in educational theory, praxis, and policy. Dystopia takes one to the edge, and forces an analysis that more unmistakably reveals the means that were utilized and exploited to create such ends. Dystopia as a "method of exaggeration," clearly exposes that which is often veiled in righteous justification and paternalism set in motion to save children from themselves.[1]

Before leaving you to the reading, we would be remiss in not making two comments about our title. First, we hope the reader sees the irony in *Dystopia and Education,* a play on John Dewey's classic text, *Democracy and Education.* We chose this title with the suspicion that Dewey would be sympathetic to this project: can valuable democratic educational practice be maintained within the confines of dystopian theory, praxis, and policy? We, of course, think not. Second, we wrestled mightily over the post-colon word of the title. We settled on *Insights* because we claim no canned resolution to these dilemmas, or easy-to-implement solutions to undo the current educational malaise. What we hope, instead, is that in reading these essays, insights can be gained and, more importantly, further questions will be raised. It is, we think, only in finding and asking insightful questions that dystopian visions of the world can be stemmed and resisted. We hope this book inspires such a search and aids in discovering those questions.

NOTES

1. We are indebted to Günther Anders (see VanDijk, 2000; and Anders & Eatherly, 1989) for the phrase "method of exaggeration." He proposed this type of philosophical inquiry, as an "occasional philosophy" to overcome human apathy and indifference to social catastrophes. His ideas were deeply influenced by his anguish over the dropping of nuclear bombs on Hiroshima and Nagasaki at the end of World War II. Although his aims were to bring about the end of nuclear proliferation, we feel his philosophical contributions shed light on this inquiry into dystopia.

REFERENCES

Anders, G., & Eatherly, C. (1989). *Burning conscience: The guilt of Hiroshima.* St. Paul, MN: Paragon House.

Atwood, M. (1986). *The handmaid's tale.* Toronto: O. W. Toad.

Burgess, A. (1986). *A clockwork orange.* New York, NY: W.W. Norton and Company. (Original work published 1962)

Chicago police sound cannon: LRAD "sonic weapon" purchased ahead Of NATO protests. (2012, July 15). *Huffington Post.* Retrieved from http://www.huffingtonpost.com/2012/05/15/chicago-police-sound-cannon-lrad-nato-summit_n_1518322.html

Collins, S. (2008). *The hunger games.* New York, NY: Scholastic.

DeLillo, D. (1986). *White noise.* New York, NY: Penguin.

Fromm, E. (1981). *On disobedience and other essays.* New York, NY: Seabury Press.

Fukui, I. (2008). *Truancy: A novel.* New York, NY: Tom Doherty Associates.

Fukui, I. (2009). *Truancy origins.* New York, NY: Tom Doherty Associates.

Greene, M. (2000). *Releasing the imagination: Essays on education, the arts, and social change.* San Francisco, CA: Jossey-Bass.

Hegel, G. W. F. (1977). *Phenomenology of spirit.* (A. V. Miller, Trans.) Oxford: Oxford University Press. (Original work published 1807)

Huxley, A. (1998). *Brave new world.* New York, NY: HarperCollins. (Original work published 1932)

Ionesco, E. (1960). *Rhinoceros and other plays.* (D. Prouse, Trans.). New York, NY: Grove Press.

Levine, K. (2007). *Bioshock.* Boston, MA: 2K Boston.

Linson, A., Chaffin, S., & Bell, R. G. (Producer), & Finger, D. (Director). (1999). *Fight club* [Motion picture]. USA: 20th Century Fox.

Lowry, L. (1993). *The giver.* New York, NY: Random House.

Orwell, G. (2001). *Nineteen eighty-four.* New York, NY: Harcourt. (Original work published 1949)

Protests spur sonic blaster sales boom. (2012, January 9). *Homeland Security News Wire.* Retrieved from http://www.homelandsecuritynewswire.com/dr20120109-protests-spur-sonic-blaster-sales-boom

Mill, J. S. (1868). *Speech to the House of Commons.* Retrieved from http://hansard.millbanksystems.com/ commons/1868/mar/12/adjourned-debate

Plato. (1968). *The republic of Plato* (A. Bloom, Trans.). New York, NY: Basic Books.

Shelley, M. (2003). *Frankenstein: Or, the modern Prometheus.* London: Penguin. (Original work published 1831)

Vonnegut, K. (1968). Harrison Bergeron. In *Welcome to the monkey house* (pp. 7-13). New York, NY: Delacorte Press.

Whitehead, A. N. (1979). *Process and reality.* New York, NY: Free Press.

Young, M. (1961). *The rise of the meritocracy 1870-2033: An essay on education and equality.* New York, NY: Penguin Books.

Dreyer, E., & Lebeko, J. (2009) *Dystopia.* Retrieved from http://www.unisa.ac.za/default.asp?Cmd=ViewContent&ContentID=22064

VanDijk, P. (2000). *Anthropology in the age of technology: The philosophical contribution of Günther Anders.* Amsterdam, The Netherlands: Rodopi.

ACKNOWLEDGMENTS

First and foremost, we want to thank our contributing authors who have patiently put up with our comments, our editing suggestions, and the numerous starts and fits of this project, and remained our friends throughout. In particular, the philosophical community of Southeast Philosophy of Education, who has endured multiple panel presentations on the topic of dystopia and education. To Information Age Publishing and series editor, John E. Petrovic, we extend our appreciation for taking a chance on this project when others balked at the idea, and for the painstaking editing and conceptual input as the book took shape. Finally, to Stefan, Ezra, Charlie, and Bella, our continual quiet sources of inspiration: you remind us daily why schools should not reflect the qualities of dystopia.

Dystopia and Education:
Insights Into Theory, Praxis, and Policy in an Age of Utopia-Gone-Wrong, pp. xxvii–xxvii

SECTION I: THEORY

DYSTOPIAN THEORY: CAN WE SEE WHAT WE HAVE NOT YET THEORIZED?

Jessica A. Heybach and Eric C. Sheffield

There is a widely shared myth that as Christopher Columbus approached the shores of the (brave) "new world," rumors of his arrival spurred a native spiritual leader to travel to the coast with the purpose of welcoming Columbus to his ancient lands. This Shaman, as the story goes, sat for several days peering out into the sea tirelessly searching for the "boats" that were certainly soon going to arrive. However, this Shaman, having never experienced or even imagined that seafaring vessels such as those captained by Columbus could exist, was unable to see these huge sailing ships until they were very nearly on the shore. Of course, there may be little to no narrative truth to this story. On the other hand, myths are important not because of their accuracy, but because they contain important insights into human endeavors.

Kurt Lewin (1952) famously suggested, "there is nothing more practical than a good theory" (p. 169). The above myth seems to say much the same: theory is not simply helpful, theory is necessary for "seeing" the human endeavor in newly creative, critical, and constructive ways. And given this, theory is the most practical of endeavors. The authors of this first section of our collection present various dystopian theoretical perspectives—perspectives meant to accomplish just this theoretical aim—to aid the reader to see "schooling" in different ways thereby making it possible to more insightfully examine both policy and praxis from fresh dystopian, perspectives.

CHAPTER 1

AN AESTHETIC OF HORROR IN EDUCATION

Schools as Dystopian Environments

Kerry Freedman

INTRODUCTION

Visual culture is the realm of humanly created objects, images, and environments that shape our ways of thinking and behaving. This includes fine art and popular culture, such as film, painting, fashion, television, architecture, sculpture, graphic design, advertisements, landscape design, computer games, and crafts. Visual culture has the capacity to powerfully influence emotions, beliefs, knowledge, and even self-worth (Freedman, 2003). In contemporary life, people experience a wide range of visual culture every day, often without reflecting on those experiences. However, because visual culture forms can work in insidious, as well as entertaining, uplifting, and educational ways, it is important to understand their influence on the ways we think and act.

Visual culture images produce a cognitive response through the pyschobiological mechanisms in the human brain that are influenced by visual aesthetics (e.g., Dissanayake, 1995; Efland, 2002). With regards to

Dystopia and Education:
Insights Into Theory, Praxis, and Policy in an Age of Utopia-Gone-Wrong, pp. 3–13

the visual arts, aesthetics refers to the way things look. As well as its content, the aesthetics of an image influence our responses to the image and our responses can be kinesthetic, such as those that accompany pleasure or fear.

A critical aspect of visual culture is the use of aesthetics in a determined manner by artists and designers to produce an emotional response. Not all intended responses occur; in fact, as will be discussed later in this chapter, many different responses are likely to occur when viewers encounter any particular example of visual culture. However, good artists and designers understand the functionality of lines, shapes, and colors to attract viewers and initiate emotional states.

For example, artists and designers know how to use aesthetics to illustrate utopian conditions that both support a sociocultural critique (of, for example, political situations) and give people a sense of well-being. One of the key aspects of the utopian is an aesthetic of beauty tied to nature. For over a century, utopian environments have been visualized and described in popular culture in terms of natural beauty that contrasts with industrial development. Utopian aesthetics typically involves images of beauty in nature, such as a season of growth with lush greens and other colors that indicate a robust world. Humans in such environments are depicted as ideally happy and relaxed, away from the stresses and other unhealthy conditions of industrial life.

In the 20th century, a humanly made aesthetic of clean geometric or organic forms has been considered utopian by some people because they find it a relief from chaotic visual, urban environments. Emerging from several Western sources, as well as Russian Futurism in the 1910s and influenced by Asian aesthetic traditions, modern art and the international architectural style had a visual simplicity of design that often gave the eye a sense of rest in an increasingly complex visual world. Modern design was based, in part, on a futuristic, technological vision and it challenged both the political and visual fussiness of the Victorian decorative arts in the early 20th century. Human brains and eyes are made to look for edges and the visual simplicity of modern design became popular, in part, because it gives us what we seek.

However, notions of beauty change over time and both natural and Modern design conceptions of beauty seem outdated in a time of postmodern eclecticism, hyperreality, and 6½ feet tall, female "supermodels" who would have been labeled "freaks" at an earlier time in history. The postmodern period is characterized by both a rejection of the idea of beauty and an extreme fascination with the concept, including the contradictions of its extremes. This is seen quite clearly in media culture. Consider the use of computer software to make models' skin look more beautiful (but less natural) and the example of "reality" television programming in which people are as likely to be young as old, or slender as overweight. But, even in the context of an increased awareness of the complexities in its meanings, beauty by whatever definition one holds will tend to produce a sense of pleasure. That is the idea behind a utopian aesthetic—it is to suggest a perfect world, one that both "pleases" and "excites" the eye and the body.

Utopias and their opposites, dystopias, have been visually represented in science fiction since the early 20th century and have precursors centuries earlier in fine art paintings. Dystopian aesthetics is used in art and design to illustrate visualizations of frightening environments and terrible acts. Often, this form of aesthetics is used to show humans or fictional beings hurting one another or destroying the health and beauty of a natural environment, leaving a wasteland of overuse and ruin. At times, dystopian environments are represented as an extreme version of Modernist architecture where industrial institutions have overtaken nature to become the controlling force in human life. In contemporary visual culture, utopian forms of beauty tend to comfort viewers, whereas dystopian aesthetics produces a sense of discomfort in most people.

In real-life, when students see challenging images, they usually feel a similar sense of discomfort, isolation, or even fear. The same is true when they live or study in spaces where architecture is in ruins or diminishes the importance of the people who reside there. Visual evidence of real neglect or injury to people, animals, or the environment can act as a form of oppression and is didactic in character. The dystopian aesthetic of many schools in the United States and the challenging images students see outside of school, require a formal education in the reflective critique of images and environments that can lead to constructive action.

In this chapter, I will first discuss a particular aspect of dystopian aesthetics referred to as the aesthetics of horror from a visual culture perspective. Second, real-life dystopian environments will be analyzed. Third, the dystopian aesthetics of school will be discussed with the necessity of an education in critical response to fiction and non-fiction visual culture that will help students understand that they can make a mark on the world.

THE AESTHETIC OF HORROR

A part of dystopian aesthetics, the aesthetics of horror, is a philosophy of art used to represent the relationship between beauty and fear. In a seminal work by aesthetician Noel Carroll (1987), the author referred to the type of horror that can be seen in visual culture as "art-horror," as opposed to a natural horror of something; that is, the aesthetics of the genre called horror is intended to evoke the psychological response of art-horror through its visual and kinesthetic qualities and may be considered a classification determined by the intention to achieve this type of response. As Carroll points out, this type of art form functions in this manner because "in works of horror, the humans regard monsters as abnormal, as disturbances of the natural order" (p. 52). And, because the emotional responses of the characters in the art form cue those of the audience, the acceptance of an abnormal character as normal goes a long way to enabling viewers to accept that character. Carroll observes on this point,

> The character's affective reaction to the monstrous in horror stories is not merely a matter of fear, i.e., of being frightened by something that threatens danger. Rather, threat is compounded by revulsion, nausea, and disgust. The monster is so unwholesome that its very touch causes shudders. And this corresponds as well with the tendency in horror novels and stories to describe monsters in terms of, and associate them with, filth, decay, deterioration, slime and so on. (p. 53)

In this way, even the negation of beauty in visual culture can make a comment on beauty and, therefore, show us something about our relationship to beauty and our fear of its loss (in our own bodies, in our natural environment, and so on).

Several characteristics of horror may attract us at the same time that they repel; horror has a seductive quality (Hallie, 1969). We are intrigued and also may sympathize or empathize with, for example a mutant, because although this condition is not considered a natural category, we experience variations on the human condition in real life. And, horrifying images can affect students in the same way whether or not they are about real events.

Humans continually live with the fear that beauty can cross the line into something terrible. For example, when considering human features, even a slight exaggeration of their shape or size can produce an emotional response in viewers. And, a greater change can seem other-worldly, as seen in the prosthetic and make-up design used in television and movie series *Star Trek* (Roddenberry, 1966-1969), *Star Wars* (Kurtz, 1977-2008), and other popular science fiction visual culture.

However, from an educational standpoint, I consider one of the most interesting characteristics of the aesthetics of horror is that although humans are initially repulsed by and reject the aesthetic, many people seem to get used to it and actually find it exciting to see in an art form. Although extreme changes in the general arrangement of human facial features can seem monstrous and difficult to accept at first, we can become accustomed to facial and body changes as part of a costume in science fiction visual culture, accepting them as plausible and even beautiful over time (especially when other aspects of a character are made to be attractive). The film industry has proven this through the creation over 100 years of zombie, alien, monster, and other movies that terrify and make billions of dollars for producers, actors, and designers. Like seeing a car wreck, people look out of concern, empathy, and the fascination that arises in us when powerful forces collide; we also look as a strategy to learn what not to do.

Although people are repulsed by such imagery, we seem able to submit to horror in a film or game because it is controlled; it does not actually threaten us. Usually, films end with monsters being destroyed or zombies are sent back to their graves and even when we are given a surprise ending where the monsters win, we can walk out of the theater knowing it was just a film.

For example, the effect of humanoid beings in films and computer graphics that look eerily real, but also unreal, is called the "uncanny valley" (e.g., Weschler, 2011). Originally coined by robotics scientist Masahiro Mori in 1970, and an extension of early 20th century psychologists' idea of the uncanny, the uncanny valley refers to the moment of recognition when representations stop becoming fictions, but have yet to become real. There is a type of representation that is too real to be accepted as a fiction, but not real enough to be believed. In the psychological state that the uncanny valley produces, viewers may feel ill or cannot look because the image is extremely disturbing. Computer animations are particularly notorious for being unable to convince when attempts to make figures look alive are unsuccessful. Some films like *Polar Express* (Zemickis, 2004), which was expected to be a holiday blockbuster, bombed because the eyes of the characters looked dead. And, because the uncanny valley works when it is unintentional, film and game makers use it to their advantage when making deliberately scary or creepy imagery confident that some viewers will enjoy the temporary state of revulsion knowing they can walk away from it at the end of the film. Often, frightening films, such as zombie films, include a dependence on humor to admit their campy quality, but also to broaden their audience by counteracting the nausea that could follow if too much attention is given to the imagery without some relief.

Visual extremes of any sort on a large scale can become oppressive because such images, objects, and environments alter human experience. This is why films can seem to be more powerful in a theater than on a television screen. The large scale of images on a movie screen is hard to assimilate and viewers' experience of reality is altered as they suspend disbelief and become part of the imagined world. But, the experience of becoming part of this new world for the short period of the film's duration can be enjoyable because although it is frightening, safe fear can be exhilarating.

Not so in real life. For most people, images of real, terrifying acts are much more difficult to look at and, in fact, it is probably an indication of psychological health that viewing such images is a challenge. When viewers know that horrific images are records of actual events, emotions leave the art-horror realm and become authentically frightening.

DYSTOPIAN ENVIRONMENTS

When architecture is used to take over a space in such a way as to diminish the importance of the humans who reside in that space, people may feel a level of either awe or discomfort. An extreme example can be found in a European cathedral, such as the cathedral in Koln, Germany, the scale of which can diminish the people inside it, but also can inspire awe and an uplifting feeling of being part of something larger than oneself. Cathedrals were originally designed for this purpose and, because of their complex engineering, cathedrals worked didactically to convince a largely illiterate population that a supernatural force enabled their scale and beauty. Cathedrals can engage human response through the use of the art and design of sculptures, paintings, mosaics, and stained-glass windows.

But, there is another type of architecture that diminishes people and resists human engagement in an industrial environment intended for social control. This type is easily seen in large-scale work environments or institutional architecture, such as schools. Most public high school architecture has characteristics similar to prison architecture, such as a lack of windows, cement walls, long hallways that direct people into small rooms, and few public gathering spaces or lounge areas. The environment created through the design of many such schools emphasize social control, but it is often the neglect of this architecture, particularly in urban and lower socioeconomic areas, that can be most oppressive. And, when schools and their local communities are in this condition, students cannot walk away from this dystopian aesthetic.

The phrase "dystopian aesthetics" is a contradiction. The modern use of the term "aesthetics" refers to both the branch of philosophy that deals with art and beauty and the sense of appearance people get from artistic and natural forms. The term was an appropriation from the Greek word for sensation by German philosopher Alexander Baumgarten in the early 1700s. Baumgarten's use of the term specifically referred to beauty, and his argument that good taste involves a desire for beauty (Baumgarten, 1954). However, the variety of contemporary uses of the term have led to its opposite also being referred to as aesthetic. Dystopian aesthetics contradicts both natural and socialized desires. It may be a representation of chaos, but since even a chaotic state can excite, a dystopian scene usually is the visualization of the aftermath of chaos; that is, what chaos leaves in its wake. Such an aesthetic typically suggests death and destruction. It is an aesthetic of horror, illustrating things that terrify human beings regardless of age, gender, cultural background, and so on. Unlike the term terror, horror knows no politics—it reaches down to subliminal human fears, such as the possibility of the total destruction of humanity and the certainty of our own deaths.

One of the primary purposes of dystopian aesthetics in art is didactic. The roots of the aesthetic may be found in ancient imagery representing various cultural mythologies that were intended to teach people how to behave through fears of terrifying, supernatural beings or eternal suffering in an afterlife. And, certainly some contemporary dystopian uses of aesthetics are deliberately intended to teach people to change behaviors that damage natural systems. This form of aesthetic in contemporary visual culture is used as a warning of ecological disaster.

Such images impact us, in part, because they reference real life and teach us how to act. Science fiction images of dystopia suggest potentially real catastrophic futures that may be posthuman in character, illustrating the possibility of our self-destruction. Such environments look frightening because humans could not survive in them.

Contemporary dystopian environments are typically those that have had beauty, but have lost it to misuse or neglect. Such environments look run-down, dirty (not in terms of natural areas of soil, but of something once meant to be clean that is now not as it should be), and lonely. This includes damaged and desolate natural environments and humanly designed environments with architectural features that may be ruined, and ones that can produce a sense of isolation and sadness because people cannot (or should not) be living there any longer. It also includes landscapes that look as though nature has been taken over by intelligent machines, sometimes with various sorts of mechanical debris, as in *The Matrix* (Wachowski & Wachowski, 1999) or *WALL-E* (Stanton, 2008) movies.

DYSTOPIAN AESTHETICS AND THE VISUAL CULTURE OF SCHOOL

I have been in many culturally and environmentally diverse environments, including spending time in dilapidated former Soviet institutions and yurt dwellings in Kyrgyzstan, a country with very few natural sources of water, little vegetation, and limited building resources. I remember considering the efforts of the yurt dwellers to make their homes beautiful by draping clothes of various prints and colors about their tent walls and over furniture. Even in this sparse countryside with few resources at hand, these structures were comfortable and visually attractive. They had not been neglected, but rather beautified.

In contrast, urban schools in the United States often look like part of a wasteland that has been allowed to disintegrate without consideration for those who study in that space. Without question, the worst visual environments I have ever worked in are inner city schools where young children are expected to learn in spaces that have, for example, decomposing walls, active mold, unsafe stairways, dark hallways, poorly lit classrooms, and broken fixtures. Furthermore, most of the schools I am referring to have all of these; they look as if humans could not be sustained within their walls. Such an aesthetic involving the neglect of real life public institutions and children's spaces, surely illustrates a society in decline. What are students to learn in such spaces? That they are not valued? Not worth the money it takes for adults to care for schools? Not good enough to have the privilege of beauty? Perhaps that education itself is unimportant?

This type of neglect of children's environments is a form of intellectual oppression, and like dystopian science fiction, is didactic visual culture. If people do not resist such oppression, they may be considered participants in it, which means that adults who do not help children to avoid such environments are participating in their negative effects. Resistance to manipulative visual techniques must be learned, as for example people must learn to "read" below the surface of an advertisement to reveal the particular ways that the image is able to stimulate emotions that can make us want to buy. It is the responsibility of educators to ensure that students do not have to encounter dystopian images and environments without the faculties they need to constructively respond to these.

In order to provide a response to dystopian visual culture, students need to be taught how to critique such images and environments. One of the purposes of contemporary education must be to provide students with hope for the future. This idea is based on the belief that people can change things for the better and that positive change occurs when individuals improve themselves and their surroundings. It is the basis of contemporary education; education should enable students to envision a better future and participate in its construction. Instead, although hard-working teachers provide the best education possible in these environments, many schools, particularly urban schools, have become places of stifling depression and testing with few opportunities for students to learn how to envision a future that is different from their present.

As a result of recent education policies, and although people who support such policies argue that they enable possibility by improving student learning, the beauty of possibility has been taken from school. Even if children are able to improve their test scores in some subjects, those tests do not demonstrate a capacity to envision and create. The truly frightening aspect of this condition of dystopian aesthetics—this condition of not enabling students to see past the deadening character of 21st century schooling—is that it is now taken-for-granted.

The current political environment leading to the No Child Left Behind Act (NCLB) and other policies has resulted in efforts to eliminate any type of aesthetic education from school. At an alarming rate since the NCLB began (and although its first iteration included art as a core subject), arts education resources have shrunk, arts teachers have been forced to teach to standardized tests, and whole high school arts departments have been closed resulting in a lack of work preparation in art and design. As the curriculum has been narrowed to a "common core" of subjects (reading and math), the possibility of learning about and through creativity has been taken away from students. The dystopian educational system of constricted curriculum, mechanistic learning, and standardized assessments are supported by the dystopian visual and kinesthetic environment in school. Without opportunities to create, what chance do students have to imagine alternative worlds? How are they to create better futures?

To create a visually literate population, socially conscious art educators support the reconstructive ideals that have been the foundation of progressive education for 100 years (while accepting that those ideals will not always be achieved), which should be a part of any democratic education (Freedman, 2000). These ideals help students to learn to challenge visual culture that is manipulative and create an alternative point of view. Research has demonstrated that visual culture can be used to help with this project and that art can play an important role in learning important life lessons where reading and math may fail. For example, Cohen-Evron (2005) has demonstrated that art education can reveal the reproduction of wartime stereotypes and hatred, but it can also help to stop that cycle. But, widespread use of art for such purposes is difficult when acceptance of a dystopian aesthetic is prevalent in some schools and the courage to address challenging issues and topics in school needs to be nurtured.

CONCLUSION

Aesthetics is one of the ways that people learn about reality from fictions and learn about possibilities from reality. We must break the chain of acceptance or disregard of an aesthetic of horror that students find both interesting and frightening. By addressing the aesthetic, we can promote the wellness of children, give them hope, and aid them in establishing a sense of agency for constructive action.

This can only be achieved if creativity is valued and practiced in educational environments. Part of the process of learning in and through creative practices involves students learning about and criticizing aesthetics in its many forms and influences. Images and environments that challenge students will continue to exist even if creativity is eliminated from school and as students become older, they will need an increasing level of sophistication in their criticism and agency in order to meet these challenges. But, moving away from institutionalized dystopian physical environments and oppressive curriculum structures may help students to envision the alternative of a brighter future.

In order to help students develop aesthetic literacy in general, and visual literacy in particular, teachers who are knowledgeable about the visual arts and aesthetic education are vital in school. In the early 21st century, it has become popular for policymakers and school district administrators to act as if aesthetics is an optional area of study. This behavior is shocking in the context of the increase in aesthetic information produced and distributed through increasingly pervasive visual technologies. For example, these "leaders" seem to believe that the visual arts are not essential learning and can be ignored or adequately addressed in after-school programs that are not held to the same standards of learning required in schools. This belief is delusional at best, and may even be a deliberate attempt to oppress creativity and the critique of visual information, particularly among those who cannot pay for an art education outside of school. Not only do the arts directly or indirectly make up about a third of the economy (Florida, 2002), but also visual literacy is as important as textual literacy in a contemporary culture so heavily dependent on pictorial and other visual sources of knowledge. Art teachers are needed in school to help students learn the concepts and skills required for the types of knowledge development discussed in this chapter and for artistic production. However, all teachers should be responsible for ensuring that students are as visually literate as they are literate in words and numbers. If all students were taught the conditions of aesthetics, including how important aesthetics is to human health and welfare, we could possibly move closer to a utopian vision and farther away from the dystopian reality so many students are forced to live within.

REFERENCES

Baumgarten, A. (1954). *Alexander Gottlieb Baumgarten: Reflections on poetry.* (K. Aschenbrenner & W. B. Holther, Trans.). Berkeley, CA: University of California Press.

Carroll, N. (1987). The nature of horror. *The Journal of Aesthetics and Criticism, 46*(1), 51-59.

Cohen-Evron, N. (2005). Students living within violent conflict: Should art educators "play it safe" or face "difficult knowledge?" *Studies in Art Education, 46*(4), 309-322.

Dissanayake, E. (1995). *Homo aestheticus: Where art comes from and why.* Seattle, WA: University of Washington Press.

Efland, A. (2002). *Art and cognition: Integrating the visual arts in the curriculum.* New York, NY: Teachers College Press.

Florida, R. (2002). *The rise of the creative class: And how it's transforming work, leisure, community, and everyday life.* New York, NY: Basic Books.

Freedman, K. (2000). Social perspectives of art education in the U.S.: Teaching visual culture in a democracy. *Studies in Art Education, 42*(4), 314-329.

Freedman, K. (2003). *Teaching visual culture: Curriculum, aesthetics, and the social life of art.* New York, NY: Teachers College Press.

Hallie, P. (1969). *The paradox of cruelty.* Middletown, CT: Wesleyan University Press.

Kurtz, G. (Producer). (1977-2008). *Star wars* [Motion picture series]. San Francisco, CA: Lucasfilm.

Lewin, K. (1952). *Field theory in social science: Selected theoretical papers by Kurt Lewin.* London: Tavistock.

Roddenberry, G. (Producer). (1966-1969). *Star trek* [Television series]. Los Angeles, CA: Desilu Productions and Paramount Productions.

Stanton, A. (Director). (2008). *WALL-E* [Motion picture]. Emeryville, CA: Pixar.

Wachowski, A. & Wachowski, L. (Directors). (1999). *The matrix* [Motion picture]. Burbank, CA: Warner Brothers.

Weschler, L. (2011). *Uncanny valley and other adventures in the narrative.* Berkeley, CA: Counterpoint.

Zemickis, R. (Director). (2004). *Polar express* [Motion picture]. Burbank, CA: Warner Brothers.

CHAPTER 2

YOUTH, THE SELF, AND VIOLENCE

A Hegelian Analysis of *Fight Club*

Kip Kline

In short, the subject of utopian desire in the dystopia is politics itself—of agency and of a kickstarting of the engine of history in a moment when it seems to many to be terminally stalled.

—Phillip E. Wegner (2009, p. 119)

CRITICAL DYSTOPIA AND HENRY GIROUX'S CRITIQUE OF *FIGHT CLUB*

In the epigraph above, Phillip Wegner (2009) describes an animating feature of what Tom Moylan (2000) has dubbed "critical dystopia" (Diken & Laustsen, 2002). In this subgenre, dystopian narratives do not necessarily abandon certain versions of modern notions of hope and transformation, rather, they seek to infuse the social and cultural status quo with critiques that unveil the ways in which utopian impulses have bankrupted political economies. This critical dystopia subgenre that grew out of a backlash

Dystopia and Education:
Insights Into Theory, Praxis, and Policy in an Age of Utopia-Gone-Wrong, pp. 15–30

against Reagan/Thatcher era politics in the 1980s has continued into the 21st century alongside the advancement of neoliberal ideologies in the West and in the United States in particular. Critical dystopian literature has, among other things in the past few decades, attempted to explore the dire consequences of the continuing concentration of wealth and power into fewer and fewer hands and subsequent reduction in agency for most people.

Certainly David Fincher's cult-classic film, *Fight Club* (Linson, Chaffin, & Bell, 1999), based on Chuck Palahniuk's 1996 novel, has been widely read as such a "critical dystopian" text in academic literature. It has been labeled by Diken and Laustan (2002) as "Marxism for dummies" and a platform for critique of "microfascism," which, is a "line of flight with respect to the social bond" (p. 349). Elsewhere it has been noted as having lifted the veil from the "crisis of capitalism" and the "cultural contradictions of late capitalism" (Lizardo, 2007, pp. 221-243; Ta, 2006, pp. 265-277). Additionally, there has been no shortage of treatment of the film in the *Journal of Men's Studies*, some of which discusses the film as a critique of the emasculating effects of consumerism (cf. Clark, 2002, p. 65). This body of work positions *Fight Club* firmly in the critical dystopia subgenre; specifically, it highlights the ways in which the story critiques the deleterious impact of the utopian impulses in late capitalism.[1]

Henry Giroux (2001) recognized the film's ostensive critical dystopian aims, but trenchantly critiqued it for falling short. In fact, he asserted that the film ultimately reinscribed the ideas and themes it may have seemed to, on the surface, criticize. Giroux stated,

> Ostensibly, *Fight Club* appears to offer a critique of late capitalist society and the misfortunes it generates out of its obsessive concern with profits, consumption, and the commercial values that underline its market driven ethos. But *Fight Club* is less interested in attacking the broader material relations of power and strategies of domination and exploitation associated with neoliberal capitalism than it is in rebelling against a consumerist culture that dissolves the bonds of male sociality and puts into place an enervating notion of male identity and agency. (p. 5)

Giroux viewed the film as ultimately only making "a superficial gesture toward social critique" (p. 5). This gesture, for Giroux, ended up obfuscating the reality that the actual social problems of late capitalism are rooted in neoliberal ideologies that have come to dominate the political/social/cultural landscape in the United States and have subsequently created structures that do agentic, social, and financial violence to already marginalized peoples, and instead suggested that the real issue was the regrettable emasculation of men in an age of consumerism. This idea that the ultimate problem of consumerism, exemplified in the film by the

IKEA lifestyle, is the damage it has done to men (e.g., made them too passive, etc.) was problematic for Giroux since it seems to be driven by nostalgia for an outdated notion of masculinity that has done violence to women in a number of ways—violence he claimed was essentially sanctioned by the messages in *Fight Club*, evidenced by lines from the narrator that claim that Marla (the female lead) is the root of all his problems.

Beyond this, Giroux (2001) was concerned with the resultant public pedagogy of the film that includes the message that

> repressed white masculinity is thrown into a crisis by the eruption of an ultra-conservative version of post-60s femininity that signifies both the antithesis of domestic security, comfort and sexual passivity—offering only neurosis and blame in their place. (p. 22)

In the end, he was convinced that any level of social critique that *Fight Club* may have seemed to offer on the surface was overshadowed by its actual function of reinscribing dangerous notions of masculinity and violence. Giroux (2001) concluded that *Fight Club*

> functions less as a critique of capitalism than as a defense of authoritarian masculinity wedded to the immediacy of pleasure sustained through violence and abuse. Once again, *Fight Club* becomes complicitous with the very system of commodification it denounces since both rely upon a notion of agency largely constructed within the immediacy of pleasure, the cult of hyper competitiveness, and the market-driven desire of winning and exercising power over others. (p. 15)

I am quite sympathetic to Giroux's (2001) critique of *Fight Club*. Although I am not sure that the relationship between the narrator and Marla demonstrates as much patriarchal violence as Giroux seems to suggest. At the end of the film (discussed further below), the narrator becomes self-determining in a way that does not completely negate Marla. Though, admittedly, at the same time, Marla is completely gender-colored through this same scene, operating as a symbol for humankind's moral side. That said, I am not interested in arguing against Giroux's critique of the film, nor am I unconcerned about public pedagogies that turn a blind eye to the structural forces of violence that are part and parcel of advanced neoliberalism. I am also bothered by media messages that end up reinscribing problematic iterations of masculinity. Because of this, I hope that my own analysis of *Fight Club* is not read as too celebratory. Yet, I want to be clear that I am engaged in a different kind of analysis than Giroux. That is to say, I am treating *Fight Club* philosophically. My purpose in discussing Giroux's critique is to establish that the film is, no doubt, a complex and variably understood contribution to the critical dystopian subgenre. All of its possible shortcomings as a piece of trenchant social critique notwithstanding, there are notable philosophical themes in *Fight Club* that are worth exploring. More than this, I argue that the exploration of these themes can, in turn, help to establish certain critiques of the status quo. For this reason, I examine issues of selfhood that are articulated in the film through Hegel's ideas about the self. Ultimately, I am concerned to turn this analysis onto youth and their experiences with adults in schools.

FIGHT CLUB AND THE STRUGGLE FOR SELFHOOD

Contrary to perhaps the most quoted line from the movie, the first rule of Fight Club is actually that you *have* to develop a self. At least this is the implicit rule of the film in which the narrator (Edward Norton) struggles with and against his alter ego, Tyler Durden (Brad Pitt), toward a kind of integration of self that plays out literally and graphically in bare-knuckled, bar basement brawls. The more explicit first rule of Fight Club is, "you do NOT talk about Fight Club." However, this rule is perhaps a bit tongue-in-cheek since it is clear that the point is to actually tell like-minded people (exclusively men in this case), so the club can grow. Likewise, the implicit philosophical rule of *Fight Club* that one must develop selfhood also acknowledges the existence of pitfalls in the struggle for self and integration of self. This is evidenced through certain developments of the plot and characters.

In the beginning of the film we are introduced to the narrator who is so bored and discontent with his white-collar job that he has developed insomnia. He seeks medical relief from his sleeplessness, but his doctor is unsympathetic. When the narrator tells the doctor that he needs help and is "in pain," the doctor suggests he visit a support group for men with testicular cancer if he wants to see what pain really looks like. The narrator complies and after he fools the rest of the group into thinking that he has testicular cancer, too, the emotional response he is able to feel with and from the others somehow cures his insomnia. He subsequently becomes addicted to attending all kinds of support groups for people in great physical anguish, always posing as a victim of the relevant affliction. The relief from the insomnia is interrupted by the presence of Marla, who seems to be doing the same sort of thing the narrator is doing—pretending to have a number of different ailments and attending their corresponding support groups. The narrator is angry with Marla, but begins a relationship with her.

On a flight home from a business trip, the narrator meets Tyler Durden. They part ways after the flight and the narrator finds his apartment has been demolished in an explosion. He calls Tyler and they meet at a bar. Tyler then engages the narrator in a passionate conversation about the damage done to them (men) by a consumer society. after a few drinks, they walk out to the parking lot where Tyler asks the narrator to hit him. This leads to a fistfight between the two that both end up finding somewhat fulfilling or exciting or attractive. At the end of the night, the narrator moves into Tyler's completely run-down house across town. The two return to the bar parking lot on subsequent nights and recruit other men into what becomes the Fight Club and it eventually moves into the basement of the bar.

Marla eventually becomes involved with Tyler sexually while the narrator continues to harbor negative feelings toward her and with the development of the sexual relationship it becomes clearer that Tyler and the narrator are two sides of one self struggling to integrate. This is also demonstrated through the development of Tyler as an underground anticorporate ringleader. He and the narrator organize the growth of Fight Clubs across the country and eventually develop a series of anticorporate efforts called "Project Mayhem." While the narrator originally is in agreement with the organization and content with his role in it, he eventually wants more power than Tyler is willing to yield to him. Then, in the final phases of Project Mayhem, the narrator sees Tyler as spiraling out of control as some of the anticorporate demonstrations go awry. In the middle of all this, we see that the narrator does feel something like care for Marla, but is conflicted by Tyler's relationship with her. In the last scene, the narrator, Tyler, and Marla sit in the top floor of a building at a safe distance from the bombs that are about to explode in several other buildings holding sensitive credit card information. The narrator wants to stop the bombing and this is a part of his struggle for self. He finally realizes integration by pulling the trigger of a gun that was originally held by Tyler until the narrator realizes that Tyler is, indeed, himself. The film ends with Marla and the narrator holding hands as they watch the bombs go off.

HEGEL, SELFHOOD, AND *FIGHT CLUB*

The dialectical structure of *Fight Club* begins to show through the ways in which violence gets linked up to the objectification of human experience that the narrator's job (some kind of insurance actuary navigating the world of product recall formulas) reveals.[2] The movie argues that for the narrator to both end the sort of violence he participates in perpetrating with his job and the sort of violence he is the victim of in the pressures on him to define himself in terms of consumer values, he must face violence directly in the Fight Club. Fighting as a specific form of violence is not necessary for development, but facing fear and pain is; especially fear.

And the ultimate fear is the fear of death. This is the case for Hegel and for Tyler Durden.

In a poignant scene when Tyler is teaching the narrator the importance of facing fear/death, he takes a young convenience store clerk into the back parking lot, holds him at gunpoint and asks for his wallet and tells him he is going to die. He addresses the clerk by name, Raymond (after reading it from his driver's license), and asks him what he really wants to do with his life because it clearly cannot be working in a convenience store. Raymond says he wanted to be a veterinarian but had to drop out of school because he needed money. Tyler pulls the gun away and tells Raymond that he is coming back in 6 weeks. If Raymond is not on his way to becoming a veterinarian, Tyler is going to kill him. Tyler explains to the narrator that Raymond can now really live after really experiencing fear.

For Hegel the life and death struggle can be interpreted in many ways, but perhaps the most convincing is to interpret it as a pre-historical common event that led to the first forms of culture (culture, as soon as it is on the scene, regulates relations between people and already has the processes of position-taking with others and internalizing otherness established). However, facing death in a physical sense in order to more fully experience one's essence as something beyond the body is common enough for some groups of people, and for some individuals in any society or culture. This does not need to take the form of a struggle with another person in a life-and-death way, literally. Yet, struggles with other people in ways that seem to totally threaten the self do occur quite commonly in the course of many people's lives. I argue that such struggles occur most often in our contemporary historical moment with young people who find themselves enmeshed in nonsymmetrical relationships with adults and adult-run institutions. In what follows, I will examine these relationships and their connection to youth self-formation and maintenance using some of Hegel's (and others') insights about unequal social relations and the desire for recognition.

HEGEL AND SELFHOOD AND MEAD'S SOCIAL THEORY OF SELF

The human desire for recognition stems from theories of selfhood, its development, and theories of self-consciousness that are fundamentally social in nature. Hegel, followed by others, was onto this. As Brandom (2007) has noted, for Hegel, "Self-consciousness is essentially, and not just accidentally, a *social* achievement" (p. 136, emphasis in original). That selfhood is constructed out of the social, then, means that other selves are necessary and this necessity comes in the form of acknowledgement and recognition. Hegel (1807/1977) famously stated that,

> Self-consciousness exists in and for itself when, and by the fact that, it so exists for another; that is, it exists only in being acknowledged.... The detailed exposition of the Notion of this spiritual unity in its duplication will present us with the process of Recognition. (§ 178)

It is this kind of ultimate dependence on recognition and acknowledgement by another that makes the development of selfhood an essentially social endeavor. As Majid Yar (2001) puts it, "It is only by seeing how others see me that I can come to apprehend and 'take possession' of myself" (p. 59). The achievement of selfhood or of self-consciousness, this seizing of the self that Yar discusses is, for Hegel, an entirely mediated process and that mediation comes in the form of another self. In this way, selfhood strictly depends on others. Yar says that Hegel denied, "the notion of a self-subsistent, *a priori* ontologically differentiated, monadological consciousness, seeing it as instead depending upon exteriority for its existence" (p. 58). Or, as Hegel (1807/1977) himself said,

> But according to the Notion of recognition this [that a self consciousness' certainty of itself have truth] is possible only when each is for the other what the other is for it, only when each in its own self through its own action, and again through the action of the other, achieves this pure abstraction of being-for-self. (§ 186)

The American philosopher and sociologist, George Herbert Mead articulated another thoroughly social theory of the development of selfhood that can also prepare the way for more discussion about the desire for recognition. Mead's (1934) theory begins with the idea that the self develops out of social and symbolic interaction and that this interaction is constituted by the construction of and interaction with "the generalized other" (p. 34). Mead describes this by saying, "[it is] the organized community or social group which gives to the individual his unity of self" (p. 34). He illustrates this idea with the analogy of a baseball team. Each individual player's actions are influenced by the internalization of an expectation of how all other players playing the various other positions might act under a given set of circumstances.

Phil Carspecken (1999) explains the process by saying that the formation of the "generalized other" develops in conjunction with gaining "consistent understandings of one's self from the perspective of others" (p. 193). This leads to a differentiation of the self into what Mead (1934) calls the "I" and the "me." The "me" reflects the "generalized other" and the "I" is a kind of response to the "me." This "I/me" distinction reflects the dialectical relationship between the society and the individual. So we can say that the "me" is the part of self that is capable of being objectivated in ways the "I" is not. In fact, the act of objectivation requires distinction from the "I" which is, in part, the reason why the "I" cannot be objectivated since each objectivation has an "I" necessarily distinguished from it. In other words, the "I" is never an object of immediate experience. We cannot observe the "I" directly, we can only "know" it as an awareness of the past, never as the subject of present experience. Mead says, "If you ask, then, where directly in your own experience the 'I' comes in, the answer is that it comes in as a historical figure. It is what you were a second ago that is the 'I' of the 'me'" (p. 174).

The "I" and the "me" have to exist together, but once both are in place, the "I" is only a limit case to privileged access but is within privileged access only as a trace. One cannot even really notice or think of the "I" without actually bringing the "me" into play because the "I" is the pure subject that resists any effort to represent it. Put another way, the "I" essentially has no qualities. Once we begin to speak or think of it in any context, it instantly becomes the "me" and so the "I" behaves like Derrida's (1998) "trace."

Both Hegel and Mead clearly establish the essentially social nature of the construction of selfhood. For Mead, especially, the struggle for selfhood and the integration of self is a social process even when the struggle seems to be internal, like the one that is dramatized by the narrator and Tyler Durden in *Fight Club* (1999). That is to say, even when human beings are involved in the construction or maintenance of a self when not in the physical presence of another, we are imagining another consciousness and its response to our meaningful acts. This is precisely what Mead meant by the "generalized other." It explains human phenomena with which we are familiar enough. It is not uncommon, for example, for a person to blush when she or he does something that might be considered embarrassing (e.g., tripping or clumsily falling down) if done with others watching, even if it is done without anyone else around. Or, we are familiar with the idea of rehearsing important conversations in private before we have them with others and we can feel certain things in response to our own rehearsed words based on imagining how the other person might respond.

Having discussed the wholly social nature of the construction and maintenance of a self, it is now possible to come back more directly to the fundamental human desire for recognition. To that end, I discuss the connections between what Charles Taylor called "expressivism" and Paul Willis's (1977) reworking of praxis theory in his seminal ethnographic work, *Learning to Labor.*

THE DESIRE FOR RECOGNITION: REFORMULATED PRAXIS THEORY AND EXPRESSIVISM

Phil Carspecken (1999) argues that Paul Willis's (1977) ethnography of working class boys in England, *Learning to Labor*, constitutes the paradigmatic study that became a breaking of new ground, paving the way for those that followed to use the phrase "critical ethnography." Its importance with regard to youth and self-formation lies primarily in its reshaping of praxis theory (tacitly) and therefore it will be important to explore praxis theory as it was conceived by various groups around the time of Willis's study. It will then be possible to interpret the impact of *Learning to Labor* with respect to praxis.

The context for this reformulation begins with the concept of power and agency versus structure debates of the 1970s between three major Marxist camps: Marxist-culturalists (mostly connected to E. P. Thompson), Marxist-structuralists (largely associated with Althusser), and the traditionalists. It is not necessary for the purposes of this chapter to rehearse all the details of the conflict between these camps and it has been done in a sophisticated manner elsewhere (Carspecken, 1999). Here, I am concerned with the way in which power was treated in these debates and the resultant implications for praxis theory.

In order to understand how Willis (1977) picked up praxis theory and reformulated it in ways that have significance for youth self-formation and the struggle for integration of self it is important to summarize Marx's use of praxis (Marx & Engels, 1845/1998). The Marxist-culturalists insisted that Marx consistently made use of praxis theory throughout his corpus while Althusser and the structuralists claimed that while the early Marx used a theory of human agency, the later Marx moved away from subjectivity and instead adumbrated structuralism.

In the earlier writings of Marx such as *Theses on Feuerbach* that the culturalists referred to for their arguments about human agency, praxis was discussed within the Hegelian context that held sway at that particular historical moment (Marx & Engels, 1845/1998). Thus, Marx made use of Hegelian categories such as "self-production," "alienation," and "objectification" in his discussions of praxis. Hegel's idea was that *Geist* produces itself through expression of its nature in objective forms even while no objective form can actually fully express it and so each expression contains a contradiction that leads to new expression and this process is known as a dialectic. Marx, on the other hand, located these same ideas within the human subject as opposed to *Geist*, that is to say he thought human beings, not *Geist*, expressed themselves in objective forms in order to produce themselves. Being human is being an expressive entity whose existence is more like a process of self-formation through objectivation than like the existence of physical things. This was an indispensable move for praxis theory but, in his attempt to completely shed himself of Hegel's idealism, Marx limited the concept to human action oriented toward the physical world. According to Carspecken (1999), this was a damaging move that "truncated the core insight" (p. 38). Willis would later repair the damage, at least implicitly, with his tacit reformulations.

Marx's general idea was that human beings are motivated to express themselves or to actualize themselves through work oriented toward the physical world. This is why the artisan was the paradigmatic case for him. In this way, humans create themselves or create a self through the products they produce skillfully and artistically. This kind of activity engenders pride and satisfaction. However, such actualization depends upon certain conditions. The tools and other materials, the modes of production, the entire process must be under the control of the particular human agent creating the product, otherwise she will experience "alienation" because she is essentially cut off from the products she creates. The working class of a capitalist society becomes "alienated" in this way since it is not its own ideas that are being used to create products, but rather those of designers or other employers that use them only for their labor. Additionally, workers do not own the products they produce, nor do they own the tools with which the products are made and this also contributes to their "alienation."

Carspecken (1999) refers to the kind of motivation human beings have to actualize in this way as an attempt to fulfill "expressive needs," by which he means, "the need to become a self, maintain a self, and grow as a self through expressive activity" (p. 38). That praxis theory is ultimately about the desire to meet these expressive needs leads Carspecken to group Hegel, Marx, and Herder together as having sophisticated, though tacit, theories of human motivation.

Human beings, motivated by the desire for recognition seek to meet their "expressive needs" of forming and maintaining a self though production. This is Marx's praxis theory, but he lost key insights from Herder and Hegel along the way when he focused exclusively on action oriented purely toward the physical world. The desire for recognition that Hegel formulated is fed by human-to-human relations. This is the kind of reformulation of praxis theory that Willis's (1977) *Learning to Labor* does, albeit implicitly.

Willis's (1977) "lads" willingly participated in permanently locking themselves into their fathers' working class, shop-floor culture and rebelled against their teachers' urgings about the importance of school. They did so because they were first and foremost cultural producers; their socially constructed identities were of higher importance than goal-oriented action and plans for the future. The primacy of identity and the reality that human beings are motivated by the desire for recognition are part and parcel of Willis's reformulated praxis theory. Original Marxist ideas about "alienation" remain in Willis's tacit re-workings, but he also recaptures insights from Hegel and Herder by replacing Marx's paradigmatic artisan and her actions solely oriented toward the physical world with a more thoroughgoing understanding of human self-expression that includes the notion that it is not the material products that are self-expression in and of themselves but rather, they become self-expressive in the sense that other people might *recognize* the person through her creation. Since the "lads" were "alienated" by the culture of the school that did violence to their "expressive needs," they responded by creating cultural forms in opposition to such "alienation," and this was of greater importance for them than anything,[3] including making future plans based on goal-oriented action that might increase their vocational choices or even provide them with opportunities to change their socioeconomic status. With this reformulation of praxis theory, "expressive needs," for Willis, are resituated within human-to-human actions, not action oriented toward the physical world.

One manifestation of the desire for recognition and the desire to meet expressive needs comes in the form of humans pursuing communicative goals. Carspecken (1999) discusses this intersection between communicative goals and desire. In action oriented toward consequences, the level of success of the goal is observable in the objective world, while goals related to action oriented toward understanding are observable only in nonobjective, subjective states. Carspecken adds that "communicative goals often are not clarified in terms of the exact understanding that is desired until after the communicative act is completed" (p. 88). This has significance both for identity claims and, notably, for communicative goals that are bound up in expressive needs.

As Carspecken (1999) says, it is not uncommon to hear someone say, "I didn't know what I really needed to say until after I said it!" (p. 88). This is so because agents often have implicit and holistic understandings of that which they wish to communicate that come prior to the explicit content that comes in the form of words, gestures, or performances. There is a kind of uncertainty that the actor feels in this prior moment of holistic understanding about the significance or validity of the content. This uncertainty becomes the impetus for expressing what the actor has understood implicitly and holistically. It is important to note that people can feel that the expression falls short of the prior holistic understanding. This often leads to a person saying something like, "No, I guess that's not really what I meant," or "That's not quite it." On the other hand, the expressions can sometimes exceed what was grasped holistically and prior to the articulation and in these cases the actor often mentions surprising herself.

This is also the moment at which recognition enters the scene. The success of a communicative act is often the result of the agent recognizing her own act. Indeed, she will also notice a sense of shortcoming if the act is unsuccessful. After the act is completed, the actor will find a match between holistic, implicit understandings and the expression or not. Carspecken (1999) points out that this idea is connected to the concept of expectation. "Among the many expectations constituting any meaningful act are always a cluster that anticipate what the act will bring out *for the actor*" (p. 92, emphasis in the original). Recognition is also a desire to be recognized as an autonomous agent by others. Desire manifests itself in the identity claims that are a part of every meaningful human act at various levels of foregrounding or backgrounding. It is clear that this desire for recognition from others indicates a need for human beings to construct a social self. It also leads to identity claims, and these claims are often attached to the fulfillment of expressive needs.

One way of thinking about *Fight Club* with regard to the critical dystopia subgenre mentioned above is the theme of the fear that looms from the threat of the annihilation of the self in late modern/postmodern society. For the narrator in the film there is a kind of Hegelian struggle for selfhood that includes not only fear of death (made clear by memorable lines like, "This is your life and it's ending one minute at a time;" and, "We just had a near-life experience!") but also a "fighting" with forces of alienation (i.e., the meaninglessness of consumer culture). Not unlike Willis's lads, there are ways in which the character in the film fervently seeks to meet expressive needs and to fulfill the desire for recognition. This happens clearly in the character's addiction to attending support groups for people dying of a variety of causes ("When people think you're dying, they really, really listen to you").

Fight Club's portrayal of the struggle for self has many iterations in modern institutions, such as schools, that are populated by youth and under the control of adults. Many critical scholars of education have noted the kind of dissatisfaction students feel in schools, much of it having to do with the extremely truncated notions of self that the institution makes available to them. It is also well established in critical studies in education that youth often feel a pronounced sense of "alienation" owing to a feeling of not being listened to, something the narrator in *Fight Club* was only able to remedy by convincing other people he was dying.

There is a final idea from *Fight Club* that can be made sense of in light of Hegel's notions of self. That is, as noted above, in the process of struggling for selfhood or integration of self, violence can loom as a threat. Again, perhaps not physical violence, but it is certainly not uncommon for human beings to have their sense of self threatened in a totalizing way.

VIOLENCE AND SELF-FORMATION

In *Fight Club*, we see the depiction of a kind of Hegelian master-slave relationship. The master-slave relationship is one in which the person in the slave position regards the master as the full embodiment of her or his own essence. In this way, the slave only finds validation through being in the slave position with regard to the master. We are familiar enough with these kinds of unequal social relationships. The person in the master position is significantly insecure and can have extreme reactions to any suggestion that the slave might possibly value another person or even to the slave showing some hint of development of independence. The slave position is also in need of continuous maintenance. It is never ultimately secured. This maintenance usually takes the form of the person in the master position feeling the need to negate the person in the slave position through the use of verbal put-downs, explicitly degrading the worth of the slave, and always having the last word. The person in the slave position sometimes shows growth, while the master ultimately does not because, in the end, the slave is less dependent on the master than the master is on the slave. Yet, we can also think of other master-slave relationships in which the submissiveness of the slave is more pronounced and the person in the slave position is terrified of developing any independence, sometimes even in cases where physical abuse is present.

Hegel's insight is at play in *Fight Club*. When the narrator, meets Tyler Durden toward the beginning of the film, we see the start of a Hegelian master-slave relationship. The narrator is at first a willing and, in some ways, delighted slave to his own "other," Tyler. This plays out in a number of scenes after the narrator moves into the boarded-up, abandoned house with Tyler and immediately adopts his lifestyle, which is in various ways quite different than the lifestyle the narrator had previously grown used to. In this initial phase, the narrator takes on a number of Tyler's qualities. But, later in the film, there is conflict between the two characters and the narrator must individuate himself from the relationship. Here the dialectic mentioned above that starts with the linking of violence to the objectification of human experience in the product recall formulas becomes clear. All of this happens after a series of conflicts over "Project Mayhem" as the narrator begins to feel less and less comfortable with Tyler's tactics.

By the end of the film, this conflict has become a life-and-death struggle, but the narrator soon realizes that Tyler is actually also himself and that the relationship to Tyler as his dominant half and him (the narrator) being the subordinate half is part of an identity he (the narrator) is clinging to. So as mentioned above, at the very end of the film, the narrator turns a gun on himself, which produces a kind of identity integration. Whereas Tyler Durden was only self-determining in the negation of others, the narrator ends up being both self-determining and somewhat caring (with regard to Marla, the female lead), demonstrating the complex role that violence can play in the struggle for selfhood.

YOUTH, SCHOOLS, AND SELFHOOD

It makes sense that the ideas about selfhood and violence are portrayed in *Fight Club* with young characters. To be sure, the characters are not school-aged, but they seem youthful in many ways, ultimately owing to their struggle for selfhood and integration. My contention is that a particularly noticeable place where violence is at play in the struggle for self for youth is in schools. Perhaps not actual, physical violence (although this is certainly a part of the schooling experience for some youth), but at least symbolic violence exists in the form of alienation and grossly asymmetrical power relations. These kinds of relationships between adults and youth characterize schools. There is a sense in which schools have made any measure of success in the struggle for selfhood and the integration of self for young people at best extremely difficult and at worst impossible.

Many adults who work in or are in positions of authority in schools spend much energy on the maintenance of control of youth. It is one of a number of ways in which relationships between adults and youth in schools exhibit characteristics of the initial stages of the master-slave. Adult power and control over children animates processes and interactions in schools in ways that often lead to alienation on the part of young people. The hypercontrol that adults seek to exercise over students comes in various forms of the wielding of arbitrary power or the creation of arbitrary rules (which often do not apply to the adults).

In addition to excessive control, some youth also experience threats to self in the form of marginalization of difference and psychically violent responses on the part of adults to certain ways in which they seek to meet their expressive needs. For the most part, uniformity and/or conformity is largely rewarded in schools while many forms of expression that deviate from established norms (almost always middle class, white norms) are met with admonition, punishment, or ridicule. I have argued elsewhere that adults in authority positions in schools and in the media create and sanction an extremely limited set of choices of canned identities that can be taken up by youth in schools (Kline, 2011). For some students, the canned identities available do not provide for their particular expressive needs. Others are unable to access any of the sanctioned identities. In both cases, these youth can experience violence to self by certain reactions to their inability to meet expressive needs within the boundaries of the norms of the school. They can also experience real threats to selfhood, sometimes in totalizing ways. Perhaps an argument that such violence to self is necessary or even desirable in the process of youth constructing and maintaining selfhood should be considered. Recall the scene from *Fight Club* mentioned above in which Tyler Durden violently threatens the convenience store clerk in order to get him to pursue the life he really desires. Could this amount to an argument that violence is a useful tool in helping a young person find her or himself and pursue an identity? I think not. My reading of the scene is that the kind of violence to self that is analogous to what schools and the adults who run them do to young people is the same kind of violence that convinced the convenience store clerk he could not or should not pursue his desire to be a veterinarian in the first place. Yes, it took the threat of violence to persuade the convenience store clerk to pursue his dream, but this was a threat *for* selfhood (or in support of selfhood, or something like that) and not *to* selfhood. The struggle *for* selfhood is difficult enough (and sometimes, perhaps, necessarily violent) but it is made unnecessarily difficult when adults and adult-run institutions are involved in constructing threats *to* selfhood.

The struggle for self and its integration is an essentially social phenomenon. Schools are by and large social institutions. Youth have a particular interest in the quest for self. Schools are institutions that ostensibly serve youth. The connections seem obvious. Yet, in the most intuitive place where adults might provide some kind of nurturing or stable environment for young people to struggle toward selfhood, we unfortunately find significant alienation, violence, and threats to self.

NOTES

1. It is not my intention to be reductionist here. Each of the articles mentioned has its own unique response to *Fight Club* and each is certainly more complex than the generalization I make. It is simply beyond the scope of this chapter to peel back every layer of the sophisticated arguments in each of these articles.
2. The dialectic begins to fully take shape later in the relationship between The narrator and Tyler Durden. That relationship takes on a form that is reminiscent of a certain reading of Hegel's master-slave dialectic. This idea is explored in a section below.
3. Willis's original title for what became *Learning to Labor* was *The Main Reality*.

REFERENCES

Brandom, R. B. (2007). The structure of desire and recognition: Self-consciousness and self-constitution. *Philosophy and Social Criticism, 33*(1), 127-150.

Carspecken, P. F. (1999). *Four scenes for posing the question of meaning and other essays in critical philosophy and critical methodology.* New York, NY: Peter Lang.

Clark, J. M. (2002). Faludi, *Fight Club*, and phallic masculinity: Exploring the emasculating economics of patriarchy. *Journal of Mens Studies, 11*(1), 65.

Derrida, J. (1998). *Of grammatology*. Baltimore, MD: Johns Hopkins University Press.

Diken, B., & Laustsen, C. (2002). Enjoy your fight!—"*Fight Club*" as a symptom of the network society. *Cultural Values, 6*(4), 349.

Giroux, H. (2001). Private satisfactions and public disorders: Fight Club, patriarchy, and the politics of masculine violence. *JAC: A Journal of Rhetoric, Culture, and Politics, 21*(1), 1-31.

Hegel, G. W. F. (1977). *Phenomenology of spirit*. (A. V. Miller, Trans.) Oxford, England: Oxford University Press. (Original work published 1807).

Kline, K. (2011). Radical hermeneutics, adolescence, and twenty-first century critical pedagogy. In C. Mallot & B. Porfilio (Ed.), *Critical pedagogy in the twenty-first century: A new generation of scholars* (pp. 53-67). Charlotte, NC: Information Age Publishing.

Linson, A., Chaffin, S., & Bell, R.G. (Producer), & Finger, D. (Director). (1999). *Fight club* [Motion picture]. USA: 20th Century Fox.

Lizardo, O. (2007). *Fight Club*, or the cultural contradictions of late capitalism. *Journal For Cultural Research, 11*(3), 221-243.

Marx, K., & Engels, F. (1945/1998). *The german ideology*. Amherst, NY: Prometheus Books. (Original work published 1945)

Mead, G. H. (1934). *Mind self and society from the standpoint of a social behaviorist*. Chicago, IL: University of Chicago Press.

Moylan, T. (2000). *Scraps of an untainted sky: Science fiction, utopia, dystopia*. Boulder, CO: Westview Press.

Palahniuk, C. (1996). *Fight club*. New York, NY: W. W. Norton.

Ta, L. (2006). Hurt so good: *Fight Club*, masculine violence, and the crisis of capitalism. *The Journal of American Culture, 29*(3), 265-277.

Wegner, P. E. (2009). *Life between two deaths, 1989-2001: US culture in the long nineties*. Durham, NC: Duke University Press.

Willis, P. (1977). *Learning labor: How working class kids get working class jobs*. New York, NY: Columbia University Press.

Yar, M. (2001). Recognition and the politics of human(e) desire. *Theory, Culture, and Society, 18*(1), 57-76.

CHAPTER 3

MERIT, DEMOCRACY, GOVERNING

Benjamin Baez

INTRODUCTION

I will be discussing here two visions of the role of schooling in the United States, and I will argue that these two visions, opposite in motive and political effects, present to us (more or less intentional) dystopian visions of governing. The two visions of schooling I will discuss here are those presented to us by two texts: Michael Young's *The Rise of the Meritocracy: 1870-2033* (1961) and John Dewey's *Experience & Education* (1938/1997). These might seem like odd choices because I imagine that readers of this chapter would be imagining as "dystopian" something literary along the lines of texts by Bradbury, Burgess, Huxley, and most definitely, Orwell. My choice of these two texts, particularly Dewey's, is especially odd because I also imagine that readers of this volume would assume a dystopia to be one that was intentionally meant to be a dystopia. By traditional definitions of dystopia, I suppose neither of these qualify. Yet, I hope to stretch those traditional definitions to capture a more contemporary idea of texts that attends to their narrative functions, and that when read for the stories they are espousing begin to look very much like those texts we generally imagine as literary. With this caveat, I chose Young's and Dewey's texts for three specific reasons.

Dystopia and Education:
Insights Into Theory, Praxis, and Policy in an Age of Utopia-Gone-Wrong, pp. 31–49

The first reason is that both texts tell stories about the role of schooling in shaping our lives. Schools are spaces in which dreams and fantasies of utopian futures abound, and attempts to make those utopias practicable via schooling can have nightmarish consequences for children. The second reason for my choice is that I am following the definition of dystopia put forth by our editors, Jessica Heybach and Eric Sheffield (preface), which indicates that a dystopian text conjures up an "imaginary place or state in which the condition of life is extremely bad, as from deprivation, oppression, or terror." Schools, of course, are imagined as spaces full of risk (think gun violence, bullying, teen suicide, adolescent sexual behavior, failing, *A Nation at Risk*, high-stakes testing, teacher ineptness, etc.); they are also imagined as laboratories for putting into practice various utopias (think democracy, merit, global competitiveness, etc.). As spaces for imagining risk and utopias, schools allow us to conjure up multiple and diverse forms of control.

The last reason for my choice is that via ostensibly oppositional strategies, each text I privilege here offers an example of what I will mean when I use the word "governing." As I explain in greater detail in the next section, by "governing" I mean to refer to the various ways in which practices and rationalities gear themselves to the shaping or directing of individual conduct. Some forms of governing come from above, so to speak, either via ways we ordinarily understand as being oppressive, that is, through the use of force or threats, or, given our problematic, via rationalities associated with scientific expertise. These governing practices coming from above illustrate what Michel Foucault (1988) called the "technologies of power" (p. 19). Young's (1961) text will offer me a point of departure for elaborating on these forms of directing conduct. But not all forms of directing conduct are oppressive; some are directed at creating particular kinds of citizens, ones empowered to take care of themselves and others. These forms of governing come from below, that is, via attempts at shaping the voluntary action so that one behaves "as one should." I will argue that the practices associated with democratic education illustrate these latter kinds of governing techniques, and I will use Dewey's (1938/1997) text as emblematic of such forms of governing.

And so this will be my main argument about Young's (1961) and Dewey's texts (1938/1997): all forms of directing individual conduct via schooling practices require rationalizing the governing of individuals who have little say in the matter. All attempts at making practicable any such rationalizations are *impositions*, directing the behavior of children by inventing a society whose future can be conjured up as meritocratic or democratic (as in the case of our examples). I will also suggest, however, that to the extent "democratic" utopias give up on the idea that theirs are morally sound, they might offer us a better dream about the world we live in now, one currently governed by the nightmarish uses of quantifiable information to relegate us to varying levels of social inequality.

In the next section of this chapter, I will discuss in greater detail what I mean by "governing" and the role that schooling plays in it. I then turn to Young's (1961) text, reading it via an understanding of the role of scientific expertise in directing conduct with the use of information that makes up students with varying levels of worth. I then turn to Dewey's (1938/1997) text and read it via an understanding of how pedagogic techniques promoting democratically-minded individuals also invent students in order to direct their actions toward specific ends. I end with a discussion of how scientific expertise and "democratic" pedagogy might be read as technologies for governing children from above and from below, even if justifying their impositions in the name of "freedom," "democracy," "progress," "global competiveness," or heaven knows what else. These techniques of governing determine in advance what those children, or the adults those children will become, are going to be, and thereby constrain avenues for their own inventions about how best to live their lives.

GOVERNING

By governing, I am not intending to be understood as referring to anything associated with the political divisions of the state. I follow Michel Foucault in using the term "government" to refer to the "conduct of conduct," where the first use of the word *conduct* means to lead or guide and the second use to refer to action and behavior. The essence of the phrase, then, is that in governing one is directing the activity of individuals and populations by shaping the way they act (Dean, 2003, p. 119). In other words, the "conduct of conduct" entails ways in which not only the state (formal or political government) but myriad institutions, both "public" and "private," or "state" and "nonstate," seek to guide, shape, or affect the conduct of individuals (Gordon, 1991, pp. 2-3). Governing, then, refers both to the rationalities and techniques social institutions use to guide, shape, and direct the behavior of individuals *and* to the rationalities and techniques individuals themselves use to govern their actions. The rationalities of government address themselves specifically to the shaping of conduct, and they are directed at making particular forms of reality thinkable and practicable both to practitioners and to the persons to whom their practices are directed (pp. 2-3).

Governing can be done by the use of force or coercion, but such forms of governing in so-called advanced liberal societies are inefficient in the long run. More effective are governing practices directed at the individual's freedom to act. Thus, techniques for governing in advanced liberal societies are often disciplinary, individualizing subjects through hierarchical and lateral observation, surveillance, and normalizing judgments (cf. Foucault, 1977). Modern forms of governing individualize in such a way that individuals understand their actions as based in autonomous choice to act. "Freedom" thus becomes crucial to social administration, which, in turn, appears to produce "freedom" (Popkewitz, 1999, p. 25). In other words, as Foucault (1993) said, "the contact point, where [how] individuals are driven by others is tied to the way they conduct themselves, is what we can call, I think, government" (p. 203).

Enter the school, which, along with the family and the community, has played a significant governmental role in advanced liberal societies (cf. Popkewitz, 2003). The school has become the site in which, and an object for which, governing is furthered by a scientific and pedagogical expertise that is motivated by an ethic of promoting in children the ability for self-realization, self-reflection, and self-responsibility (Hunter, 1996). Modern pedagogical practices thus seek to make the child a self-regulated actor whose agency is inscribed in being "educated," "studious, "meritorious," "civically-minded," "democratic," and a responsible member of various communities. Not that these things are generally agreed-upon; in no way do I intend to suggest universality of motives or intentions. Schooling serves particular (though highly contested) ends and as creating particular (though highly contested) kinds of citizens. But despite these contested aims, governing via the school gains legitimacy by aligning a vision of a social good with individuals' personal orientations in such a way that the social good "structure[s] the possible field of action of others" (Foucault, 1983, p. 221).

For all this to occur, of course, requires that the family's role be supplanted (or augmented) by the school's in order to ensure individual progress, and, consequently, the nation's progress. Education is now deemed an essential function of the state. What counted as "education" was originally within the purview of the family before it became "schooling" within the purview of the state (Tyack, 1988, pp. 43-44). The reasons for the state's role in education have been contested, of course, but it seems that a system of public education was deemed necessary for the transmission of cultural heritage, the furtherance of social and economic policies, and the maintenance of social order (Drake, 1961; Tyack, 1988;). Indeed, governing techniques in school often frame education as serving "the public interest," but there are no objective or legitimate meanings for concepts such as "education," "public," and "interests." Thus, it is crucial to ask instead fundamental questions about how curricular practices will create, and then govern, individuals and communities who will come to see themselves as "educated," with "public" identities and interests.

I must stress here that governmental technologies are not by definition oppressive. Indeed, we should, following Nikolas Rose (1999):

> differentiate the exercise of power in government from simple domination. To dominate is to ignore or to attempt to crush the capacity for action of the dominated. But to govern is to recognize that capacity for action and to adjust oneself to it. To govern is to *act upon action*. (p. 4, emphasis mine)

With regard to the school, governing entails understanding what motivates and mobilizes children (and parents, teachers, etc.) to be governed and to act upon these forces, to instrumentalize children (and parents, teachers, etc.) and their actions so as to redirect them toward desired aims, often by enticements rather than coercion (Rose, 1999, p. 4.). These noncoercive enticements enable what Foucault (1991) called the "art of government," the creation of continuity between the ideals of the state and the actions of citizens so that all subjects govern themselves effectively, "which means that individuals will, in turn, behave as they should" (p. 92). I want to conclude this section by also stressing that I am not intending to imply that any form of governing is better, more efficient, and so on. My argument focuses on *techniques* for conducting conduct and the rationalities that undergird them, not on their ideological underpinnings or on the efficiency of any particular technique. Having given this quick overview of governing via schooling, let me turn to the texts at hand.

MERIT

Originally published in 1958, *The Rise of the Meritocracy* is Michael Young's (1961) satire on the reorganization of British society through educational testing. This book is actually more like a sociological study of postwar Britain, but it qualifies as a dystopian text because of the negative vision of the future it presents. In Young's tale, the year is 2033 and the use of intelligence tests had culminated in a meritocracy that replaced an inefficient and unpopular social order allocating rewards and status on the basis of a hereditary system (cf. Baez, 2006). The meritocracy allocated rewards and status on the basis of this formula: Merit = IQ + effort. This, however, had catastrophic consequences on people's lives and on a democratic form of government. Eventually, the masses revolt in a revolution that led to the death of the narrator himself. Young's tale rings true today—and less like a satire—for the dystopian view of the role of standardized testing in education has indeed come about.

Young's (1961) tale was a warning about the consequences of various practices in postwar Britain. He questioned, specifically, three such practices: (1) relegating children to schools on the basis of intelligence testing; (2) using different curricular offering for each child so as to prepare each for different kinds of work (what I imagine we would now call "tracking"); and, (3) using education as the means to obtain employment rather than as an end in itself. In this tale, practice #1, the use of standardized testing (i.e., IQ tests), justifies practice #2, tracking, which purportedly leads to a merit system that allocates social rewards differentially, which in turn legitimizes (or is legitimized by) practice #3 as the philosophy for justifying public education. As Young's tale indicates, the beauty of such a system is that we

> have an élite selected according to brains and educated according to deserts, with a grounding in philosophy and administration as well as in the two S's of science and sociology.... Today we frankly recognize that democracy can be no more than aspiration, and have rule not so much by the people as by the cleverest people; not an aristocracy of birth, not a plutocracy of wealth, but a true meritocracy of talent. (p. 21)

It appears the public support of education today, in the United States at least, is no longer premised on, say, a republican fantasy of the kind that Horace Mann (1846) imagined, as much as on rewarding talent and effort, which, of course, justifies the social disparity we have in the levels of income and prestige. And this differentiation of individuals, and consequent stratification of society, can now claim legitimacy not only on the grounds of economic and bureaucratic efficiency, but also on moral grounds, since individuals tend to believe that merit is the basis for "both material and symbolic benefits," which, when possessed, seem genuinely earned and deserved (Breen & Goldthorpe, 2001, p. 81). Rationalities associated with merit also work at the psychological level. The techniques rationalizing and putting into practice ideas about merit work at the individual level because they fixate on children's "ideological mind;" that is, a mind always looking to develop an identity approved by society (Erikson, 1993, p. 356).

Notions of merit in the United States play a more contested role in schooling than they do in other countries. Americans have always juggled an elitism premised on an economic/scientific bases for determining social rewards with an egalitarian (anti-intellectual) fantasy that "anyone can pull himself up by his own bootstraps" and achieve his dreams if he works hard enough. Young's (1961) meritocracy and U.S. egalitarianism both account for effort, to be sure, but the former places greater emphasis on intelligence, while the latter values effort above all else. Still, there is no question that notions of merit are central to American schooling, and their operationalization in standardized (and "high stakes") testing is becoming the norm in American schooling—a norm that has come to define what aptitude, achievement, learning, and, in short, education, will mean. Rumblings about this are also taking place now. And so the kind of stratification legitimated by educational testing that Young warned about in the world he imagined for Britain in 2033, and the bubbling of dissent in the masses that he narrated, seems very much like the world Americans are experiencing in 2012.

I think readers of this chapter will be very familiar with arguments about the psychological and social oppression to which high-stakes testing leads, and so I will not spend any time rehashing those arguments here. I want to focus instead on a point Young (1961) made about the role of science (particularly what we would now call psychometrics) in the world order he warns against. This allows me to transition to the kinds of governing techniques that come *from above*, so to speak. These kinds of techniques constitute disciplinary forms of power that rely on scientific expertise for knowing, individualizing, and normalizing individuals.

If standardized testing has become a key governing strategy in society, then the creators of these tests will be the kinds of "scientists [who] have inherited the earth" (Young, 1961, p. 109). Pierre Bourdieu (1993) argued that "scientists generally are social *engineers* whose function is to supply recipes [in the form of theoretical rationales] to ... [the] governing élite [that] needs a science capable of ... *rationalizing* its domination" (p. 13). I am not as certain as Bourdieu seems to be that the connection between science and elitism involves a kind of conspiracy, since that implies an intentionality that may be difficult to demonstrate empirically, and, besides, such intentionality is unnecessary for understanding the kinds of disciplinary forms that power now takes. Regardless, standardized tests offer rationalizations for certain kinds of governing techniques, particularly those ensuring differential distribution of resources and the kind of acquiescence necessary to ensure that.

The proliferation of psychometricians, at any rate, has profound consequences for our social order. They manipulate tests to ensure discrimination among test takers, and while, following Bourdieu (1984), "claiming disinterestedness ... use their theoretical knowledge to install their mode of domination" over society (p. 153). That theoretical knowledge looks like it uncovers knowledge of innate phenomena, but in fact it will reconstruct the social order, and consequently psychometricans will give themselves the authority to dictate what is worthy and legitimate in society; for, scientific theories have particular authority in a society because of what Bourdieu (1991) calls their "theory effects" (p. 133). This means that by expressing in coherent and empirically-valid language that which is supposedly implicit (such as ability, aptitude, or intelligence), psychometrics transforms the representation of the social world (for instance, to one that can be measured via normed instruments), and, consequently, transforms the social world itself to match those representations (such as an educational system based on merit). Such scientific theories, therefore, do more than simply tell us what we cannot observe directly; they bring into existence that which they declare.

For psychometrics to dictate what counts as achievement, aptitude, intelligence, and so on, to legitimate the individual and social definitions of worth by doing so, and thus to direct the actions of individuals toward particular ends, there had to be a radical change in what counted as knowledge (cf. Baez & Boyles, 2009). Society had to be deemed knowable via statistical analysis. The enumeration of people via statistical analysis brought into existence laws carrying with them the connotations of normalcy and of deviations from the norm (Hacking, 1990). Because of such statistics, we now have numerous classifications of children in schools, such as the "gifted," the "intelligent," the "high achiever," and so on. All these labels, of course, come with their corollary: the "ADHD," the "at-risk," the "doesn't-want-to-learn," and so on, leading to a slew of institutional practices to "fix" these children. One can see, therefore, how institutional violence is legitimized by scientific knowledge. These statistics "make up people" and can be understood, according to Hacking, along two levels of analysis: the level of labeling—pressing from above by statisticians who create a "reality" that people make their own; and, the level of the autonomous behavior of the persons so labeled, which presses from below, creating a reality statisticians face (p. 234).

Statistics then become the techniques for governing, for they allow us to normalize children in schools. These techniques, therefore, can be used not only to impose homogeneity but individualization as well; that is, they make it possible to measure gaps, to determine levels, to fix specialties, and to render the differences useful by fitting them one to another (Foucault, 1977, p. 184). Standardized testing, spurred on by statistics, thus addresses itself both to the population and to the individual. Foucault (1977) explains that the examination "is a normalizing gaze, a surveillance that makes it possible to qualify, to classify and to punish," establishing "over individuals a visibility through which one differentiates them and judges them" (p. 184-185) He argues that of all the mechanisms for controlling and disciplining bodies, the "superimposition of the power relations and knowledge relations assumes in the examination all its visible brilliance" (p. 184-185). In other words, according to Foucault:

> The standardized test, therefore, opens up two correlative possibilities: firstly, the constitution of the individual as a describable, analyzable object, not in order to reduce him to "specific" features ... but in order to maintain

> him in his individual features, in his particular evolution, in his own aptitudes or abilities, under the gaze of a permanent corpus of knowledge; and, secondly, the constitution of a comparative system that made possible the measurement of overall phenomena, the description of groups, the characterization of collective facts, the calculation of the gaps between individuals, their distribution in a given population. (p. 190)

With the plethora of standardized tests to which schools and children are subjected, we now have the evidence of where children and schools actually are, where they should be, what they should earn, what they are worth, why they belong, and so forth. And we can direct their actions accordingly. Psychometrics thus directs itself to individual subjectivities, not for their own sake, but for the overall system of governing toward self-responsibility in advanced liberal societies. It is an economy of social administration.

The privileging of quantitative data that we see all around us in schooling now makes absolute sense; they allow the reduction of individual and population phenomena to statistically generalizable data that permit the objectification of individuals as individuals and as parts of a host of populations (e.g., racial, national, etc.); and which is ultimately used to manage and administer individuals, to shape their identities and their actions. As Thomas Popkewitz (1999) explains, once individuals were objectified in such a way that their inner characteristics could be represented as statistical data, irrespective of the feelings and values of the observer, strategies could be developed to order them systematically and taxonomically within a functional system that was administrable (p. 19). And the pyschometrician could think of herself as being neutral, simply explaining human behavior with information called "data." In fact, she must think herself neutral, as only furthering the imperatives of a science that is always in search of truth, for to think otherwise is to rethink objectivity in science, and thus science itself and her role in it.

Jean-François Lyotard (1979/1984) wrote that the nature of knowledge in the postmodern age has undergone (and is undergoing) dramatic change, largely as a result of the proliferation of information-processing machines: "knowledge" is being transformed into "quantities of information," easily translatable into databases, easily used by anyone with a computer, and easily exchanged and sold (p. 4). This "informationizing" of knowledge, if you will, also transforms relations between and among myriad institutions and individuals, all of which are being converted into "data" that can be manipulated to expose all kinds of patterns and to justify all kinds of social administration. So knowledge must now fit new economic/political channels and become operational only if translated into quantities of information. We may conclude this part of the chapter by proposing that Young's (1961) tale offers a dystopia very relevant to education, a vision of a highly symptomatic form of control in the information age: the creation of a cadre of experts that converts individuals into information that becomes the basis for governing them in all kinds of ways.

DEMOCRACY

In 1938, John Dewey published *Experience & Education*, which came almost 20 years after his most famous elaboration of his philosophy of education, *Democracy and Education* (1916/1944). In *Experience & Education*, a very short book based on the Kappa Delta Pi Lecture Series, Dewey took exception with what he called "traditional" and "progressive" education. The former is what we might now call the "banking-model" of education in which students simply relate back information deemed by educators as being "tried and true" and necessary for future success. Progressive education seems to be that which cultivates individuality, focuses on learning via experience, and emphasizes the present. Dewey, however, argued against progressive education's tendency toward an inchoate curriculum shaped by excessive individualism. In the book, therefore, Dewey rejected the either/or mentality associated with these philosophies and argued instead that some parts of both philosophies can ground effective educational practice. Dewey's elaboration of education, like Young's, attributed a large role to science, except that for Dewey (1938) science was not used for sorting individuals in a hierarchical social system (the kind that Young warned against in his text); science allowed instead our "getting at the significance of our everyday experiences of the world in which we live ... and provides a working pattern of the way in which and the conditions under which experiences are used to lead ever onward and outward" (p. 88). School, in other words, would become a laboratory for living in the world.

Why would I read Dewey's text as a dystopia? While Young may not have opposed labeling his tale a dystopia, I would guess that Dewey (and perhaps some readers of this chapter) would object to his text being labeled such. But a close reading of Dewey's text reveals particular narrative patterns associated with dystopias. It uncovers, for example, that without progressive education in his tale, the future envisioned by Dewey was one of stagnation. Moreover, Dewey's concern in the text was with having educators recognize children's freedom to act, and to work on that freedom in such a way that they would act in particular ways. As such, unlike Young's text, which illustrates the ways that governing works from above—scientific expertise creating individuals—Dewey's text illustrates governing from below—recognizing the individual's capacity for freedom and rationalizing the use of that freedom for directing individual action toward certain ends. I must stress here that my argument is not with Dewey's philosophy of education as such; my concern here is with the ways that such a text can be read as illustrating a form of governing that is different from the one I discussed above. The previous one using scientific expertise may be said to characterize the ways domination happens in advanced liberal societies in the so-called information age. The form of governing I uncover in the Dewey (1938/1997) text is one that cannot be called domination in a simple sense. This form of governing, following Rose, recognizes individuals' capacity for action and adjusts itself to it; it involves working on the actions of individuals capable of acting otherwise; it works on the individual's freedom.

Given this understanding, it might be useful to attend to Dewey's (1938/1997) notion of freedom. In Dewey's text, true "freedom" was only the "freedom of intelligence," which appears to mean the "freedom of observation and of judgment exercised in behalf of purposes that are intrinsically worthwhile (p. 61). If "intrinsically" here refers to a psychological state, then Dewey relied on the emerging science of psychology to rationalize acting upon action, which then would make his text very much like Young's (1961); that is, a text elaborating upon the power of scientific expertise in directing individual behavior. But if "intrinsically" here does not refer to a psychological state, then it must have some social reference. Indeed, I think this seems a more likely reading of the text. For Dewey opposed the "freedom of intelligence" to the "freedom of movement," by which he meant the latter to explain the external or physical side of activity without purpose (p. 61). And when combined with what he said about "social control," which suggests that control resides in the nature of the work being done, in which individuals have an opportunity to contribute and in "which all feel a responsibility," one can read Dewey's text as rationalizing the direction of the educator's conduct in order to shape the children's freedom, so that both educators and children behave *as they should* (p. 56).

I now want us to read all this in line with Dewey's (1916/1944) concern in *Democracy and Education* and the texts by others who have elaborated on what democratic education means and how it can be put into effect. Schools are social institutions that are subtended by a fantasy of democracy (cf. Baez, 2011). For Dewey, democracy can never be subject to external authority; it can only be created by education (p. 87). Democracy entails a mode of participation with one's fellow citizens that is animated by a sense of responsibility for one's society (Elshtain, 2000, p. 117). Democracy in this sense is not fundamentally tied to political government. It relates to civic society writ large and entails a certain disposition, a "personal way of life, signifying possession and continual use of certain attitudes, forming personal character and determining desire and purpose in all relations of life" (Dewey, 1939/1986, p. 148). Democratic education, if you will, must concern itself with the skills and dispositions that will enable children to function in a society imagined as democratic. It is the idea that notions of democracy can rationalize acting upon dispositions that I read as entailing governmental rationalities.

So, in the traditional model of education that Dewey (1938/1997) elaborated upon in *Experience & Education*, democracy would only entail formal political action, and so only a "future-oriented" education would be necessary. Since children cannot participate directly in the democratic process, they can only learn about this process abstractly, in books, and understand it as something they will do *in the future*. But in the progressive model of education as Dewey imagined it in the same text, children would be able to construct their own education as a stage for democracy (e.g., today, they might debate the political issues of the day; they might support the environment; they might meet with policymakers; they might learn about other cultures; etc.). Democracy can now be imagined via a theory of experience, for only via direct experience in democracy can children really come to *know* it and become "democratic."

In this way, one might see how a theory of experience that treats its object (e.g., democracy) as undeniably empirical can now be read as one that actually treats its subjects (i.e., students) as entirely technical. For students' experiences can now be manipulated in the name of society. The "life of the child becomes the all-controlling aim" of the school (Dewey 1902/1990, p. 36). But not just schools, of course; all political institutions must be assessed for the contribution they make to the "all-around growth of every member of society" (Dewey, 1920/1957, p. 186). Indeed, social institutions, laws, and arrangements are not simply means for progress and welfare; "they are the means of *creating* individuals;" only in physical bodies "is individuality an original datum. Individuality in a social and moral sense is something to be wrought out" (p. 194, emphasis in original).

Democratic education thus rationalizes the intrusion of the school into the psyche of individuals, since "democratic schools," James Beane and Michael Apple (1995) wrote, "Like democracy itself, do not happen by chance. They result from explicit attempts by educators to put in place arrangements and opportunities that will bring democracy to life" (p. 9). Democratic schools create democratic structures that allow children to participate in making decisions that affect their lives, and to ensure this, there must be "selective intervention of the state, especially where the process and content of local decision making serve to disenfranchise and oppress selected groups of people" (p. 10). The conduct of teachers must also be changed. They must be made into "transformative intellectuals" (Giroux & McLaren, 1996, p. 303) or "critically transitive teachers" (Boyles, 2000, p. 173) who treat students as critical agents who understand the connection between the personal and the social and strive for emancipation. It should be noted here, then, that both the governors and the governed are caught up in these rationalities of governing.

When compared to the administration of individuals in the so-called meritocratic system that Young warned about, the differences associated with the administration rationalized by progressive education, democratic education, and the theories of experience subtending them, are ones of degree, not kind. That is, they are similar in that they narrate two forms of governing; they are different, of course, in elaborating the motivations and political ideologies that undergird their rationalities and techniques for directing behavior. But in both texts discussed here, what is being narrated is the rationalization of schooling as a field for the elaboration of technologies directed toward the creation of individual citizens (meritocratic or democratic, in our particular examples), which entails working on their "freedom" so as to direct them toward certain (more or less authoritarian) ends. And all these technologies gain their legitimacy by aligning a vision of the social good with individuals' personal orientations in such a way that the social good, following Foucault (1983), "structure[s] the possible field of action of others" (p. 221).

We may conclude this part of the chapter by saying that Dewey's (1938/1997) tale is dystopian to the extent it can be read as narrating a vision of schooling as a key location in which children are invented as would-be citizens, and thus as subject to manipulations that will teach them to be autonomous, intelligent, responsible, and democratic. It is a vision that when viewed this way is just another form of imposition onto the lives of subjects who have no say in the matter. This kind of vision entails inventing children as having bad (or, more accurately, "miseducative") experiences, and then working on those experiences so as to direct them toward certain beliefs, capabilities, and motivations (toward "educative" experiences), arguably in the name of their progress (and the nation's). This imposition is framed as serving democracy, as logical and good. However, there are no objective meanings in concepts like "experience," "autonomy," "responsibility," "democracy," or even "freedom." These must be given content by curricular practices that will invent and then administer individuals and communities who will come to see themselves in those things and this is the important point, to behave accordingly.

GOVERNING, REVISITED

The texts by Young (1961) and Dewey (1938/1997) may be read as dystopias, and my reading of them offers yet another kind of dystopia itself. For I have read those texts as elaborating governmental rationalities, which operate above the school (as in the case of normalizing techniques) or within the school (in the case of democratizing techniques, if you will) in ways that rationalize and put into practice techniques for governing children to direct their conduct in specific ways. Such analysis of schooling, it is important to note, attends, not to the effectiveness of schooling practices, or to the intentions and motives of teachers (their conduct too is being directed), but to the ways ostensibly empirical notions like intelligence, aptitude, democracy, might actually be rationalities that make particular forms of reality thinkable and practicable, both to educational practitioners and to the children to whom their practices are directed.

The contemporary school is a site full of practices for governing the soul, for experimenting with the social environment and the identity of subjects in order to achieve individual freedom and responsibility. It is a site, Popkewitz (1999) argued, where political rationalities are converted into pedagogies (p. 22). My point here probably seemed clear with regard to the use of scientific expertise (in the form of psychometrics), but perhaps was less clear with regard to democratic education. But as Beane and Apple (1995) argued, democratic education links the school to political sovereignty, and so they require impositions to direct the conduct of schools, and actually to redirect that conduct toward "democratic structures and processes by which life in the school is carried out ... [and toward developing] a curriculum that will give young people democratic experiences" (p. 9). For these democratic rationalities, the impositions onto the conduct of schools and its individuals do not promote the market in the name of society, as one might say with regard to neoliberal projects associated with high-stakes testing, but promotes the individual and the school in the name of democracy.

To the extent that Dewey's (1938/1997) text can be read as espousing education for democracy or democracy for education, then, as Popkewitz (1999) pointed out, even John Dewey was complicit in this linking of individualism and science with social administration (p. 19). In *Experience & Education*, Dewey argued that the "methods of science also point the way to the measures and policies by means of which a better social order can be brought into existence" (p. 81). In this way, Dewey, Popkewitz argued, inscribed political/moral assumptions of progress into his conception of personal development within the idea of "community." The idea of "community" embodied a Protestant notion of hard work, a commitment to science as a problem-solving device in a democracy, and an Emersonian notion of citizen "voluntarism" in social affairs (p. 19).

What we see in any attempt at rationalizing schools for particular ends is a rationalization for particular governmental relations, no matter how well-intended. And ultimately this is why I choose to call both these texts dystopias. The "student" they narrate is not just an empirical reality, but a *political field* of practice and knowledge, where scientific classifications and political inventions will hold great sway. With scientific expertise and democratic inventions, the "child" is not deemed a natural phenomenon with natural laws guiding its natural development for its own sake, but one deemed so for the sake of inventing it as a political space for the production of categories, classifications, rationalities, and techniques (cf. Baker, 1998, p. 138). The child becomes a site for governing rationalities and techniques that will, following Foucault (1977), "invest it, mark it, train it ... force it to carry out tasks, to perform ceremonies, to emit signs" (pp. 25-26). In governing, the relations between those who govern and those governed depend on the manner in which the governed see themselves as subjects (Gordon, 1991, p. 48). Therefore, neither the creation of subjects via meritocratic nor democratic rationalities can be deemed morally or pedagogically sound; they are impositions whose inventions have particular directives: governing children in ways determined by motivations, ideologies, or rationalities that come from elsewhere, but that very much look like they come from within.

We might attend, therefore, to how ideas about merit and democratic education mirror each other in the ways they seek to govern the conduct of children; one via homogenizing and individualizing techniques of standardized testing, and the other via a manipulation of individual experiences via particular pedagogies. They seek to act on individuals' freedom for particular purposes and aim to create subjectivities that will act and reason as intended. These forms of governing are both different and similar to the ones in the dystopian visions of Orwell, Huxley, and others. On the one hand, they are unlike traditional dystopias in that they do not involve the actions of authoritarian states, for in liberal forms of government such authoritarian actions have only but limited and temporal effects. On the other hand, they are like traditional dystopias in that they entail forms of control that are subtended by the production of knowledge and the creation of dispositions that ensnare us all insidiously, making it seem as though we act on and by our own free will.

Indeed, the differences between governmental rationalities associated with merit and those associated with democracy illuminate a shift in the "conduct of conduct." Schooling entailed the state's usurpation of the private sphere, a reconstituting of what counted as education, then a reworking of the spheres' purviews, so that education became a public matter that can greatly shape conduct in both public and private spheres. Thus, the school is a crucial investment in the art of governing. The school holds an interstitial space between political and nonpolitical forms of governing, and thus it replaced the family as the model of governing par excellence. At least since the progressive school movement of the early twentieth century, we are to understand that through "their school experiences, children would experience the world vicariously" (Finkelstein,

1991, p. 465). The school is imagined to be about life itself, a laboratory for shaping and directing life itself. This is an invention, a way of making certain realities practicable and administrable, but this invention permits myriad forms of control via rationalities permitting more or less authoritarian and empowering impositions onto the lives of actual children.

Those of us on the left might tend to struggle with analyses of governmental rationalities like mine, since they sidestep questions of intention, ideology, domination, and so on. But such concepts fail to account for how the "conduct of conduct" takes place through self-government, through freedom, through responsibility. Technologies of government in advanced liberal societies are not always premised on domination—on subverting the will of the individuals governed. Such domination is effective only temporarily and in the long run is inefficient in societies deemed to be made up of "free" individuals. More efficient forms of governing conceive of individuals as *active* in making choices that will further their own interests; therefore, governmental rationalities are focused on conducting behavior in such a way that individuals themselves become active in their own governing (Rose, 1999, p. 142). This does not mean that governing techniques cannot be understood via notions of domination; I mean only to say that they should not be solely understood under such a logic. It is the autonomy of individuals that is the target of governing, not necessarily their domination.

Having said all this, I will say that particular configurations of governing rationalities are historically contingent, and so we must constantly use the tools available to us, conceptual and practical, with an eye for the moment when the limits of their utility become evident (Bové, 1988. pp. xxvii-xxviii). I share with Rose (1999) a "profound unease about the values that pervade our times ... and a suspicious attention to the multitude of petty humiliations and degradations carried out in the name of our best interests" (p. 60). So, the point of my dystopia here, for the logic of my analysis entails seeing my story here as also dystopian, is not to put myself, or to justify putting others, in the service of those who believe they can govern better, but to open ourselves to understanding how we create subjects of children via governmental rationalities, and to how those children are entitled to "contest the practices that govern them in the name of their freedom" (p. 60). I ask that we look skeptically at the justifications and techniques we espouse via notions of merit and democracy (and perhaps this will also require that we look skeptically within ourselves). This means too that we will always be in the uncomfortable position of justifying, not the elimination of the exercise of power, but a redirection of it. This point of mine, then, seems rather dystopian.

Rather than argue completely against democratic rationalities, however, I would like us to consider the spaces it opens up for *inventiveness*—for those moments in which we refuse what is determined for us and invent new ideas about ourselves. (The meritocratic rationalities foreclose such spaces via their individualizing and homogenizing gaze.) We might consider as very important in resisting current political realities the self-government of individuals, a self-government that is always vulnerable to technologies of power but is never captured entirely by them. My overall conclusion with regard to Young's (1961) and Dewey's (1938/1997) dystopias is that such tales offer us, if we look carefully, avenues for self-reflection and inventiveness, for understanding the power we exercise when we seek to rationalize children's behavior in the name of economic progress, democracy, or freedom. Attending to the power we exercise via such rationalities might mean letting students refuse our expertise, and to allow them the "freedom of movement" that Dewey rejected, a freedom without purpose (or, more accurately, without *our* purpose). This freedom risks our expulsion from schools by those very children, but it is one we should take in order to open doors for inventiveness, both the children's and ours.

REFERENCES

Baez, B. (2006). Merit and difference. *Teachers College Record, 108*(6), 996-1016.

Baez, B. (2011). Democracy. In N. Lesko & S. Talburt (Eds.), *Keywords in youth studies* (pp. 153-157). New York, NY: Routledge.

Baez, B., & D. Boyles. (2009). *The politics of inquiry: Education research and the "culture of science."* Albany, NY: State University of New Press.

Baker, B. (1998). "Childhood" in the emergence and spread of U.S. public schools. In T. S. Popkewitz & M. Brennan (Eds.), *Foucault's challenge: Discourse, knowledge, and power in education* (pp. 117-143). New York, NY: Teachers College Press.

Beane, J. A. & M. W. Apple (1995). The case for democratic schools. In M. W. Apple & J. A. Beane (Eds.), *Democratic schools* (pp. 1-25). Alexandria, VA: Association for Supervision and Curriculum Development.

Bourdieu, P. (1984). *Distinction: A social critique of the judgment of taste* (R. Nice, Trans.). Cambridge, MA: Harvard University Press.

Bourdieu, P. (1991). *Language and symbolic power.* In J. B. Thompson (Ed.). (G. Raymond & M. Adamson, Trans.). Cambridge, MA: Harvard University Press.

Bourdieu, P. (1993). *Sociology in question.* (R. Nice, Trans.). Thousand Oaks, CA: SAGE.

Bové, P. A. (1988). Forward. The Foucault phenomenon: The problematics of style. In G. Deleuze, *Foucault* (pp. vii-xliv). (S. Hand, Trans.). Minneapolis, MN: University of Minnesota Press.

Boyles, D. (2000). *American education and corporations: The free market goes to school.* New York, NY: Falmer Press.

Breen, R., & J. H. Goldthorpe. (2001). Class, mobility and merit: The experience of two British birth cohorts. *European Sociological Review, 17*(2), 81-101.

Dean, M. (2003). Powers of life and death beyond governmentality. *Cultural Values, 6*(½), 119-138.

Dewey, J. (1990). *The school and society* and *The child and the curriculum.* Chicago, IL: The University of Chicago Press. (Original work published 1902)

Dewey, J. (1944). *Democracy and education.* New York, NY: Free Press. (Original work published 1916)

Dewey, J. (1957). *Reconstruction in philosophy.* Boston, MA: Beacon Press. (Original work published 1920)

Dewey, J. (1986). Democracy as a way of life. In J. Gouinlock (Ed.), *Excellence in public discourse: John Stuart Mill, John Dewey, and social intelligence* (pp. 146-151). New York, NY: Teachers College Press. (Originally published in 1939)

Dewey, J. (1997). *Experience & education.* New York, NY: Touchstone. (Original work published 1938)

Drake, W. E. (1961). Some implications of the institutionalization of American education. *History of Education Quarterly, 1*(1), 41-47.

Elshtain, J. B. (2000). Democracy on trial: The role of civil society in sustaining democratic values. In D. E. Eberly (Ed.), *The essential civil society reader: The classic essays* (pp. 101-122). Lanham, MD: Rowman & Littlefield.

Erikson, E. (1993). Youth and American identity. In C. Lemert (Ed.), *Social theory: The multicultural & classic readings* (pp. 355-358). Boulder, CO: Westview Press.

Finkelstein, B. (1991). Dollars and dreams: Classrooms as fictitious message systems, 1790-1930. *History of Education Quarterly, 31*(4), 463-487.

Foucault, M. (1977). *Discipline and punish: The birth of the prison.* (A. Sheridan, Trans.). New York, NY: Vintage Books.

Foucault, M. (1983). The subject and power. In H. L. Dreyfus & P. Rabinow (Eds.), *Michel Foucault: Beyond structuralism and hermeneutics* (pp. 208-226). Chicago, IL: The University of Chicago Press.

Foucault, M. (1988). Technologies of the self. In L. H. Martin, H. Gutman, & P. H. Hutton (Eds.), *Technologies of the self: A seminar with Michel Foucault* (pp. 16-49). Amherst, MA: The University of Massachusetts Press.

Foucault, M. (1991). Governmentality. In G. Burchell, C. Gordon, & P. Miller (Eds.), *The Foucault effect: Studies in governmentality* (pp. 87-104). Chicago, IL: The University of Chicago Press.

Foucault, M. (1993). About the beginning of the hermeneutics of the self: Two lectures at Dartmouth. *Political Theory, 21,* 198-227.

Giroux, H., & P. McLaren. (1996). Teacher education and the politics of engagement: The case for democratic schooling. In P. Leistyna, A. Woodrum, & S. A. Sherblom (Eds.), *Breaking free: The transformative power of critical pedagogy* (pp. 301-331). Cambridge, MA: Harvard Educational Review.

Gordon, C. (1991). Governmental rationality: An introduction. In G. Burchell, C. Gordon, & P. Miller (Eds.), *The Foucault effect: Studies in governmentality* (pp. 1-51). Chicago, IL: The University of Chicago Press.

Hacking, I. (1990). *The taming of chance.* United Kingdom: Cambridge University Press.

Hunter, I. (1996). Assembling the school. In A. Barry, T. Osborne, & N. Rose (Eds.), *Foucault and political reason: Liberalism, neo-liberalism and rationalities of government* (pp. 143-166). Chicago, IL: The University of Chicago Press.

Lyotard, J.-F. (1984). *The postmodern condition: A report on knowledge*. (G.Bennington & B. Massumi, Trans.). Minneapolis, MN: University of Minnesota Press. (Original work published 1979)

Mann, H. (1846). Tenth annual report of the Secretary of the Massachusetts State Board of Education. Retrieved from http://amhist.ist.unomaha.edu/Source_DocHorace%20Mann%20Report%20to%20MA%20Board%20of%20Education%201846.rtf.

Popkewitz, T. S. (1999). A social epistemology of educational research. In T. S. Popkewitz & L. Fendler (Eds.), *Critical theories in education: Changing terrains of knowledge and politics* (pp. 17-44). New York, NY: Routledge.

Popkewitz, T. S. (2003). Governing the child and pedagogicalization of the parent: A historical excursion into the present. In M. N. Bloch, K. Holmlund, I. Moqvist, & T. S. Popkewitz (Eds.), *Governing children, families, and education: Restructuring the welfare state* (pp. 35-61). New York, NY: Palgrave Macmillan.

Rose, N. (1999). *Powers of freedom: Reframing political thought*. Cambridge, England: Cambridge University Press.

Tyack, D. B. (1988). Ways of seeing: An essay on the history of compulsory schooling. In R. M. Jaeger (Ed.), *Complementary methods for research in education* (2nd ed., pp. 35-69). Washington, DC: American Educational Research Association.

Young, M. (1961). *The rise of the meritocracy 1870-2033: An essay on education and equality*. New York, NY: Penguin Books.

CHAPTER 4

DYST(R)OPIA

A Tropological Argument for Dystopia and Education

F. Tony Carusi

INTRODUCTION

The combination of literature and the philosophy of education is a critical avenue of interpretation and analysis as articulated in Maxine Greene's *The Dialectic of Freedom* (1988). She argues that her frustration with "the notion of a finished, predetermined, objective reality" urged her towards an engagement "with multiple modes of interpretation, [and] with all that fed into interpretation from lived lives and sedimented meanings" (p. xii). More recently, Artiles (2011) has called for renewed interest in interdisciplinary approaches to educational research that focus on the underpinning justifications for practices of exclusion and inclusion. What follows spans the disciplines of education policy analysis, discourse theory, and tropology to examine a work of dystopian literature and suggests an avenue of analysis motivated by what I term a dyst(r)opian logic. I will highlight the genre of dystopian literature as both reliant upon, and disruptive to, the sedimented (and sedimenting) meanings produced

Dystopia and Education:
Insights Into Theory, Praxis, and Policy in an Age of Utopia-Gone-Wrong, pp. 51–67

through education policy discourse, that is, those meanings that become commonsensical through their repetition and duration both logically and practically. By taking a dystopian stance toward education policy discourse, I will argue, critics can consider policies and practices that serve to fragment or disintegrate the cohesion and naturalness of the inclusive and exclusive practices of a particular discourse.

This approach requires a number of novel moves to arrive at its final suggestion for what the dystopian genre offers to critiques of education policies and practices. In the following section, I will offer a framework that draws upon the field of tropology, particularly the tropes of synecdoche and irony, and situates dystopian literature as a middle ground that turns a systematized discourse into an object of reflection for interrogation and disintegration. In order to arrive at this point, I first pay some attention to discourse to describe synecdoche and irony as operations of discourse. I then offer a logic of dystopia through these tropes to highlight the transition between a discourse cemented by synecdoche and one disintegrated by irony. Situating dystopian literature within a tropological framework is a novel combination, and, as such, I forward the term dyst(r)opia to synthesize this arrangement conceptually.

With the tropological framework outlined, the second section provides a brief summary and analysis of Eugène Ionesco's play *Rhinoceros* (1960) as a quintessentially dystopian play that gives insight for the role of the dystopian genre in education policy analysis. While this play is read generally as a statement against totalitarianism and mass conformity, I examine the main protagonist's role not as a hero of individuality, but instead as the product of individualization. When understood in this light, *Rhinoceros* affirms the role of the individual outside of a discourse as produced by and constitutive to that discourse. In other words, whereas a discourse represents itself as unified according to a set of rules, practices, and ideas, it is only capable of accomplishing this appearance of unity through the identification of what exists outside of it. This becomes salient for analysis of education policy discourse in the context of exclusionary practices as extreme as school closures for failing to meet adequate yearly progress (AYP) or as common as current high-stakes standardized testing practices.

In order to bridge policy with dystopia, in the third section I attend to Foucault's (1995) claim that homogenization and individualization operate conjointly in the larger process of normalization. Where homogenization reconstitutes subjects into the larger whole, individualization isolates the parts of the whole, allowing for indices of normality and aberration often to the pathologization of the latter (pp. 193 & 199). Moreover, I will draw upon Ernesto Laclau (1996) to show that discourse bases inclusion upon exclusion. This entailment of exclusion with inclusion poses a problem for those who argue for a widening of inclusive practices and greater access to resources in education policy, namely, that a discourse requires the exclusion of some group, often as aberrant individuals, in order to include others. Reading *Rhinoceros* in this manner elicits the tactics of homogenization and individualization cooperating within a single discourse, one that adheres to the part/whole configuration of synecdoche. Following this reading, I take the No Child Left Behind Act of 2001 (NCLB) as an example of education policy discourse to argue that the practices of standardized testing and school sanctioning engendered by NCLB run parallel to two main themes in *Rhinoceros*: respectively, the homogenization of a townspeople into rhinoceroses and the individualization symbolized in the character of Berenger, the only person who remains unchanged by the end of the play. Rather than arguing for the heroism, or antiheroism, of Berenger's nonconformity, I fold his character into the discursive individualization that is a function of the very conformity he resists. In terms of NCLB, I argue that the double process of homogenization and individualization typified by standardized tests and school sanctioning requires that effective, specifically ironic, responses take place in terms that do not fall along the conformity/individuality dichotomy due to the organization and mastery of this dichotomy by NCLB. Finally, through a tropological framework, I suggest that the function of dystopian literature is particularly suited to describing and prescribing the transition between a totalizing discourse and its fragmentation and represents a tool for education critics to counter current practices and policy guidelines.

THE PLACE THAT TOOK A WRONG TURN: DYST(R)OPIA

Considerations of tropes are found predominantly in literary and rhetorical studies. In their most innocent guise, they are stylistic devices that add flourish and pizzazz to poetry, prose, and oratory. Etymologically, trope comes from the Greek *trepein* meaning "to turn." To trope something in this sense means to use a word or phrase in a figurative rather than literal way. While tropes have a long history as literary and rhetorical devices of style, my use of tropes in this chapter focuses on a particular philosophical treatment that highlights their sociopolitical dimensions. To this end, I align my use of tropes with the work of Giambattista Vico and Ernesto Laclau. Each of these philosophers reworks the role of tropes as a means of identifying social formations. For Vico (1948), the four master tropes—metaphor, metonymy, synecdoche, and irony—make up the "poetic logic," of his new science, that is, the framework for his philosophy of history according to which these four tropes structure the laws, actions, and individuals of a civilization over time. For instance, when irony is the primary structuring trope, philosophy makes its appearance in the history of a particular civilization, Vico claims, due to the reflection both irony and philosophy require (pp. 116-119).

For Laclau, tropes are figurative of discourses and their attendant socio-political consequences. Relying on Lacan's (2005) theory of the unconscious and Jakobson and Halle's (1956) two-fold tropology of metaphor and metonymy, Laclau bridges discourse and social movement theory. For instance, Laclau argues that the chaining together of demands performed by the members of a growing social movement is primarily a metonymic process. While each philosopher's use of tropes is different, even contradictory at points, they both contribute to a theory of tropology that pertains to sociopolitical phenomena—a pertinence foreign to more classical uses of tropes.

While there are manifold tropes within the Western literary and rhetorical tradition, I isolate synecdoche and irony as particularly salient to the structuring of the dystopian genre. Recalling trope's etymology, the tropes of synecdoche and irony are particular ways of "turning" language to mean something other than what the literal word entails. The trope of synecdoche turns by identifying a part with a whole or vice-versa. For example, when I refer to the ships in port as 30 sails, I am using a part of the ship, the sail, to stand for the whole ship. Differently, the trope of irony turns by disidentifying a term with itself. Irony can be expressed in the formula A is not A. Sarcasm is one example of this, for instance, saying it is very cold when it is, in fact, quite hot. Specifically, I use tropes here as devices which "turn" discourse. As a result my analysis entails the use of discursive synecdoche and discursive irony. While still adhering to the part-whole relationship and the A is not A formula, respectively, at the level of discourse tropes offer opportunities for analysis of the discursive moves and turns within texts such as education policy.

This approach insists that education policy is an exercise of discourse. There exists a small body of literature detailing the advantages gained when understanding policy as discourse (cf. Bacchi, 2000; Bowe, Ball, & Gold, 1992; Gale, 1999; Levinson, Sutton, & Winstead, 2009; Staton & Peeples, 2000). Rather than looking at policy as an unwavering set of rules to which its target populations adhere more or less effectively, policy as discourse manifests actors who engage in the formation of policy as well as those who interpret and implement policy, including those who are subject to it and, sometimes unwillingly or unwittingly, become actors in that discourse. Taken together, policy as discourse considers the production of policy texts with an emphasis on the constructed nature of the problems and solutions policy offers. By emphasizing the construction of problems and solutions, policymaking becomes an inventive exercise rather than a process of discovering problems that exist "out there" without regard to the policies that address them (Bacchi, 2000, p. 48). In other words, the problems and solutions identified by policy are produced by that policy thus constituting both the problem to be solved and its solution.

One difficulty this presents for critics is how to respond to the problems addressed by a policy when the policy has constructed the problem and already offered the solution. Once a critic adopts the problems constituted through policy, he or she is beholden to offer a solution to that problem that is somehow an improvement upon the solution offered by the policy. This causes the critic to perpetuate the discourse exemplified by the policy because the critic is taking up the problems that are the invention of that discourse to the exclusion of those contexts and concerns that fall outside of the focus of that discourse. For instance, Boyles, Carusi, and Attick (2009) emphasize the distinction between distributive and social justice to argue that teachers and researchers can use the concept of social justice to address oppressive relationships that distributive models, often perpetuated through education policy, do not recognize. They show that arguing for a more equitable distribution of resources across education institutions according to the paradigm of distributive justice fails to contest discourses that form and perpetuate the structural and normative logics underpinning practices of social oppression. The distributive justice approach misses the ways in which its paradigm, while useful in considering the allocation of property, cannot address the issues of justice surrounding practices such as recognition and self-respect.

In terms relevant to this chapter, when critics take up the problem of resource distribution, they accept and perpetuate a problem that state and local education agencies and policies produce, particularly in terms of what counts as resources. This is not to dismiss issues of distributive justice as irrelevant or unimportant, but to show the way in which critics can assail one practice as unjust, resource distribution, while perpetuating another practice, policies defining what counts as a resource, that supports that injustice. What remains, then, is to ask in what ways a discourse structures its problems and what critics can do to challenge the status of the problems that policy identifies without falling back into the terms defined by that discourse. I contend that one of the primary ways in which a discourse constitutes its problems is through the deployment of tropes that operate according to different logics with different effects. In particular, this chapter looks at the contrasting logics and effects of synecdoche and irony at the level of discourse.

Discursive tropes organize strategic conceptualizations of reality. For discursive synecdoche, some discourse represents the whole, neoliberalism for instance, and the parts include the institutions and agents who participate, willingly or not, as the instruments of the discourse: schools, teachers, and students, for example. The discursive strategy embedded in this exercise of synecdoche, then, is to represent schools, teachers, and students as constitutive, even natural, parts of neoliberal discourse. Alternatively, discursive irony functions by disintegrating the cohesive unity of a discourse by turning A (the discourse) into not A. Taken together, discursive synecdoche works to establish, maintain, and propagate a discourse's organization by folding in more and more parts to the whole represented by that discourse, and discursive irony fragments a discourse's synecdochic integrity by disidentifying a discourse with itself, that is, by representing the discourse as something other than itself and what it promises.

Consider the transition in federal education policy discourse from the Elementary and Secondary Education Act of 1965 (ESEA) to the Reagan administration report A Nation at Risk (ANR). The former, a centerpiece of Lyndon Johnson's War on Poverty, conceives of education as remedial to economic inequalities; the latter argues for education as a primary determinant of the United States' standing in a globally competitive economic market. While both operate within an economic discourse, ESEA premises its actions on the concept of equalization of economic disparities between students, and ANR on the concept of economic competition.[1] One could approach these texts comparatively to point out a historical and discursive shift from education as remedial to economic inequality to education as a process for separating economic winners from losers. However, this approach overlooks the particular operations through which such a shift occurs, operations that a tropological approach elicits. In other words, the comparative approach can show us the beginning and end of a discursive shift, the A and B term, so to speak, but nothing of the in between, i.e., the pathways along which the shift occurs. Differently, a tropological approach can isolate those operations that move between the terms of the analysis that yield a discursive shift manifesting the pathways along which one discourse moves toward, away from, and into another discourse to various effect.

As a brief illustration of what a tropological analysis can offer, recall the "rising tide of mediocrity" ANR cautioned the American public about in 1983 (National Commission on Excellence in Education, 1983, p. 5). This maritime warning pertained to "all students, whether they are gifted or less able, affluent or disadvantaged, whether destined for college, the farm, or industry" (p. 37). Read as a statement of discursive irony, the populations that appear in the latter part of the comparisons are those singled out by Lyndon Johnson's "Great Society" and his ESEA of 1965. ANR is identifying a prior discourse, the discourse of the Great Society, and disintegrating its cohesiveness by emphasizing that the population the Great Society was supposed to help, in fact, has not been helped. In other words and ironically, the Great Society is not so great after all.

What, then, can dystopian literature offer those of us disciplined in philosophy of education given this brief sketch of discursive tropes? From the Greek, "dys" means bad or abnormal and "topia" comes from "topos" meaning place. Dystopia is a bad place—a place that took a wrong turn. It is in this manner that dystopia becomes dyst(r)opia. In one moment dyst(r)opia, recalling Greene, draws upon a sedimentation, requiring that its audience recognize and identify with the depiction of society it provides—synecdochically, the parts and whole must be familiar. However, a turn must take place, and a bad one at that. In a second moment dyst(r)opia projects that society into a future that, while adhering to its own rules, holds repressive and dehumanizing consequences, a projection that operates through discursive irony—the utopia promised by a discourse is not a utopia. Orwell's *1984* (1949/1983) is so salient because of how much it reminds us of our increasingly surveillable existence. The hyperbolized systematization of Huxley's *A Brave New World* (1932/2006), the despondent isolation of DeLillo's *White Noise* (1986), and, in the case that follows, the bestial conformity of *Rhinoceros* each in their own way both reflects what we are and projects what we can become. It is this middle passage, between what is and what might be, identity and projection, unity and fragmentation, synecdoche and irony, that dyst(r)opia is situated.

Dyst(r)opia, then, relies on an already extant system; one which I argue systematizes itself through discursive synecdoche—mapping its wholeness onto more and more parts. Constructing a dyst(r)opia simultaneously describes and prescribes reality in ways that urge alternative ways of living, knowing, and interacting. And this, I argue, is one value of dyst(r)opia for philosophical and discursive considerations of education policy. When creating dyst(r)opian visions of education in ways that persuasively describe and prescribe, critics may approach particular policy texts in at least two ways. First, they may analyze policy texts to elicit the ways in which shifts in particular discourses construct and are constructed by policy. Second, critics may work strategically to ironize the already synecdochized discourse present in the institutions and practices of public education and reflect the limits of that discourse. With this in mind, I now turn to an analysis of *Rhinoceros* through Foucault's (1995) notion of normalization in order to sketch a dyst(r)opia of education under NCLB.

TO RHINO OR NOT TO RHINO[2]

"Blue sky; harsh light; very white walls. The time is almost mid-day on a Sunday afternoon in summertime" (Ionesco, 1960, p. 4). The protagonist Berenger is late to meet his friend Jean at the café. Jean, who is a deontological paragon, proceeds to berate his hung over friend for his disheveled appearance, lack of willpower, and misguided sense of duty. Berenger wants a drink. A scuffling noise comes faintly from offstage. The noise grows louder until the conversation between Jean and Berenger is inaudible. Jean, always the categorical one, jumps from his seat and is the first to exclaim "Oh, a rhinoceros!" Then, in rapid succession the surrounding town square dwellers exclaim the same. Berenger remains visibly unperturbed. This phenomenon of a rhinoceros running through the town occurs several more times to the townspeople's dismay. Trying to find answers to explain such a monstrous event, a group of actors converge on stage. There is the Old Gentleman, the Logician, the Grocer and the Grocer's Wife, the Proprietor of the café, and several others, including Jean and Berenger. Jean is excited by the appearance of the rhinoceros and chiding Berenger for not being likewise impressed. He says, "But you must see it's fantastic! A rhinoceros loose in the town, and you don't bat an eyelid! It shouldn't be allowed!" (p. 13).

As the play progresses another rhinoceros runs across stage. A large cloud of dust blows across the scene and the scuttlebutt recommences with most people figuring this rhinoceros was the same one as before. Jean, however, knows better. He impresses upon his fellow citizens the difference between the first rhinoceros, an Asiatic, two-horned, rhinoceros, and the second, an African, one-horned rhinoceros. Berenger argues that there is no way Jean could have detected a difference in such a quick scene, and the conversation among all the performers shifts toward questioning whether it is in fact the Asiatic that has two horns and the African one, or the other way around. The Logician helps square the terms of the debate for everyone until the question being asked is sufficiently logical. Upon the proper formulation of the question, the Logician quickly exits the stage, the townspeople are left to hold the debate, and Act I ends.

While not quite yet dyst(r)opian, this first act is somewhat humorous and pleasingly recognizable. The straightman/oddball dualism between Jean and Berenger saturates popular media narratives allowing the members of the audience to identify themselves through their familiarity with that narrative. Ionesco presents readers with qualities in the exchanges between the aloof Berenger, the eager mob, and the authoritative Jean that are commonplace. This is the point, at least initially. The construction of a dyst(r)opia must first align itself with that which the audience is already familiar. It must seduce its reader to say, "your situation is not so different from this." Thus with Act I, readers are so beckoned.

Act II represents the transitional act where readers are once again placed in a familiar situation, the office, and introduced to the vehicle through which the bad turn of dyst(r)opia takes place. Berenger arrives late to work and enters in the middle of an ongoing conversation among his workmates about the recent rhinoceros sightings. In many ways the characters and their dialogue mirror the characters of Act I's townspeople so I will jump to the critical moment of the rhinoceros's appearance in the office. Again, a scuffling is heard, this time upon the heels of Mrs. Boeuf's entrance into the office. She complains of a rhinoceros following her to work. A loud trumpeting is heard by the workers, and they all rush to the stairs, which have been destroyed, to see a rhinoceros plowing through their lobby. While the workers are dealing with their own surprise according to their character, Mrs. Boeuf lets out a "terrible cry" and identifies the rhinoceros as her husband, Mr. Boeuf. It seems there is a rhinovirus that has begun to spread through the town turning people into rhinoceroses. Mrs. Boeuf pledges her love to Mr. Boeuf and jumps down to be with him, riding on his grey-skinned back offstage, presumably to become a rhinoceros herself. In the next scene a similar transformation takes place. Berenger calls upon Jean at his apartment to apologize for his behavior the other day. Jean admits him and tells Berenger that he is not feeling well. As the scene progresses, Jean changes both his opinion of rhinoceroses relative to humans and his appearance from a human into a rhinoceros.

By reading Jean's role as a categorical critic of the Kantian ilk from his very first line of dialogue up to this moment, his character represents a critic whose own discourse is shaped by and operates within an already established discursive set of rules, namely, the rules of Enlightenment Reason as idealized in Kant's *Critique of Pure Reason* (1781/2003), and shows the consequences of his immersion within that discourse. In other words, as Jean deduces the logic of being a rhinoceros (rhinontology?), his transubstantiation into a rhinoceros becomes a categorical imperative.

Act III makes this transition more explicit through the character of Dudard who comes to visit Berenger at his apartment. Dudard, according to Berenger, has several diplomas and recommends Berenger "must learn to be more detached, and try and see the funny side of things" (Ionesco, 1960, p. 78). Dudard begins this act as diffusive to Berenger's outbursts, telling him that he worries too much, that, with time, he will get used to it, and so on. While Dudard initially insists that he values his humanity over the potential to be a rhinoceros, as he and Berenger recognize more and more people who have "turned," his resolve weakens in seeing those he respects as rhinoceroses. Eventually Dudard reasons that he cannot justifiably evaluate the question of being a rhinoceros without being one himself. As he leaves the apartment, he transforms into one. Berenger is left in his apartment with his newfound love Daisy, who eventually becomes a rhinoceros as well. Left all alone, Berenger performs his concluding monologue with the realization that he is now the monster and is disgusted by his sagging skin and hornlessness. He declares, "people who hang on to their individuality always come to a bad end." And in a final statement of resistance says, "I'm the last man left, and I'm staying that way until the end. I'm not capitulating!" (p. 107).

Ionesco's readers are left with a vision of a society that has conformed to what was initially considered a monstrosity. Berenger remains as the last human, the individual who refused to give in to the "rhinocefication" of humanity. Along the lines of a tropological reading of dystopian literature, this last act projects a future world in which rhinoceroses are the norm and those who resist are, ironically, monstrous precisely because of their humanness. Many critics of the play analyze its content as a testament to nonconformity though there is debate as to whether Berenger is to be read as a hero, antihero, or even villain (Brustein, 1961; Clurman, 1961; Davies, 2002; Howe, 2004). These readings, however, maintain a split between Berenger and the rest of the characters in the play. This is not the reading I provide. I read *Rhinoceros* as purely dystopian in that the resistance offered by Berenger is not one that extricates him from the problematic of conformity, but instead reinscribes him into a position of alienation upon which the larger system of conformity and individuality is founded. In other words, Berenger's refusal to capitulate, rather than excluding him *from* the system, excludes him *as a part of* the system—as the individual. Furthermore, by understanding conformity and individuality as two sides of the same coin, critics of a system that establishes such a dichotomy must locate disruptive strategies outside of this binary, or else have their criticism folded back in to the system they seek to escape.

THE CONSTITUTIVE GROUND OF EXCLUSION

I liken this system that houses the binary of conformity and individuality to Michel Foucault's notion of normalization. In *Discipline and Punish*, Foucault (1995) claims that, "the power of normalization imposes homogeneity; but it individualizes by making it possible to measure gaps, to determine levels, to fix specialties and to render the differences useful by fitting them one to another" (p. 184). In effect, normalization utilizes the techniques of homogenization and individualization to create the broader normative system. We are given this process at its most basic by Ionesco. In his dystopia, one is either a rhinoceros, homogenous up to the horn, or a Berenger, individualized at the other side of the gap. The differences between the rhinoceros and Berenger are clear, which is to say they are not clear at all; as the rhino becomes the central referent in the play, Berenger becomes more and more a failed rhino. By the end of the play Berenger's character is incapable of identifying himself as anything other than not a rhino, that is, his exclusion from rhinoceros status constitutes the rules of inclusion. In his final monologue, Berenger begins to examine himself in the mirror lamenting, "I haven't got any horns.... A smooth brow looks so ugly. I need one or two horns to give my sagging face a lift. Perhaps one will grow and I needn't be ashamed any more" (Ionesco, 1960, pp. 106-107) and proceeds to imitate rhinoceros sounds. He is individualized as *the* individual; however, his individuality is the point upon which conformity is founded.

Of interest to this chapter, then, is the seemingly contradictory concept that a system, a discourse in this case, bases its inclusion upon exclusion. That is to say, there is an apparent contradiction when claiming that the homogeneity of the rhinoceroses founds itself upon the individuality of Berenger; that what something *is* produced by what it *is not*. However, this is the claim of contemporary discourse theory: it is exclusion that constitutes the foundation for what a discourse includes. As Laclau (1996) explains, "if the systematicity of the system is a direct result of the exclusionary limit, it is only that exclusion which grounds the system as such" (p. 38). In order for a discourse to be a discourse, to establish those parts that belong, a founding gesture of exclusion must take place. Extending from Saussurean linguistics, Laclau's theory emphasizes that a discourse must first articulate what it is not and, through that exclusion, is capable of constituting its ground for further articulation of what it is. For a critic of a particular discourse, then, what a discourse is, what it includes, is as important to its constitution as what it is not, what it excludes. As such, the individual Berenger, that single human who is not a rhinoceros, is the ground upon which the discourse of the rhino builds itself. Berenger is as much a constitutive element of the discourse as the rhinoceroses and, as such, does not stand outside of the discourse as a hero or anti-hero, but as that exclusionary limit upon which a discourse bases itself. Rendering exclusion as the constitutive ground for a discourse, and reading Berenger's role as the firmament for that constitution, the following section analyzes NCLB as an articulation of education policy discourse that includes and excludes with the effect of producing a binary of individuality and homogeneity that constitutes the problems it addresses. Additionally, as discussed above, criticism that falls within that binary, to the favor of one or the other, risks perpetuating the very discourse it seeks to critique by offering new solutions that do nothing to question the normative system based on and invented by that discourse.

THE NCLB DEADLOCK

Foucault renders normalization as a two-part process whereby homogenization and individualization function in tandem, and, I argue, provides a framework for understanding education policy in a dyst(r)opian context.

In *Rhinoceros,* the individual, Berenger, is the relief out of which the normalized template, the rhinoceros, emanates and homogenization operates. *Mutatis mutandis,* schools undergoing the sanctioning mandates of NCLB constitute the ground from which the normalized template of schools emanates and homogenization operates. To arrive at this claim, I will briefly summarize the salient features of NCLB; offer an example of how a critical intervention may perpetuate that which it critiques in this policy; and, finally, elicit some of the discursive operations of NCLB through a dyst(r)opian analysis. Briefly, NCLB establishes an accountability system according to which students' test scores determine whether or not a school is performing its duties as an institution of education. NCLB requires that states implement a measure of schools' progress to proficiency, referred to as AYP, in the subject areas of mathematics and reading. Schools that continually fail to meet their AYP metric undergo a series of sanctions that increase in severity over time, resulting finally in restructuring which includes the dismissal of school staff and the closure of the school. According to the U.S. Department of Education, there were 5,776 schools in this final stage for the 2009-10 school year. This represents an increase of more than sixty percent from the 2007-08 school year (Hoff, 2008). Furthermore, Ravitch (2010) argues this trend will continue primarily because of how individual states structure AYP.

One approach to this trend of states sanctioning schools could be to focus on the "worst" schools and, rather than closing their doors to students, trying novel interventions that will turn schools around and increase test scores. However, such an approach exhibits the difficulties outlined above, namely, the discourse of NCLB has invented the problem of the "worst" schools and part of that invention is to use the test score-based AYP metric as proof of the problem. Interventions that seek to "improve" schools and look to rising test scores as evidence of their success ultimately perpetuate the discourse of NCLB by continuing to rely on AYP and test scores as the measure of a school's success.

A dyst(r)opian analysis takes a different approach, one which focuses on the rules of the discourse that foster the larger normative system into which schools fit and policy articulates. This analysis claims that failing schools are necessary "Berengers" for the schooling structures to sustain their normalizing practices upon mainstream students. More bluntly, in order for education policy to prove that it is working, some schools must fail. The logic that some schools must fail in order for others to remain in operation finds its support in the discourse of neoliberal economic theory as represented in the work of Hayek (1944) and Friedman (1962) and the accountability systems borrowed from business and applied wholesale to public education in NCLB (Betebenner & Howe, 2005; Haertel & Herman, 2005). There exists a body of research that ties current trends in education policy discourse to neoliberal economic theory, some favorably and others critically (Apple, 2004; Boyles, 2000; Chubb & Moe, 1990; Hess, 2010; Hursh, 2007; Whitty & Power, 2000). That the success of some schools requires the failure of others requires supplementary logics wrapped up in the discourse of free market competition and meritocracy; in order for there to be a competition, there must be winners and losers, and policy can codify that distinction based on test scores which represent the merit of student work.

As an example of Foucauldian normalization in schools, consider the link between standardized testing and school sanctioning mandated by NCLB. For standardized testing to operate successfully—that is, to indicate educational progress (AYP) and point to impediments to that progress—the test scores that it yields must be placed into a meaningful context, and, in the case of NCLB, that context is the ability to determine the success or failure of a school and apply the appropriate sanctions. Schools undergoing the sanctioning processes are individualized according to the duration of their inability to meet AYP, and each sanction provides a menu of choices: parents may choose other schools; administrators and parents may choose from a variety of supplementary educational services; and, local educational agencies may choose from a number of "restructuring" plans. All of these sanctions make possible a multiplicity of combinations and permutations of reform to change individual schools according to the particular contexts of that specific school. What, then, about the other schools that succeed in meeting their AYP metric? At the level of NCLB, these schools make up a homogenous pool of successful schools. The policy is silent on these schools other than to say that all our schools should meet AYP. This is not to say there is no difference between schools meeting AYP, but, when analyzed at the level of federal education policy discourse as articulated in NCLB, the policy's silence on these schools affords them a normal status. Said differently, as long as schools are meeting AYP, they will continue to receive funds appropriated under NCLB without discrimination, that is, homogenously.

Because of the reliance of normalization on both homogenization and individualization, efforts to resist one in favor of the other, ironically, serves to bolster both. In other words, the dichotomy of normalization that NCLB engenders is recursively self-sustaining. The more one attacks the homogeneity of schooling and supports more individualizing strategies, or vice versa, the stronger both become and, as a result, the less anything other than this dichotomy is attainable, much less imaginable. This, then, is the process whereby sedimentation occurs; where the processes of homogenization and individualization, contradictory yet in support of one another, provide normalization and systematization through their mutual support of one another, that is, their recursivity. And this is precisely the work of discursive synecdoche. Students, teachers, and schools under NCLB are parts brought into the policy's totalizing discourse of accountability, measurability, and competition that culminates in an overall definition of what schooling *is*. The more these individuals and institutions perform according to the rules of this discourse, the more sedimented these practices become, not only through their historical and habitual inertia, but also through the fixity of meaning this produces to the exclusion of alternative concepts of schooling.

DYST(R)OPIAN POLICY ANALYSIS

With this depiction of the deadlock into which education policy currently situates schools and students, the question comes, what to do? If education policy has fixed the meaning of schooling into an ossified binary between uniformity and individuality, then what other avenues are available to those of us concerned with articulating a policy climate geared towards accepting broader sets of questions in the formulation of policy? This, I argue, is where dyst(r)opian renderings and disintegrations of such deadlocks come into play. While there are a number of phenomena that point to the failures of the system NCLB propagates and maintains (for instance, "zero-tolerance" policies, the correlation between test scores and socioeconomic status, and the overrepresentation of African-American males in special education classes, to name three), these phenomena are primarily used only as direct critiques of NCLB. While this is certainly an important avenue of redress, the deadlock of uniformity and individuality goes unnoticed in such critiques. Consequently, the solutions in response to critiques risk being folded back into the larger normative discourse that produces the problems in the first place.

What a dyst(r)opian project adds to these critiques is, first, an emphasis on the seduction of the world NCLB has made familiar, that is, its synecdochic normalization; and second, the ironic turn that disintegrates the world that NCLB promises, a world without an achievement gap. In other words, rather than seeking individual redress from a system, a dyst(r)opian approach emphasizes ironically the impossibility for a system to be a system; the issues named above cannot be addressed by the system because it is inherent in the system's success. This is not to say that dyst(r)opian projects alone will bring about the sort of change in education policy for which many philosophers of education argue. However, it does offer a different tack, through the use of the genre of dystopian literature, to highlight alternative approaches to the criticisms that have yet to bring about change in education policies.

By taking into account modern dystopian literature, such as *Rhinoceros*, in educational contexts, philosophers of education can employ a critical narrative that both encapsulates the system in its synecdochic homogeneity (unity) and depicts avenues of resistance that irony (fragmentation and disintegration) provokes. As education scholars practicing philosophy, we are in a position to create such synechdochic/ironic narratives at least to the degree that Greene sought the processes of sedimentation by turning to literature. Dyst(r)opias not only offer a salient depiction of a system as it currently stands, but also counter-narratives that fragment and disintegrate the sedimentation such systems enforce.

NOTES

1. This is not to valorize ESEA over ANR or vice-versa, but to point out how texts relate discursively through their different sets of assumptions which yield different rules for what is central and worthy of policy attention and what is peripheral to that attention. For an excellent treatment of the ways in which the U.S. government discursively constructed "poverty" and "the poor" in the authoring and implementation of ESEA, see Sandra Stein's *The Culture of Education Policy* (2004).
2. Due to the relative unfamiliarity of *Rhinoceros* to the field of education, I offer material from the play sufficient to acquaint the reader with its general outline in addition to a tropological analysis of the play.

REFERENCES

Apple, M. W. (2004). Creating difference: Neo-liberalism, neo-conservatism and the politics of educational reform," *Educational Policy, 18*(1), 12-44.

Artiles, A. J. (2011). Toward an interdisciplinary understanding of educational equity and difference: The case of the racialization of ability. *Educational Researcher, 40*, 431-445.

Betebenner, D., & Howe, K. (2005). On school choice and test-based accountability, *Education Policy Analysis Archives, 13*(41), 1-22.

Boyles, D. (2000). *American education and corporations: The free market goes to school.* New York, NY: Falmer Press.

Boyles, D., Carusi, F. T., & Attick, D. (2009). Historical and critical interpretations of social justice. In W. Ayers, T. Quinn, & D. Stovall (Eds.), *Handbook of social justice in education* (pp. 30-42). New York, NY: Routledge.

Bacchi, C. (2000). Policy as discourse: What does it mean? Where does it get us? *Discourse: Studies in the Cultural Politics of Education, 21*(1), 45-57.

Bowe, R., Ball, S. J., & Gold, A. (1992). *Reforming education and changing schools: Case studies in policy sociology.* New York, NY: Routledge.

Brustein, R. (1961). The enormous sum of zero. *New Republic, 144*(5), 22-23.

Chubb, J., & Moe, T. (1990). *Politics, markets, and America's schools*. Washington, DC: Brookings Institution Press.

Clurman, H. (1961). Theatre. *Nation, 192*(4), 85.

Davies, T. W. (2002). Rhinoceros [Theatrical production]. *Theatre Journal, 54*(4), 645.

DeLillo, D. (1986). *White noise*. New York, NY: Penguin Books.

Friedman, M. (1962). *Capitalism and freedom*. Chicago, IL: The University of Chicago Press.

Foucault, M. (1995). *Discipline and punish: The birth of the prison* (A. Sheridan, Trans.). New York, NY: Vintage Books.

Gale, T. (1999). Policy trajectories: Treading the discursive path of policy analysis. *Discourse: Studies in the Cultural Politics of Education 20*(3), 393-407.

Greene, M. (1988). *The dialectic of freedom*. New York, NY: Teachers College Press.

Haertel, E., & Herman, J. (2005). *A historical perspective on validity arguments for accountability testing*. Los Angeles, CA: National Center for Research on Evaluation, Standards, and Student Testing.

Hayek, F. A. (1944). *The road to serfdom*. New York, NY: Routledge.

Hess, F. (2010). Does school "choice" work? *National Affairs, 5*(Fall), 35-53.

Hoff, D. (2008, December 18). Schools struggling to meet key goal on accountability. *Education Week*. Retrieved from http://www.edweek.org/ew/articles/2008/12/18/16ayp.h28.html.

Howe, T. (2004). Ionesco and me. *American Theatre, 21*(7), 30-32.

Hursh, D. (2007). Assessing No Child Left Behind and the rise of neoliberal education policies, *American Educational Research Journal, 44*(3), 493-518.

Huxley, A. (1932/2006). *A brave new world*. New York, NY: HarperCollins.

Ionesco, E. (1960). *Rhinoceros and other plays*. (D. Prouse, Trans.). New York, NY: Grove Press.

Jakobson, R., & Halle, M. (1956). *Fundamentals of language*. The Hague, The Netherlands: Mouton.

Kant, I. (2003). *Critique of pure reason* (rev. 2nd ed.). (N. K. Smith, Trans.). London, England: Palgrave Macmillan. (Original work published 1781)

Lacan, J. (2005). The instance of the letter in the unconscious, or reason since Freud. In Ècrits (pp. 412-444). (B. Fink, Trans.). New York, NY: W.W. Norton.

Laclau, E. (1996). *Emancipation(s)*. London: Verso.

Laclau, E. (2005). *On populist reason*. London: Verso.

Levinson, B. A., Sutton, M., & Winstead, T. (2009) Education policy as a practice of power. *Educational Policy, 23*(6), 767-795.

National Commission on Excellence in Education. (1983). *A nation at risk: The imperative for educational reform*. Washington, D.C.: U.S. Government Printing Office.

Orwell, G. (1983). *1984*. London, England: Penguin Group. (Original work published 1949)

Ravitch, D. (2010). *The Death and life of the great American school system: how testing and choice are undermining education*. New York, NY: Basic Books.

Staton, A. Q., & Peeples, J.A. (2000). Educational reform discourse: President George Bush on "America 2000." *Communication Education, 49*(4), 303-319.

Stein, S. (2004). *The culture of education policy.* New York, NY: Teachers College Press.

U.S. Department of Education. National Snapshot. (2009-2010). Retrieved from http://www. eddataexpress.ed.gov/state-report.cfm?state=US

Vico, G. (1948). *The new science of Giambattista Vico* (T. Bergin & M. Fisch, Trans.). Ithaca, NY: Cornell University Press.

Whitty, G., & Power, S. (2000). Marketization and privatization in mass education systems, *International journal of educational development, 20*(2), 93-107.

CHAPTER 5

TESTS, CONSUMERISM, AND THE CRUEL DRONE OF *WHITE NOISE*

Andrew N. McKnight

INTRODUCTION

What follows looks at current educational policy specifically with regard to how high stakes tests and the public reporting of scores has added to the commoditization of public schools. Pursuant to this analysis, this chapter deploys a few vignettes from Don DeLillo's (1985) dystopian novel, *White Noise*, along with theoretical counterpoint mostly provided by critical theorist and psychoanalyst Erich Fromm, to illustrate educational policy and practice within larger social contexts. Specifically, I will address Fromm's (1981) concept of *homo consumens*, or the pattern of how our society has shaped us into humans whose primary purpose is to consume and who thus look at most things through the filter of whether something advances us in our pursuit of the objective and the material rather than the interpersonal. In the present context American schools have certainly become a commodity with reference to grades, various test scores, and what privileges these may bestow on the successful as related to individual mobility and to relative perceived prestige of the schools in question.

Dystopia and Education:
Insights Into Theory, Praxis, and Policy in an Age of Utopia-Gone-Wrong, pp. 69–80

The parallels with *White Noise* come with a comparison of how one of the characters, Babette, becomes so beholden to a belief in a particular nostrum's capacity to maintain mental health that her attachment in the end makes her do things that are both physically and interpersonally objectifying. Our obsession with scores and school prestige and related rankings and real estate values similarly precludes us from thinking about the public good of education as connecting us to the larger human community. This positions schools, and the success of the students therein, as a commodity fetish. I, however, would be remiss if I did not acknowledge that there are legitimate concerns to be had with the quality of schools, for example, instructional resources, adequate staffing in numbers and in quality, violence, and other cultural attitudes and practices that affect how young people encounter school.

White Noise provides a good canvas for analysis in that it explores some familiar dystopian themes, and presents them against the backdrop of a bleak, socially alienated—yet socially stable—landscape. The characters are middle class and not at all in want of the basic necessities or comforts of life. Their troubles are entirely socially and psychologically created against a vista of consumerism, mass media, and technology. It is in this confluence where *White Noise* helps to provide context for why so many parents in the United States tacitly support aspects of present education policy that cause their children emotional and intellectual harm. This is not the sweeping dystopia of Zamyatin (1972/1999), Huxley (1932), or Orwell (1949), but closer to the steady hum of a cynical and alienated culture of consumer-technology on autopilot. This is their white noise, found in the day to day mundanity of their lives, yet with certain facets of the human condition always looming in the background. It is something so embedded within the characters' consciousness that even having to flee an "airborne toxic event" in the middle of the novel does not fundamentally alter the fear of death they already had or disrupt the lives they led (pp. 109-163). These habituations are the extra-rational sides of consciousness (e.g., fear, doubt, regret, sadness) that even traumatic events cannot dislodge. My connection of this to educational policy lies in what potentially destructive policies find support, not because of evidence and logic or ethics, but because they touch the bottom flares of our raw emotionality and are congruent with our learned behavior.

Using Fromm's (1990), some might say deterministic, idea of normative humanism as a set of general ideas concerning what is "conducive to health and happiness," I will construct a criticism of the present set of circumstances and will discuss alternative narratives that might yield a more humane intersubjective form for public education, one that does not force parents and children into unhealthy and ultimately objectifying relationships (p.14). This chapter follows the trajectory of our historical faith in tests which are now explicitly tied to corporate production models; how these tests drive fears and aspirations among parents; and, the personal and social sacrifices that result.

FAITH IN TESTING

Faith has proved an interesting phenomenon in the history of human society. It has variously given people personal solace, brought groups together in fellowship around shared moral beliefs and spiritual rituals, acted as a surrogate for cosmology in prescientific times, and also manipulated people into ignorance, hatred, discrimination, war, and servitude: a mixed bag, if we are honest. Faith also operates at the level of secular civil society reflected in our beliefs about capitalism, democracy, science, and how we conceive public education—what is taught to whom, how it is taught, and how it is determined whether knowledge has been acquired. This leads us to one of the more dominant of American faith systems, namely our belief that attaching a number to something somehow makes it more meaningful or true.

Through its birth in the 19th century and aggressive expansion in the 1920s within the context of public schooling (Rugg, 1941) famously referred to this period as an "orgy of tabulation," mass scale quantitative assessment has become a perennial mainstay of our educational policy and practice (p. 182). What I find perplexing is that on the one hand most people see tests as routinized tasks, part of the ritual of schooling connected to competition for grades, class rank, grade promotion, for example, and not necessarily connected to what we actually know and can do. When I ask my students, for instance, if they have ever crammed for a test only to have not the foggiest recollection of the material two weeks later, the overwhelming answer is in the affirmative. They then usually go on to say that what they really know is usually engendered by "hands on" activity, out of personal interest, or connection to a family member or some other sort of mentor. On the other hand, they actively or tacitly support political figures who equate high test scores with what will make us economically competitive, and posit that tests are how we will hold teachers and students accountable to the general public for their performance, their merit. They are also quite deferent to the authority of psychometrics as a somewhat mystical expert culture. So it seems intuitively for most that rote methods are not how we learn and that tests do not necessarily correspond to actual knowledge, but that this is not enough cause for us to challenge their actual use in measuring knowledge and, let us be truthful, determining real estate values and making certain publishing companies a lot of money. There is also a seeming suspension of criticality concerning ramifications, such as real pedagogical inefficiency, ineffectiveness, and irrelevance, not to mention the emotional toll the testing regime takes on students and teachers.

Apparently missing among many who either actively or passively support current testing practice is an aforementioned criticality about the linear relationship between means and ends. Put another way, does the means of instruction that supports mass scale quantitative testing lead to what we would hope constitutes knowledge. Being more philosophically pragmatic, I tend to find practical everyday truth as being in the pudding, so to speak. If you know how to make an omelet, depending on what we determine the constituents of an omelet to be, and the omelet you make me meets the latter criteria, then your truth claim is borne out. If correct ingredients are properly cooked and seasoned, I will gladly eat the omelet. Experimental science finds its truth (lower case "t") in the result—in what the data reliably reveals about our natural universe. It may lead to complications, further questions, uncertainties, and complexities, but it is deemed to be true within a given parameter concerning probability, and through its continual confirmation. The remaining determination concerns whether we have produced an omelet of knowledge or something less intellectually healthy.

The question at hand is whether subject-specific multiple choice tests reflect anything more than an ancillary byproduct of applicable knowledge, knowledge in use gained through inquiry and activity, or if it is related to something else, like specific preparation for the test itself. It follows that the possibility is one can know something, and pass a quantitative test, if the test is sufficiently related to the knowledge in question. It is also possible that one might not pass the test because the experience of a pen and paper test is sufficiently divorced from the actual activity in question as to be cognitively incongruent. Third and fourth possibilities include that a student passes a test due to the specific type of preparation, for example, via short term memory acquisition, or that the student fails due to a true lack of knowledge either as defined by the aforementioned memory acquisition or actual applied knowledge. A final possibility is that a student fails due either to cognitive incompatibility with the quantitative measure itself, or to emotional reaction to the testing process (e.g., fear, anxiety, apathy, anger, etc.).

The problem is that the social scientists who propagate the various systems of testing cannot give an adequate quod erat demonstrandum concerning the connections of these tests to actual knowledge in a lived projection, hence the faith system. Although our intuition and experience may tell us one thing about the validity of such measurements, we still prop up the practice without the benefit of any evidence concerning the relationship between the methods deployed to pass these tests, the validity of the tests themselves as measures of knowledge, and the connection of each of the former to a demonstrable knowledge. For instance, there is no evidence, isolated from the massive static of other factors like general life experience and organized experimental activity, that those who pass these tests can then go out and apply the material to an extant field of inquiry or problem. There is also no evidence to suggest that those who pass these tests could do so a year later, or a decade later, begging a serious question about the nature of what passes for knowledge. What is not in debate are the effects that this faith, oblique as it is from rationality, has on where we live, what we value, and what we sacrifice in the service of other masters.

CONSUMERISM AS MASTER

It is hard for me to come to any other conclusion than that the dominant American religion is consumerism—what we are truly devoted and beholden to and by which we are subjugated. A standard neo-Marxist interpretation of our consumerist context is that while capitalism was originally designed to monitor production, it eventually had to create demand in response to a surplus of non-necessary goods brought about by the advent of technology and greater efficiency, and subsequent increases in production. Greater consumption, with demand created through advertising and other forms of manipulation, such as tying the health of the nation state to ever increasing accumulation of things, gradually became our dominant expression of self and its desires. Fromm (1981) termed this new breed of human *homo consumens*; or in plain English, the human who consumes:

> *Homo consumens* is the man [sic] whose main goal is not primarily to *own* things, but to consume more and more, and thus to compensate for his inner vacuity, passivity, loneliness, and anxiety. In a society characterized by giant enterprises and giant industrial, governmental and labor bureaucracies, the individual, who has no control over his circumstances of work feels impotent, lonely, bored, and anxious. At the same time, the need for profit of the big consumer industries, through the medium of advertising, transforms him into a voracious man, an eternal suckling who wants to consume more and more and for whom everything becomes an article of consumption—cigarettes, liquor, sex, movies, television, travel, and even education, books, and lectures. New artificial needs are created and man's tastes are manipulated. (p. 32)

Parents, and the fear implanted concerning their children's relative competitiveness, represent one of the most primal sites for this kind of manipulation. Simply put, if you do not consume completely and wisely, your children will not become the workplace commodities they need to be in order to successfully "consume." This is no more evident in how the previously discussed faith in test scores drives real estate markets. This works in tandem with an internalized idea that working hard and being financially successful means that your children deserve a more advantageous and a more richly resourced public education.

Additionally, the ideology of meritocracy, divorced from actual property and cultural inheritance and tied to certain religious beliefs connected to notions of predestination, grace, or divine intervention for the worthy among us, makes it conceptually difficult to blame the wealthy and the powerful for their success. Individual success is also divorced from others' relative economic poverty, but instead attributed to the latter's lack of industriousness or providence. The possibility of wealth, even if there is extremely limited access to opportunity, to cultural and monetary capital, justifies the system as fair. Conversely, to complain is to admit either one's failure or one's weakness. In one way this is a kind of machismo, or the irrational belief that a person's honor is not measured by his or her connection to a given community, but by their assertion of individualistic aggression without moral context or rational consistency. The cult of the individual prevents the realization of a common powerlessness. Former Republican Senator Phil Graham of Texas stated with reference to Bush's tax cuts that "the last form of bigotry acceptable in this country is bigotry to the successful" (Kessler, 2001). Any other position violates the primacy and moral rectitude of wealth and what it allows us to consume. Perhaps the most pernicious aspect of this for our schools and students is the persistent ideology of the bootstrap and its punitive implications: the myth of upward mobility based on merit and the punishment of the nonconformist based in the justification of a just and equal system, respectively. Schools force students to be good extensions of, and adherents to, the worth ethic that feeds a consumer society (e.g., time on task and assessments, or production evaluations); and those who do not conform are punished, just like in the workplace.

Marcuse (1969) adds the following context which I think is congruent with Fromm (1990) and applies to the fear of failure, and lack of competiveness that many parents fear for their children:

> The so-called consumer economy and the politics of corporate capitalism have created a second nature of man which ties him libidinaly and aggressively to the commodity form. The need for possessing, consuming, handling, and constantly renewing the gadgets, devices, instruments, engines, offered to and imposed upon the people ... has become a "biological" need.... The second nature of man thus militates against any change that would disrupt and perhaps even abolish this dependence of man on a market ever more

> densely filled with merchandise—abolish his existence as a consumer consuming himself in buying and selling. The needs generated by this system are thus eminently stabilizing, conservative needs: the counterrevloution anchored in the instinctual structure. (p. 11)

The second nature referred to saturates consciousness and guides action as if it were the only reality and also natural, the only game in town, so to speak. Pursuant to the neo-Marxist humanist ideas of Marcuse and Fromm, to be elaborated upon in the conclusion, failure within these circumstances might in many ways be seen as an unwillingness to participate in an ethically questionable or even bankrupt system and thus laudatory. Conversely, as embedded into the dominant consumerist ethos and allied consciousness, those who disobey are thought to be lazy, disturbed, criminal, and immoral "troublemakers" (lacking in work ethic).

PARALLELS IN *WHITE NOISE*

DeLillo's (1985) novel *White Noise* straddles the line between a life with no meaning in which things simply happen, banally, and one of a looming dread of impending death. The story is centered around the lives of a middle aged couple: Jack, a Professor of Hitler studies (a field he pioneered), and his wife Babette. Both worry about their general health, and are deeply fearful of death. Other concerns seem fleeting and banal, much like the portrayal of Hitler studies as reduced to something sterile, detached, and academic in the worst sense of the word. Babette, Jack's fourth wife, is a loving mother, reads tabloids to the blind, and teaches classes on posture to the elderly.

The vignette I will describe here is illustrative of a kind of obsession, a fear of death that causes self destructive behavior. This is parallel, in my mind, to how parents' fears have allowed potentially rational people to tolerate corporate-driven, marketed, accountability regimes, and an inflated real estate market. The fear of death discussed here might serve as a metaphor for all that may lead us toward despair from some unknown, (e.g., a failure in a future economy that is not known and cannot be predicted).

The vignette begins with the discovery of an empty medicine bottle marked "Dylar" by Denise, Babette's daughter from a previous marriage. She is concerned that something might be wrong with her mother but cannot find the medication in a medical index. Jack is less concerned stating that "everybody takes something," echoing a certain modern cynicism that reality is indeed better numbed by chemicals (DeLillo, 1985, p. 62). Later in the novel we see Babette lying to Jack stating that the pill she just took in front of him was actually a "Life Saver." Later still he finds her bottle taped to the underside of a radiator cover and investigates only to find out nothing about its use. Jack confronts his wife and she reveals her awful truth, namely that she answered an advertisement in the back of a tabloid to become a human test subject for a drug that was supposed to alleviate the fear of death. Babette was initially put through a battery of tests and then determined to be unsuitable for the clinical trials, such as they were. In recounting her story she states, "It involved an indiscretion. This was the only way I could get Mr. Gray to let me use the drug. It was my last resort, my last hope. First I offered him my mind. Now I offered my body" (DeLillo, 1985, p. 194).

Babette goes on to describe what happened in the motel room (where she met Mr. Gray and had sex with him) as "a capitalist transaction" (DeLillo, 1985, p. 194). The root cause of this desperation and despair? "A human condition" (p. 195). "'I am afraid to die,' she said, 'I think about it all the time. It won't go away'" (p. 196). Jack protests this admission stating that he was the one with the more pronounced fear of death; he is annoyed and dismissive of her fears, but with deep pathos for the fear itself. She replies that the man who played on her fear for sex (let's be honest) said she was "extra sensitive to the terror of death" (p. 197). They then engage in an Olympian contest of whose fear of death is more profound with Jack at one point stating "I have no body. I'm only a mind or a self, alone in a vast space" (p. 198), a commentary perhaps on the atomistic nature of self in a consumerist society.

At the end of the novel Jack sets out to find the man, Mr. Gray, who had extorted sex from Babette, *and* who also has the Dylar that Jack has come to crave as a panacea for all of his own fears. Who he encounters is Mink, a possibly Asian man who is now seemingly addled by the nostrum Dylar which he pops like candy in front of Jack while randomly spouting strange slogans from commercials—he is the personification of white noise, like the steady drone or our media culture. He intimates that he learned English from television and his answers to Jack's questions are often followed by statements that may contain symbolism, but also seem random, like the collection of facts, claims, and sentiments contained within a commercial break or by flipping through the channels. For instance, in reference to Dylar he tells Jack "this stuff fix you up" (DeLillo, 1985, p. 310) Jack replies, "I'll still die" (p. 310). Mink then states, "but it won't matter, which comes to the same thing. Some of these playful dolphins have been equipped with radio transmitters. Their far-flung wanderings may tell us things" (p. 310). Perhaps this is a accidental statement, but perhaps the playful dolphins in their travels might reveal truths concerning the conditions and parameters of our existence.

Mink then proceeds to tell Jack about how Babette wore a "ski mask so as not to kiss my face, which she said was un-American" (DeLillo, 1985, p. 310), perhaps a commentary on our problems with human connection and intimacy as well as the detached nature of the transaction. Jack intends to kill Mink and steal his Dylar. He pulls a gun on him which causes his retreat to the bathroom of the Motel room while popping as many Dylar as he can, and stating nonsensically, or perhaps with veiled purpose, "did you ever wonder why, out of thirty-two teeth, these four cause so much trouble? I'll be back with the answer in a minute" (p. 312). The long and short of it is that Jack does shoot Mink, but then is prompted by "the old human muddles and quirks … [of] compassion, remorse, mercy" (p. 313) to drive him to a hospital. Finally Jack regains a sense of connection to a human subject; it is this kind of connection that might serve to compromise the things we presently do for children, to children, in the service of an irrational fear and in the service of alienated and alienating masters. What follows attempts context where our actions might be guided by assessing the individual needs of children to freely inquire and create, but also how they might be guided into beneficial social relations with others.

BEING MORE HUMANE/CUTTING THROUGH THE WHITE NOISE

Freud (1961) posed the following dilemma with regard to striking a balance between individual human desires and the need for some kind of communal living arrangement:

> a good part of the struggle of mankind centre [sic] round the single task of finding an expedient accommodation—one, that is, that will bring happiness—between this claim of the individual and the cultural claims of the group; and one of the problems that touches the fate of humanity is whether such an accommodation can be reached by means of some particular form of civilization or whether this conflict is irreconcilable. (p. 43)

So at least can there be in some measure humane norms, a greater sanity that can be defined and pursued, even if these norms refer to general qualities of interaction rather than specific prescriptions. Fromm's position concerning normative humanism may seem deterministic, and it is in some ways, but it applies itself to a broad set of qualities concerning human interaction that are not oppressive and objectifying. Fromm (1990) states, "the criterion of mental health is not one of individual adjustment to a given social order, but a universal one, valid for all men, of giving a satisfactory answer to the problem of human existence" (p. 14). These universals are applied with an acknowledgement that social reality is socially constructed, but that human nature, generally conceived of as flourishing in healthy loving relationships, colors these interactions. For Fromm (1981), "love is union with somebody, or something outside oneself under the condition of retaining the separateness and integrity of one's self [italics omitted]" (p. 3). However, this natural state can be arrogated if the aforementioned social context, as "determined by the social arrangements under which he lives," yields to relationships of "submission and domination ... [where] both persons involved have lost their integrity and freedom" (Fromm, 1990, pp. 2 and 14).

Regarding the vicissitudes of school accountability measures, artificial and epistemologically false pedagogical arenas for competitive behavior, emotional manipulations of the real estate market, and the capitalistic distribution of resources to schools which drives the aforementioned market, Fromm (1981) might argue that the "social character" under current conditions "satisfied with submission is a crippled character" (p. 29). He continues with the insight that this less than humane manifestation of human behavior is explained within a social context that "serves the purpose of a society requiring submissive men for its proper functioning" and it "tends to produce and hold onto ideas and ideologies which fit it and are nourished by it" (pp. 29-30). It prevents us, for instance, from taking time-honored liberal positions like questioning the limit to which an individual's or group's economic prosperity should be tolerated when this wealth among some leads directly to the poverty of others. Or, it prevents us from even looking at the demonstrable cost of high stakes testing, in terms of money, actual intellectual and social/emotional growth, and of the psychological tolls for students, teachers, and parents.

As in *White Noise* it seems as though we are tormented by a life where everything urgently matters, like the sacrifices we make of ourselves and for our children to receive the "best" education. But, it also seems that we are not supposed to feel too much, and if something does connect itself too deeply to a sense of ultimate meaning, such as happiness or mortality, then we have a treatment for that, perhaps Dylar, although we often remain miserable. Nothing is allowed to get too visceral (although it generally already is), too close to something irresolvable by one's own self through sublimation, detachment, projection, or anesthesia. The former is done in denial of the kind of community that would connect us, but also leave us vulnerable in our dependence. This precludes the sacrifice of our illusions of existential independence and individual freedom to the resignation of a communal existence that in turn diminishes our individual power.

In terms of institutional educational spaces we are corrupted by the very thing that was supposed to save us, because it was sufficiently removed from what fosters healthy human relationships. Tests, what they purport to tell us about human worth, and the promise of an economically advantageous future as related to school performance sacrifices happiness and intellectual and social growth for a myth of prosperity and the canard that the more we consume the more contented we shall be. So, we are left with detached lonely dread in place of perhaps a complicated matrix of connectedness.

The question that remains unanswered concerns resistance, or perhaps a more destructive counter-narrative, one that might disrupt the whole educational enterprise and forces us to justify everything afresh. Personally, I am not sure that resistance is all that probable, given the outside influences, layers of school bureaucracy, and related entrenched privilege. However, it seems to me that thinking about strategies that might denude at least some of the most egregious structural contradictions and personal hypocrisies could not hurt.

First we might do well to dismiss outright adherence to what Bertrand Russell (1916) called "good form" (p. 163). Good form in this instance represents a passive credulity to those who control our educational institutions—bureaucrats, producers of educational materials, business interests, and elected officials. Russell (1916) defined good form as,

> A superficial open-mindedness, a readiness to hear all sides, and certain urbanity toward opponents. But it is not compatible with fundamental open-mindedness, or with any inward readiness to give weight to the other side. Its essence is the assumption that what is most important is a certain kind of behavior, a behavior which minimized friction between equals and delicately impresses inferiors with a conviction of their own crudity. (p. 164)

Those who purport to first know more than the general population about education, and second, suggest that if we dissent to present arrangements that somehow we have low expectations for children, are left-leaning radicals who hate traditional values, and that we have abandoned our strivings, to paraphrase President Clinton, to effectively compete and win in the global marketplace.

If even the "airborne toxic event" that disrupts the middle of *White Noise* did not alter the characters' general feelings about life and death—it was too embedded a mindset—then what causes apostasy? Perhaps turning toward the radical for comparison will provide enough of a contrast to spawn conversation about alternatives, and thwart the status quo and the good form programming that supports it. If, for instance we were to examine the ramifications of deschooling, as Ivan Illich (1970) proposed, seed ground might be readied for new ideas. Faced with the complete extirpation of the educational establishment as we know it, and all of the hegemonies that support it, pause might be given for reflection. The movement might be incremental and not revolutionary as Illich may have wanted; however, space might be created among those involved with schooling at its most intimate level (students, teachers, parents, elected school boards) to question institutional priorities and resources and disrupt "rituals ... [that] hide from their participants ... discrepancies and conflicts between social principle and social organization" (p. 74). Regardless, the present "white noise" that clouds our consciousness might be squelched, returning as Illich warranted, "the acid test of our response ... [to] our pinpointing of the responsibility for teaching and learning" (Gartner, Illich, Greer, & Riessman, 1973, p. 20).

REFERENCES

DeLillo, D. (1985). *White noise.* New York, NY: Viking Press.

Freud, S. (1961). *Civilization and its discontents.* New York, NY: Norton.

Fromm, E. (1981). *On disobedience and other essays.* New York, NY: Seabury Press.

Fromm, E. (1990). *The sane society.* New York, NY: Henry Holt.

Huxley, A. (1932). *Brave new world.* London, England: Chatto & Windus.

Illich, I. (1970). *Deschooling society.* New York, NY: Harper & Row.

Gartner, A., Illich, I., Greer, C., & Riessman, F. (1973). *After deschooling, what?* New York, NY: Harper & Row.

Kessler, G. (2001, May 6). Panel aims to Rejigger tax relief; senators likely to tilt cut to lower brackets. *Washington Post,* A1.

Marcuse, H. (1969). *An essay on liberation.* Boston, MA: Beacon Press.

Orwell, G. (1949). *1984.* London, England: Secker & Warburg.

Russell, B. (1916). *Why men fight.* New York, NY: Albert and Charles Boni.

Rugg, H. (1941). *That men may understand.* New York, NY: Doubleday.

Zamyatin, Y. (1999). *We* (A. Ginsburg, Trans.). New York, NY: Eros HarperCollins. (Original work published 1972)

SECTION II: PRAXIS

DYSTOPIAN PRACTICE OR PRAXIS?

Jessica A. Heybach and Eric C. Sheffield

One of the interesting and ongoing conversations we have had throughout this project has swirled around an issue of wording: are the authors in this second section examining and suggesting changes to schooling *practice* or schooling *praxis*? This question might, at first blush, appear to be simply one of semantics. On the other hand, words convey subtle differences in meaning and we settled on *praxis* mindfully: practice connotes doing-for-doing's-sake; praxis connotes a critical thoughtfulness that informs action—a deep philosophical awareness and clarity as to the impact of one's actions on the world they inhabit. These qualities are often not associated with mere practice.

In *Pedagogy of the Oppressed*, Freire (1970) writes, "Critical consciousness is brought about not through intellectual effort alone but through *praxis*—through the authentic union of action and reflection" (p. 48). That is, in praxis critical reflection informs the actions we consider and ultimately transforms the structures that dictate lived experience. Freire argues, "For apart from inquiry, apart from the praxis, individuals cannot be truly human. Knowledge emerges only through invention and re-invention, through the restless, impatient, continuing, hopeful inquiry human beings pursue in the world, with the world, and with each other" (p. 72). Given the connection between praxis and humanity, we ask you, our readers, to take this idea with you as consider the examination of contemporary schooling and the practical suggestions our authors make in the chapters that follow. And, consider which is more reflective of current schooling activity: practice or praxis?

CHAPTER 6

DYSTOPIAN LOVE MANIFESTED IN A DYSTOPIAN AESTHETIC

Insights Into Contemporary Educational Practice From *A Clockwork Orange*

Eric C. Sheffield

We long, amid a troubled world, for perfect being. We forget that what gives meaning to the notion of perfection is the events that create longing, and that apart from them, a 'perfect' world would mean just an unchanging brute existential thing.

—John Dewey (1925/2000, p. 63)

Save me from my humanity
Save me from my human self
I will submit to computer god
And give myself away to you

—Dystopia (2008)

Dystopia and Education:
Insights Into Theory, Praxis, and Policy in an Age of Utopia-Gone-Wrong, pp. 83–98

INTRODUCTION

"What's it gonna be then, eh?" So begins Anthony Burgess's (1962/1986) quintessential 20th century dystopian novel, *A Clockwork Orange* (referred to as *Orange* from here on). This opening query—one that periodically reappears throughout the book—is given voice by the narrator and hero, "Little Alex." Burgess' nightmarish tale is that of Alex, a seemingly incorrigible "chelloveck" (fellow) who, at a very tender age, along with his "droogs," (friends) commits nearly unimaginable acts of violence and terror including burglary, beatings, rape, and murder. Burgess pulls no punches in describing these heinous acts, though certainly the impact of the descriptions is eased somewhat by his use of "nadsat," the dialect spoken exclusively by teenagers and derived from Russian, various Slavic tongues, and English slang that Burgess himself created. Importantly, these acts of violence are never directed at someone "who has it coming," but rather, the wake of Alex's random waves of violence is completely awash with the old, the weak, the innocent, and the vulnerable, making it initially impossible for the reader to feel any sympathy whatsoever for Little Alex. As is the case with other such violent crime sprees, fictional or real, Alex's time is finally up as the first section of the novel closes—one of his innocent victims was found dead:

> The old ptitsa [girl] who had all the kots [tomcats] and koshkas [cats] had passed on to a better world in one of the city hospitals. I'd cracked her a bit too hard, like.... That was everything, I'd done the lot, now. *And me still only fifteen.* (p. 81, emphasis mine)

It is here, as the first section of the novel ends and the second section begins, that the truly dystopian nature of Burgess's novel takes shape.

The periodic query, "What's it going to be then, eh?" is a regular reminder to the reader that *Orange* is, beyond all else, an inquiry into the nature of human free will with special attention to doing "good" and/or "evil." More particularly, Burgess (1962/1986) takes up an essential dystopian question: do we remain human in any meaningful way when free will is severely restricted or completely eliminated? From this core question arise numerous others pondered for millennia by people from all walks of life: are humans inherently tainted (original sin)? Are we inherently good and then corrupted by society? Can humans be "taught" to do only good? Are "good" and "evil" dependent on human choice? These and other essential human concerns swirl around the tragic tale of Alex and his droogs.

Burgess's (1962/1986) response to these questions seemed to depend on whether the reader resided in Great Britain or the United States in1962. As Burgess explains in the Introduction to the 1986 reissue of the novel, his American publisher asked that the 21st chapter be dropped for the American audience, and yet it remained for the British/world audience. I do not want to give the mystery away here for those readers who have yet to finish the novel; however, Burgess makes it clear that he believes writers have a responsibility to "show the possibility of moral transformation, or an increase in wisdom" (p. xii). He continues:

> When a fictional work fails to show change, when it merely indicates that human character is set, stony, unregenerable, then you are out of the field of the novel and into that of the fable or the allegory. The American or Kubrickian *Orange*, is a fable; the British or world one is a novel. (p. xii)

In the end, Burgess preferred the 21 chapter version as it was meant to be read and as it was reissued in the U.S. some 25 years after its initial publication—one that suggests Burgess's belief that sans the 21st chapter, the novel is not "a fair picture of human life" (p. xiii).

Like many works of the dystopian genre, including those examined in this volume, *Orange* takes up politics, control, surveillance, utopian visions, dystopian realities, the beauty of human existence, its evil underbelly, and other macrosystemic, broadly human, concerns. These are typical fodder for the dystopian genre. However, *unlike* much dystopian art, the actual site of utopia-turned-dystopia is not found in these broad socioinstitutional structures but in the emotional, spiritual, cognitive, and physical existence of an individual human being: that of Alex, our "humble narrator."

In what follows, I first describe how these essential human questions are "treated" within the narrative of the actual physical space of Alex as a living, breathing, human "self." Next, I suggest that Alex's treatment in the text constitutes what I will call a dystopian aesthetic in two-parts: the first growing out of a traditional understanding of aesthetics as related to art, art education, and how experiences shape one's engagement with the arts; and, a second, more radical part, that asks us to consider the aesthetic qualities of lived experience more generally with particular reference to free will. In both cases I rely on some insights from John Dewey to help the analysis along. Subsequent to this analysis, I suggest that this dystopian aesthetic is a manifestation of dystopian love—a dehumanizing love reminiscent of what Erich Fromm (1939) calls "sadistic love"—sympathetically directed at "selves" from "not-selves" whose goal is to severely limit individual autonomy thereby saving the self from the self. Finally, I conclude with some thoughts as to the existence and impact of this dystopian love-driven aesthetic in and for contemporary school practices.

THE BODY OF ALEX AS A DYSTOPIAN SPACE

In his role as our humble narrator, it is Alex who foreshadows the journey on which he is about to embark, a journey from "sickness," to "cure," back to sickness and, ultimately, redemptive growth. In a conversation with his "post-corrective adviser," P. R. Deltoid, Deltoid asks:

> "What gets into you all? We study the problem and we've been studying it for damn well near a century, yes, but we get no farther with studies. You've got a good home here, good loving parents, you've got not too bad of a brain. Is it some devil that crawls inside you?" (Burgess, 1962/986, p. 43)

Not wanting to engage in the conversation, quietly pleading "the fifth" to Deltoid's question, Alex allows only the reader into his thinking on this troubling question:

> But, brothers, this biting of their toe-nails over what is the *cause* of badness is what turns me into a fine laughing Malchick [boy]. They don't go into what is the cause of *goodness*, so why of the other shop? If lewdies [people] are good that's because they like it, and I wouldn't ever interfere with their pleasures, and so of the other shop. And I was patronizing the other shop. More, badness is of the self, the one, the you or me on our oddy knockies [lonesome], and that self is made by old Bog or God and is his great pride and radosty [joy]. But the not-self cannot have the bad, meaning they of the government and the judges and the schools cannot allow the bad because they cannot allow the self. (p. 44, emphasis in original)

As a narrative matter, the above conversation is crucial as it comes after an evening of "phillying about" that culminates in the violent rape of a woman as her husband, an author, is forced to look on. The words penned by this author (part of a book entitled *A Clockwork Orange*) and read aloud by Alex immediately prior to the rape, drip with a not-so-veiled narrative irony:

> The attempt to impose upon man, a creature of growth and capable of sweetness, to ooze juicily at the last round the bearded lips of God, to attempt to impose, I say, laws and conditions appropriate to a mechanical creation, against this I raise my sword pen. (p. 25)

And so, we find Alex in the opening chapter of part two in the adult "zoo" serving his term for murdering the old ptitsa mentioned earlier and soon to be the very "creature of growth" imposed upon as a "mechanical creation"—precisely the kind of imposition decried by the author-victim of Alex's crime.

Not long into his imprisonment, rumors of a new treatment which can cure individual criminal behavior (and allow for a prisoner's release) are confirmed in conversations with the prison chaplain who has befriended Alex. Known simply as "Ludovico's Technique,"[1] this treatment is designed to severely limit individual autonomy thereby creating utopianized selves capable only of "good" behavior. The chaplain has grave philosophical doubts about the treatment's potential: "The question is whether such a Technique can really make a man good. Goodness comes from within, 6655321. Goodness is something chosen. When a man cannot choose he ceases to be a man" (Burgess, 1962/1886, p. 93). Of course, Alex is on an inevitable collision course with the Ludovico technique and after a skirmish in his overcrowded cell results in a dead cell-mate, he is chosen by the "not-selves" as the first "self" to receive the experimental treatment. In being administered the Ludovico technique, Alex becomes literally a dystopian space into which is implanted a dystopian virus of sorts—one meant to exorcise evil behavior out of Alex thereby saving him from himself.

The Ludovico technique consists generally of classical, associational, conditioning. The idea is that if someone like Alex will not choose good over evil, then the "not-selves" will (and should) severely limit his ability to freely choose. Over a 2-week period Alex is treated via the forced viewing of horrendously violent film and still images in tandem with a daily injection designed to cause debilitating physical illness. This is clearly a case of classical associational conditioning: pair horribly debilitating physical, emotional, and intellectual pain with images of violence, and the "self" will no longer have the choice to act violently. At the end of the two week treatment, Alex is, in fact, cured.

In one of the more nightmarish scenes of the entire book, Alex is presented to a group of the "not-selves" where he is put on display. To prove the success of the treatment, Alex is physically attacked and when he begins to respond in the way that he would choose (defending himself from the attack), he becomes horribly ill and cowers in front of his attacker. He is next presented with a scantily clad, young woman. Prior to his treatment, Alex most certainly would have tried to have his way with her; but, once again, at the very thought of a violent sexual act, he becomes paralyzingly ill and falls to her feet in submission.

This shift of the dystopian site of activity from broad systemic surveillance and control as seen in *Brave New World* (Huxley, 1932/1998), *1984* (Orwell, 1949/1977), *Hamdmaid's Tale* (Atwood, 1986), and other dystopian classics, inward to the very core decision-making capacities—physical, emotional, cognitive, and spiritual—of the individual creates a frighteningly different locus of dystopian control. If the self can be utopianized in this way, then there is no need for building and maintaining a broad overall mechanism of control; rather, that control can be fomented from the inside out by severely limiting individual human free will. Even in the torture of Winston Smith in *1984* (Orwell, 1949/1977) the goal is something different: destroy the self, and in its place insert the communal belief system of the "Party." In the case of young Alex however, there is no destruction, in toto, of Alex as a self; rather, a sickening controlling virus of sorts is inserted into him that, while severely limiting his autonomy, leaves him well aware of what is happening. There is no need for Orwellian doublethink. There is no need to rewrite history. There is no need for complete reprogramming, genetic/environmental engineering, or continual surveillance. Instead, the subject is simply restricted from acting in ways that he would prefer all the while completely conscious of the restriction. Ludovico's technique creates the perfect combination of rehabilitation and continual punishment, and Ludovico's technique is a perfect dystopian mechanism of control, from the inside out.

A DYSTOPIAN AESTHETIC IN TWO PARTS

Having described this outward-to-inward shift in the locus of dystopian control, what I want to suggest in this section is that Ludivico's treatment is an extreme manifestation of what I will call a dystopian aesthetic in-two-parts. The first of these parts is much clearer, much older and much more obvious as it is born out of classical questions of art's value, Platonic issues of censorship, and notions of how experience, particularly as John Dewey understood it, is the site wherein individual impulses, desires, and purposes are developed. This first part addresses the historic aesthetic questions of what constitutes beauty or the beautiful; and questions about how art engages the spectator emotionally. This first part is also more obviously "educational;" that is, it asks educators to consider the value art has for teaching and learning, an issue I will return to near the end of this chapter.

The second piece of this dystopian aesthetic is, I believe, more complicated, grows out of the first part, and (particularly in educational contexts) is more insidiously viral. The questions that arise out of the second piece of this dystopian aesthetic do so in light of Dewey's contention that all of experience might be seen for its aesthetic, and anesthetic, qualities. That is, if all of experience might be seen for its aesthetic qualities, what is there to say about Alex's treatment in this regard? And, what about following his treatment? Can Alex, or any human for that matter, live aesthetically—organically—when free will is so severely limited? With this brief introduction in mind, let's return to our young tragic hero.

Little Alex, though the reader never learns how it came to pass, is a bit of an oddity: a 15-year-old who loves classical music; and his love of music is closely connected to the pleasure he takes in acting out violently. In the midst of one of Alex's more heinous acts of cruelty (as it was carried out on two very young girls), he tells the reader:

> Then I pulled the Ninth out of its sleeve, so that Ludwig van was now nagoy [naked] too, and I set the needle hissing on to the last movement, which was all bliss ... then I leapt on these two young ptitsas [girls]. This time they thought nothing fun and stopped creeching [screaming] with high mirth, and had to submit to the strange and weird desires of Alexander the Large which, what with the Ninth and the hypo jab, were choodessny [wonderful] and zammechat [remarkable] and very demanding, O my brothers.... Well, if they would not go to school then they must still have their education. And education they had had.... Then they were going down the stairs and I dropped off to sleep, still with the old Joy Joy Joy [Beethoven's Ninth] crashing and howling away. (Burgess, 1962/1986, pp. 50-51)

Alex's love of classical music and its connection to violence appears throughout the early part of the novel, and becomes particularly crucial in Alex's post-Ludivico experiences. [2]

One of the unintended consequences of Alex's "cure" came about because the horrifying images he was forced to view during the treatment process were accompanied by classical music, and he was well aware of the ramifications:

> I don't mind about the ultra-violence and all that cal [shit]. I can put up with that. But it's not fair on the music. It's not fair I should feel ill when I'm slooshying [hearing] lovely Ludwig van and G. F. Handel and others. All that shows you're an evil lot of bastards and I shall never forgive you, sods [bastards]. (Burgess, 1986, p. 130)

The narrowly aesthetic experience that was constructed for Alex in the treatment process would potentially reverse all of those that came before—experiences that clearly led Alex to love classical music as an art form.

Burgess (1962/1986) himself argues that for experiences to be aesthetic, for them to be understood as art experiences, they must be dialectical (p. xiv) and other contemporary, postmodern, scholars certainly agree with him (see, e.g., Heybach, 2012). This dialectic nature of art experiences is crucial to growing both a love of the arts and an understanding of the arts as an important matter for navigating our contemporary, postmodern, visual culture context (cf. Freedman, this volume). In the case of Alex's early experiences with music, including those depicted in *Orange*, it is clear that the music speaks to him and he to the music.

The music inspires him, he calls upon it in crucial moments of his lived experience, and he is devastated at the idea that it would, for the rest of his days, no longer speak with him, but rather act didactically on him, causing unbearable physical, emotional, and intellectual pain. This aesthetic is dystopian as it puts Alex in a hard, impossible place that only hinders rather than grows his understanding, love, and appreciation of arts, particularly music.

The unintended consequence, in tandem with Alex's association of classical music with violence, harkens back to early Platonic dystopian/utopian questions: are censorship and noble lies necessary to keep a utopian peace? Plato certainly believed so (cf. Jones, this volume). In one of his more antidemocratic contentions, Plato suggested that the arts, particularly the poets (Burgess would certainly qualify), should be censored lest they inflame the passions of the citizenry such that those citizens act unreasonably, desire too vehemently, and rip apart the utopian fabric of the perfect city state.

In an ironic twist, however, Alex's treatment consists not in having art censored, but in didactically and violently bombarding him with images and music overwhelming his experiential desire to pursue them. The not-selves (government, schools, and I would add, corporations) in this case use art to restrict free will in drowning Alex with images, music, and intense pain. This twist on the utilization of arts has important educational implications that I will come back to later. Suffice it to say for now that Alex's treatment seems an apt metaphor for postmodern living: our experiences are stiflingly crammed with an onslaught of images and sounds—images and sounds that we can rarely avoid or turn off, that overwhelm us to the point of sickness, and potentially restrict choice if they are not understood critically, dialectically, or artfully.

The story of Little Alex's treatment is also an artistic rendering of a crucial philosophical and educational matter. Dewey (1938) has argued, impulse becomes desire, and purpose develops from that desire in the context of experience; and, experiences are interactive, continual, and form general habits of mind, spirit, and action:

> The basic characteristic of habit is that every experience enacted and undergone modifies the one who acts and undergoes, while this modification affects, whether we like it or not, the quality of subsequent experiences. *For it is a somewhat different person who enters into them.* (p. 35, emphasis mine)

Alex epitomizes Dewey's point perfectly—our orienting habits are born from experiences. Humans grow from one experience to the next, carrying with us what we have learned from prior and present experiences into those of the future. Importantly, Dewey goes on to suggest that we can distinguish educative experiences from miseductive ones by the degree to which they promote the desire to pursue further such experiences, and the degree to which they promote growth generally:

> Growth, or growing as developing, not only physically but intellectually and morally, is one exemplification of the principle of continuity.... There is no paradox in the fact that the principle of the continuity of experience may operate so as to leave a person arrested on a low plane of development, in a way which limits later capacity for growth.
>
> On the other hand [as opposed to miseducative experiences], if an experience arouses curiosity, strengthens initiative, and sets up desires and purposes that are sufficiently intense to carry a person over dead places in the future, then continuity works in a very different way [it is educative]. (p. 36-38)

The Ludivico treatment is clearly miseducative, didactic, and restrictive to freedom in its destruction of Alex's love of classical music. In a phrase, it is aesthetically dystopian.

There remains one more point I'd like to make regarding this narrowly art-oriented part of this dystopian aesthetic I am suggesting, and it is related to Dewey's understanding of interaction, or transaction. Dewey (1938) argues that experiences don't simply go on inside a person, they arise only in the context of a self interacting with both the objective and social factors of experience:

> An experience is always what it is because of a transaction taking place between an individual and what, at the time, constitutes his environment ... the environment, in other words, is whatever conditions interact with personal needs, desires, purposes, and capacities to create the experience which is had. (pp. 43-44)

Given these theoretical distinctions, the treatment that Alex has been convinced to endure is in fact a manifestation of dystopian, miseducative, anaesthetic experiences. Both the dystopian and miseducative characteristics of Alex's treatment are the result of "not-selves" having complete control over the environmental factors that impact the growth of selves. Needless to say, there are numerous practical implications here for art as a subject of study and educational practice generally and I will return to those in my concluding remarks.

The second, more insidiously viral part of the dystopian aesthetic I am suggesting here grows out of Dewey's (1934) understanding of experience as interactive and continual and his suggestion that "any practical activity will, provided that *it is integrated and moves by its own urge to fulfillment*, have esthetic quality" (p. 41, emphasis mine). To illustrate more completely Dewey's point with specific consideration of Little Alex, human free will, and growth-of-self, I give you two descriptions provided by Dewey of a most unlikely object: a stone. First, in *Democracy and Education*, Dewey (1916/1997) writes:

> The most notable distinction between living and inanimate beings is that the former maintain themselves by renewal. A stone when struck resists. If its resistance is greater than the force of the blow struck, it remains outwardly unchanged. Otherwise, it is shattered into smaller bits. Never does the stone attempt to react in such a way that it may maintain itself against the blow, much less so as to render the blow a contributing factor to its own continued action. While the living thing may easily be crushed by superior force, it none the less tries to turn the energies which act upon it into means of its own further existence. If it cannot do so, it does not just split into smaller pieces (at least in the higher forms of life), *but loses its identity as a living thing*. (p. 4, emphasis mine)

Dewey's contention here seems to address Burgess' reminder that *Orange* is an inquiry into the nature of human free will: "What's it going to be then, eh?" The implication of Dewey's first stone is that the essential nature of human existence is tied to the question of if, and then how, we humans act freely to turn that which is enacted upon us into the means of our own further existence. And, robbed of the freedom to do so, we lose our identity as living things. That is, when our freedom to act in experience toward growth and renewal is restricted or eliminated, we become objects; we are dehumanized; we fragment or shatter into dust; we are dystopianized.

This contention may seem to fall outside the bounds of aesthetic understandings, and as a traditional aesthetic matter, maybe it does. However, Dewey (1934) argues that, in fact, this understanding of human experience is crucially aesthetic. In *Art as Experience*, he describes a second stone—one that illustrates his aesthetic experiential point:

> A generalized illustration may be had if we imagine a stone, which is rolling down hill, to have an experience. The activity is surely sufficiently "practical." The stone starts from somewhere, and moves, as consistently as conditions permit toward a place and state where it will be at rest—toward an end. Let us add, by imagination, to these external facts, the ideas that it looks forward with desire to the final outcome; that it is interested in the things it meets on its way, conditions that accelerate and retard its movement with respect to their bearing on the end; that it acts and feels toward them according to the hindering or helping function it attributes to them; and that the final coming to rest is related to all that went before as the culmination of a continuous movement. Then the stone would have an experience, and one with esthetic quality. (p. 46)

Importantly for the educational questions addressed here and throughout this collection, Dewey (1934) describes as well those experiences that are anesthetic; that is, those experiences that deaden, rather than enliven, the engagement essential to learning experientially. About these numbing experiences, he writes:

> In much of experience we are not concerned with the connection of one incident with what went before and what comes after. There is no interest that controls attentive rejection or selection of what shall be organized into the developing experience. Things happen, but they are neither definitely included nor decisively excluded; we drift. *We yield according to external pressure, or evade and compromise*. There are beginnings and cessations, but no genuine initiations and concluding. One thing replaces another, but does not absorb it and carry it on. There is experience, but so slack and discursive that it is not an experience. Needless to say, such experiences are anesthetic. (p. 46)

I have several rather simple questions on these counts, questions I return to in my conclusion: which of these stones is "a creature of growth and capable of sweetness?" Which of these stones is being "treated" with "laws and conditions appropriate to a mechanical creation?" Which of these stones is Alex? And, most importantly, which of these stones represents students, teachers, and even administrators in contemporary schooling situations—situations increasingly indicative of a dystopian aesthetic?

DYSTOPIAN LOVE

What I have outlined thus far, and surely it is only an outline as I believe there is the need for a more complete dystopian theory of education, goes some way in informing educational practice. As Happel and Atkinson (this volume) point out in their insightful chapter, the value of a dystopian lens is that it exaggerates the contemporary context in ways that allow us to see more clearly current "goings on," and certainly *Orange* does so in important ways. However, there remains the crucial question of motivation: that is, with particular reference to Alex and his "treatment," from where does the desire on the part of the "not-selves" to "fix" Alex spring? What I want to suggest here is that the dystopian aesthetic unleashed on Alex, both as an aesthetic proper and as an aesthetic more broadly construed, is done so out of a particular understanding of love: dystopian love. In a telling scene between Alex and his probation officer, P. R. Deltoid, Deltoid (the most intimate symbol of the not-selves) says to Alex: "But I'm warning you, little Alex, being a good friend to you as always, the one man in this sore and sick community who wants to *save you from yourself*" (Burgess, 1962/1986, p. 43).

Dystopian love, as the desire to save the other from him/her self and expressed by Deltoid above, is reminiscent of Erich Fromm's (1939) concept, "symbiotic pseudolove." More particularly, dystopian love is essentially what Fromm described as "sadistic love," which "springs from the desire to swallow its object to make him a will-less instrument in one's own hands" combined with what Fromm called sympathy (p. 517). Fromm described the basic premises of love as "freedom and equality ... the strength, independence, integrity of the self, which can stand alone and bear solitude"; and, that acting out of love is "a spontaneous act" done such that the loved one's "ability to act of one's own free volition" is achieved (p. 517). It [sadistic love] can also be blended with sympathy in which case the impulse is to have the object as an instrument and, at the same time, to further him in any way excepting in one: *letting him be free*" (p. 515, emphasis mine). The subtle and crucial difference between Fromm's sympathetic-sadistic love and dystopian love is that strivings informed by sympathetic-sadistic love spring from "selves" and are directed toward other selves; dystopian love, however, is constituted of sympathetic-sadistic love directed toward selves from what Alex calls, the "not-selves": schools, governments, and increasingly, corporations.

Yes, Orwell's (1949/1977) Big Brother "loves" you, but can only do so in a particular way: with sympathy and sadistic intentions. Because dystopian love's source is institutional, rather than individual (something of a postmodern construction of George Herbert Mead's (1934) "generalized other"), it is difficult to trace and difficult to negotiate from within personal, individual, and singular conceptions of self- and other-love as Fromm describes it above. In the case of Alex, this dystopian love is manifested as a dystopian aesthetic (Lucivico's technique) operating in the physical space of Alex, with the sympathetic goal of saving him from himself by turning him into a "will-less instrument" in the hands of the not-selves, unable to act freely. A dystopian love-driven aesthetic, as an institutional manifestation of sympathetic-sadistic love, succeeds in severely limiting free will in continually pounding selves into submission, into fragments, into dust. Unfortunately, the stones being pounded into fragments seem familiar: students, teachers and administrators in contemporary schools.[3]

IMPLICATIONS FOR PRACTICE

What I have outlined here is certainly a theoretical infant; much fleshing-out remains for these ideas to fully animate discussions of how educational policy and practice might be reformed in light of them. However, that fleshing out must wait as time and space are limited as is, I suspect, my readers' patience. And so, what do these ideas imply? To get at this question I will work from more general "practical" considerations to particular matters of practice.

First, and maybe foremost, the dystopian theory I have only initially suggested here pushes us to continually inquire into our educational motivations, at every level, and at every practical turn. Why have educators instituted zero tolerance behavior policies? Why is there an increasing police presence in public schools? Why do administrators continue to regulate the school day on an outmoded factory model? How do teachers decide on the "management" approach they take in their classrooms? Why do teachers need to teach to the test? Why do administrators increasingly rely on "teacher proof" instructional methods? Scripted teaching? Why have particular state governors sought to eliminate tenure? And, why, has there been the adoption of micro-managed tracking systems for teacher "accountability?" Certainly this is a short list. However, if the answers to these and other such questions tend toward a desire to save our students, teachers, and administrators from themselves because we, as a society, sympathetically but sadistically "love" them, then the slide into dystopian educational practices has already begun.

Closely related to this question of educational motivation, is one of general educational aim: what do we hope to accomplish with and for our students, teachers, and administrators? What Burgess, Dewey, and Fromm seem to suggest is that the hallmark of human existence and, by extension, the goal of education, is a growth in freedom. Students must be allowed a guided, but increasingly free, voice in what their education should entail. Teachers must be encouraged, rather than discouraged, to freely make decisions, to freely construct educational experiences, to freely guide their students based on their students' impulses, desires, and purposes. Administrators must be free to aid classroom teachers in this essential quest rather than be hamstrung by increasingly restrictive federal and state policy.

Orange, John Dewey, and this dystopian theory remind us that the experiences we construct in schools have far-reaching impact on all involved. The value our students, teachers, and administrators place on specific activities is only in small part about the moment. These experiences are, in large part, related to past and future experiences. We must remain mindful that one bad experience can ruin a student's potential to pursue other such experiences. We must construct educational experiences with great forethought and love of subject matter, not just love of student. And we must remain patient: humans do not grow in a linear, lock-step, developmentally regulated way—read the 21st chapter of *Orange*. Not keeping these practical matters in mind, the educational experiences run the risk of becoming anaesthetizing, numbing, deadening, and vehemently inhumane: dystopian.

Finally, at the micro practical level, I want to echo Kerry Freedman's (this volume) suggestion that an education in the arts is a crucial matter if growth in freedom is our educational goal. Given the current deluge of images and sounds with which are daily pounded; given that Alex's treatment seems a frighteningly apt metaphor for contemporary existence; given that the "not-selves" are increasingly in control of our environmental existence, a critical education in the arts proper and aesthetics generally is imperative. And, as Freedman (in this volume) suggests, this education must be incorporated into all content fields because the pounding citizens receive comes from every corner of our postmodern lives, not just in art galleries.

SUMMARY AND CONCLUSION

I have argued in this chapter that Anthony Burgess's (1962/1986) *A Clockwork Orange* is an inquiry into human freedom. I have suggested that Alex's treatment at the hands of the "not-selves," (the Ludivico technique) constitutes a dystopian aesthetic in two-parts: one part an aesthetic, art proper matter, and a second more radically general aesthetic understanding of human existence. I have also made the case that this concern about Alex constitutes a dystopian love, an institutional version of Erich Fromm's (1939) sympathetic sadistic love, rather than a love meant to grow freedom in its object. I concluded by tracing how such a theoretical understanding might, as an initial matter, provide insights into sound educational practice.

Fortunately or unfortunately dystopian visions can focus our attention more pointedly at the implications for contemporary practice. Equally fortunate or unfortunate is that examining educational practice via such a lens allows us to see how incredibly dystopian, dehumanizing, and even enslaving current educational policy (and their implied practices) is for students, teachers, administrators, and even whole communities. In the end, I see staunch, organized, and energized resistance as the only way to redirect us away from this growing dystopia. And so I leave you with a question: "What's it going to be then, eh?"

NOTES

1. Burgess, never missing an opportunity for some semiotic irony, is here hearkening to the 17th century Italian Franciscan Priest, Ludovico Maria

Sinistrari, infamous for his role as adviser to the Supreme Sacred Congregation of the Roman and Universal Inquistion in Rome; and, an expert on exorcism and sexually oriented "sins."

2. The question of Alex's association of music and violence, though an important consideration, will not be taken up in much detail here. However, it is important to note that Dewey himself was aware of experiential educational direction. In *Experience and Education* he makes mention of a burglar who becomes better at his trade through experiential practice. His position on experiential direction is that ultimately this kind of experience is miseducative in that it restricts, rather than broadens, future experiences—certainly true here in the case of Alex.
3. Fromm (1939) was certainly not oblivious to these kinds of institutional mechanisms of control. Near the end of this 1939 article, he writes: "In the present era, the tendency to make of the individual a powerless atom is increasing. The authoritarian systems tend to reduce the individual to a will-less and feelingless instrument in the hands of those who hold the reins; they batter him down by terror, cynicism, the power of the state, large demonstrations, fierce orators and all other means of suggestion. When finally he feels too weak to stand alone, they offer him satisfaction by letting him participate in the strength and glory of the greater whole, whose powerless part he is. The authoritarian propaganda uses the argument that the individual of the democratic state is selfish and that he should become unselfish and socially minded. This is a lie. Nazism substituted the most brutal selfishness of the leading bureaucracy and of the state for the selfishness of the average man. The appeal for unselfishness is the weapon to make the average individual still more ready to submit or to renounce" (p. 22).

REFERENCES

Atwood, M. (1986). *The handmaid's tale.* Toronto, Canada: O. W. Toad.

Burgess, A. (1986). *A clockwork orange*. New York, NY: W. W. Norton. (Original work published 1962)

Dewey, J. (1997). *Democracy and education*. NY: Free Press. (Original work published 1916)

Dewey, J. (2000). *Experience and nature*. Mineola, NY: Dover. (Original work published 1925)

Dewey, J. (1934). *Art as experience*. New York, NY: Perigree.

Dewey, J. (1938). *Experience and education*. New York, NY: Touchstone.

Dystopia. (2008). Control all-delete. On *Dystopia* [CD]. Austin, TX: Life is Abuse Studio.

Freedman, K. (2013). The aesthetics of horror. In J. Heybach & E. Sheffield (Eds.), *Dystopia and education: Insights into theory, praxis, and policy in an age of utopia-gone-wrong*. Charlotte, NC: Information Age Press.

Freire, P. (1970). *Pedagogy of the oppressed.* New York, NY: Continuum.

Fromm, E. (1939). Selfishness and self-love. *Psychiatry: Journal for the Study of Interpersonal Process, 2,* 507-523.

Happel, A., & Atkinson, B. (2013). Education's handmaids? The role of the teacher in the age of accountability. In J. Heybach & E. Sheffield (Eds.), *Dystopia and education: Insights into theory, praxis, and policy in an age of utopia-gone-wrong*. Charlotte, NC: Information Age Press.

Heybach, J. (2012). Learning to feel what we see: Critical aesthetics and "difficult knowledge" in an age of war. *Critical Questions in Education, (3)*1, 23-34.

Huxley, A. (1998). *Brave new world.* New York, NY: HarperCollins. (Original work published 1932)

Jones, S. P. (this volume). When undergraduate students read Huxley's *Brave New World* and Plato's *The Republic* in an educational foundations course. In J. Heybach & E. Sheffield (Eds.), *Dystopia and education: Insights into theory, praxis, and policy in an age of utopia-gone-wrong.* Charlotte, NC: Information Age Press.

Mead, G. H. (1934). *Mind, self, and society* (C. W. Morris, Ed.). Chicago, IL: University of Chicago Press.

Orwell, G. (1977). *1984*. New York, NY: Penguin. (Original work published 1949)

CHAPTER 7

LESSONS FROM ELSEWHERE; OR, RETHINKING DEMOCRACY AND PUBLIC EDUCATION THROUGH LOIS LOWRY'S *THE GIVER*

Eric D. Smith and Philip E. Kovacs

INTRODUCTION

As a cultural expression of the early 1990s, a moment in which the U.S. is still flush from its recent Cold War triumph, Lois Lowry's *The Giver* (1993) invites a reading that privileges the individualist ethic of socioeconomic liberalism over and against that of a moribund Communist (read Stalinist) order. As such, we might attribute much of the novel's phenomenal success to the lingering fascination with and symbolic interment of collectivist ideology, epitomized in the period's resurgence of interest in literary dystopias like Yevgeny Zamyatin's (1924/1960) novel *We* and Margaret Atwood's (1985) novel *The Handmaid's Tale*. Yet, inasmuch as the precarious decade of the 90s may also be said to function, as Phillip E. Wegner (2009) argues, as an instance of the Lacanian "life between two deaths"—that is, of

Dystopia and Education:
Insights Into Theory, Praxis, and Policy in an Age of Utopia-Gone-Wrong, pp. 99–116

the lapse between the end of one order and its symbolic recognition—*The Giver* opens onto a range of utopian possibilities that exceeds this narrow ideological matrix (Lowry, 1993). Thus resituated, the novel reveals itself as a meditation on the anxious future of "democracy" in an era in which its defining horizon of non-identity has disappeared from view and in which alternative ways of being-in-the-world have quietly succumbed to the "end of history" and its omnivorous forces of homogenization.

We argue that in its deployment of the estranging devices of utopia and science fiction (and perhaps despite its own ideological motivations), *The Giver* (Lowry, 1993) provides a conceptual framework for rethinking the intersection of democracy and U.S. public education in the 21st century, when the traditional values of each are at risk of subsumption by a reductivist neoliberal agenda. Our reading therefore complements Kenneth Kidd's (2005) observation that *The Giver* may productively be read "against its own custodial investments" as "a cautionary tale about contemporary US culture" and specifically about "the need for a thoughtful literature of atrocity" (p. 144). Exploring the novel's thematic preoccupation with alienation, homogeneity, and the social production of the subject, we read *The Giver*'s ending as hopeful rather than hopeless, as the utopian figuration of un-alienated life tinctured with wonder and awe and as a call for an educative praxis with the capacity to manifest such a reality.

SAMENESS AS ARGUMENT FOR SECURITY

It is perhaps useful to begin our look at *The Giver* as an allegory of the contemporary crisis of democracy and education with a commentary on the astonishingly familiar curriculum that Lowry (1993) constructs for the novel's collectivist dystopia. Pursuant the community's philosophical adequation of public education and vocational training, or of learning's ultimately economic valuation, Jonas' school curriculum has been purged of all ancillary inefficiencies as well as any subjects that might inspire a dangerously individuated form of intellection. The elimination of the liberal arts is, of course, *de rigueur* in such fantasies of the "totalitarian" from Zamyatin's (1924/1960) *We* to Bradbury's (1953) *Fahrenheit 451*, yet Lowry's (1993) dystopian academy recalls nothing if not the standardized curricula of contemporary North American public schools, wherein the humanities have withstood decades of steady erosion, if not outright hostility, in the face of the neoliberal imperative. Consisting of four principal concentrations (language and communications; commerce and industry; science and technology; civil procedures and government), Lowry's fictional course of study reflects the attitudes of both the neoliberal left and right, which are today little more than opposing cultural idioms of a continuous material substructure.

For representation of the neoliberal left, one may look to President Obama's educational address from September of 2011, where he exhorts students to stay in schools so that "We'll be able to make sure the newest inventions and the latest breakthroughs happen right here in the United States of America." He exhorts students to remember that the, "first obligation is to make sure that you're preparing yourself for college and career" (Obama, 2011, para. 25). There is no mention of a commitment to community, and the word "democracy" does not appear in his address. On what might appear to be the other side of the political aisle, one hears similar arguments for techno-industrial schooling from the neoliberal right, with think tanks such as the Hoover Institute arguing that purported failure to compete on international tests is not only an indication that schools are "failing," but a justification for market based reforms such as vouchers, charters, and for-profit schools. In either case, democratic possibility is beholden to the dictates of economic rationality.

In the increasingly desperate scramble to justify curricular viability in an era of ever-attenuating state appropriations, schools (public universities included) have turned to the rhetoric of technical, professional, and vocational instruction, and the promise of gainful employment in a perpetually uncertain economy. It is this uncertainty that neoliberal educational reformers claim to eliminate via scripted schooling. Nowhere is this more evident than in the national movement towards adopting universal "common core" state standards, an initiative funded by the Bill and Melinda Gates Foundation before being adopted by the federal government as part of President Obama's Race To The Top (RTT) program. The homepage for the movement—now 44 states strong—is worth quoting at length as it speaks to the homogenizing economism undergirding public school "reform":

> The Common Core State Standards provide a consistent, clear understanding of what students are expected to learn, so teachers and parents know what they need to do to help them. The standards are designed to be robust and relevant to the real world, reflecting the knowledge and skills that our young people need for success in college and careers. With American students fully prepared for the future, our communities will be best positioned to compete successfully in the global economy. (http://www.corestandards.org/)

As the neoliberal elite impose increasingly prescriptive determinations for what "young people need for success in college and careers," three questions confront today's public schools: Why relinquish the responsibilities of curricular choice to those with the least interest in the public as such? Whose interests are served by existing choices? And finally, if we know what needs to be known, what knowledge remains forbidden or inaccessible? Asked differently, what is omitted from schooling in order to ensure that all students know the common? All three questions can be productively addressed with Lowry's (1993) help.

THE ELIMINATION OF CURRICULAR CHOICE

While Lowry's (1993) text is ostensibly a belated critique of the socialist state, much of it reads right out of neoliberal educational policy. Why should curricular choice be eliminated? For the same reason that choice has been eliminated from Jonas's community. It's safer:

> "We don't dare to let people make choices of their own."
> "Not safe?" The Giver suggested.
> "Definitely not safe," Jonas said with certainty. "What if they were allowed to choose their own mate? And chose *wrong*?
> "Or what if," he went on, almost laughing at the absurdity, "they chose their own *jobs*?"
> "Frightening, isn't it?" The Giver said.
> Jonas chuckled. "Very frightening. I can't even imagine it. We really have to protect people from wrong choices."
> "It's safer."
> "Yes, Jonas agreed. "Much safer." (pp. 98-99)

The standard answer to question one, why suspend democratic curricular choice, is that it is for the good of the country, as local school districts or empowered teachers, however well-intentioned, might make dangerously wrong choices, thereby setting the stage for purported economic collapse. Former Speaker of the House Newt Gingrich's 2004 testimony to the Senate Committee on Commerce, Science, and Transportation offers a disturbing example of the terroristic rhetoric used to justify the de-democratization of public schools. The second greatest threat to America, he warns his audience, is U.S. public education: "only the threat of a weapon of mass destruction in an American city [is] a greater danger" (Gingrich, 2002, para. 1). The rhetorical equation of public education with terroristic threat suggests more than the ravings of an ideologue appealing to his base; it intimates on the one hand a pervasive fear of the public and of democracy voiced by its presumptive (and publicly elected) stewards and, on the other, the subordination of public values to the imperatives of profit.

Therefore, as for the second question, whose interests are served, our free market democracy is not markedly different from that of Lowry's (1993) socialist dystopia, as in the former case self-appointed experts (at the behest of their corporate paymasters) oversee the good of the community and offer the increasingly impoverished terms of "democratic" choice. Thus again, apropos our own situation, Lowry's words are telling: "Our people made that choice, the choice to go to Sameness.... We gained control of many things. But we had to let go of others" (p. 95). The letting go underscores the import of our third question, what doesn't need to be known? What has been "let go" in our public schools, what is left unknown, is no different from what has been "let go" from Jonas' education. The arts and humanities, facilitators of critical thought and its modes of expression, are among the most notable curricular losses (Nichols & Berliner 2007; Smith & Kovacs, 2011). There is, however, one subject in particular that must be occluded in order to maintain totalitarian rule, and we feel that it warrants extended discussion.

THE END OF HISTORY AND THE REGULATION OF LANGUAGE

This most immediately evident curricular omission, one whose acute absence resonates throughout the novel and underpins the political and economic substructures of its Community, is that of history. Excised from public consciousness, history is entrusted to the eponymous Giver, a mysterious figure who serves the function of Jacques Lacan's (1967) *subject supposed to know,* whose informed presence, like that of the Cartesian "God," secures the structure of the social order and allows its inhabitants to carry on without concerning themselves with those questions that might unsettle its fundamental coordinates—questions that Jonas' selection as Receiver permits him to ask for the first time. Thus confronted with the terrifying deflation of his society's Big Other or defining mythos (less through the gentle person of the Giver than through the historical content, both traumatic and banal, that his office keeps at bay), the dilemma facing Jonas is whether to assume the place of this now demystified *subject supposed to know,* thereby preserving the existing social dispensation, or to risk seeking an Elsewhere that would at once restore history to the public sphere and irreparably alter, if not destroy, the Community.

Here, in particular, the novel is characterized by a curious internal dissonance or contradiction, for as Jonas discovers in his sessions with the Giver, the occluded history he is to receive is neither personal nor individual but collective and global, what the Giver describes as "the memories of the whole world.... Before you, before me, before the previous Receiver, and generations before him" (Lowry, 1993, p. 77). Paradoxically, then, what this collectivist "utopia" most lacks is not simply an ethos of healthy individualism (which Lowry does not fail to advocate throughout the book) but a totalizing historical consciousness flexible and capacious enough to accommodate the counter-histories of "them" and of Elsewhere; something which Jonas, who has heretofore known only the perpetual present of the Community, finds incomprehensible: "He tried, in his mind, to grasp the concept. 'I'm sorry, sir. I don't understand exactly. Maybe I'm not smart enough. I don't know what you mean when you say "the whole world" or "generations before him." I thought there was only us. I thought there was only now" (p. 77).

Indeed, Jonas could be speaking here for the majority of American public school students, whose history curriculum reinforces the hegemonic doctrines of American exceptionalism and Manifest Destiny by either omitting altogether those less palatable chapters of its national narrative (as well as the alterior perspectives of other global histories) or by reducing the scope and scale of that history to an episodic series of familiar, canonical tableaux, beginning with Columbus's putative discovery of the new world and ending just before the Vietnam War. "History" is thereby reduced to a kind of rote and unreflective nominalism, an inert object of knowledge bearing no meaningful relation to or impingement upon an implacable, insular present. This is of course the only "teaching" of history possible for maintaining the neoliberal economic/social order, one based on the presumption of progress and safeguarded by fear and pathological presentism. In Don Latham's (2004) Foucauldian reading of *The Giver*, he reminds us that docile bodies, subjected and regulated, are essential for transforming individuals into "a viable economic force" (p. 136). Children not subjected to a regulated history, a history not bound by the corporate sanctioned "common," are a danger to the economic imperative as an alternative, critical, teaching of history risks a population capable not only of question and critique but of innovation and creation unencumbered by the delimiting requirements of capital.

A critical historical pedagogy would arguably move our country away from what E. Wayne Ross (2007) calls a "spectator democracy" where we watch while others act and move us toward a more organic, democratic social order maintained by an engaged "public" as imagined by John Dewey (1944): "Capacities are limited by the objects and tools at hand. They are still more dependent upon the prevailing habits of attention and interest which are set by traditional and institutional customs" (p. 210). The "traditional and institutional customs" of today's public schools, and arguably the society housing them, are no different than the school and society housing Jonas. Both school for work, and by necessity the capacities called upon, are vocational rather than critical, "the prevailing habits of attention and interest" focused on (re)production rather than transcendence or transformation. Importantly, the latter are prevented both in real time and in the novel because grappling with the past requires the pain associated with knowing—for example, the pain we keep from children when history lessons omit the horrors inflicted upon natives by colonizers and fail to acknowledge what Walter Benjamin (1968) describes as the barbarism that lies beneath what we recognize as culture (p. 256).

This historical pain is precisely the pain avoided in Jonas' institutional schooling. True education, Lowry (1993) seems to suggest, is marked by the presence of physical and psychic pain. Indeed, Kidd (2005) describes *The Giver* as "a novel of the education of the senses" in which the predominant lesson is "that pain must be shared if human beings are to have authentic selves" and that the "privatization of pain/wisdom does not a legitimate culture make" (p. 144). As Fredric Jameson (1981) famously reminds us, "history is what hurts," and it is this traumatic core of historical experience that refuses full inscription into the inert and idyllic narratives of a national/cultural past (p. 102). The Giver's history has this precise effect on Jonas, who, after learning the truth about war, "did not want to go back. He didn't want the memories, didn't want the honor, didn't want the wisdom, didn't want the pain" (Lowry, 1993, p. 120). In pain we question, and when we question, the normative veneers of "order" or "democracy" melt into air.

Jonas's direct encounter with a historical content expunged from the living reality of the Community, an experience both terrifying and thrilling, therefore ruptures the normative boundaries of that reality and opens up the cognitive and perceptual possibility of its "Elsewhere," or of Utopia itself, the literal "no place" or empty set that Theodore Adorno (1970/1997) defines as "the determinate negation of that which merely is" (p. 32). Elsewhere functions not simply as a place here but as a cognitive and political practice, the impossible third "space" beyond the novel's starkly posited antinomies of the collective and the individual, security and freedom, univocality and dissonance—one actualized when young Jonas begins to "see beyond" the monochromatic limits of his world as given, when the suffocating plenitude of his reality is subject to the estranging leverage of dialectical (which is to say relational, differential) thought. The collective repression of history in Lowry's (1993) dystopia works (like all similar prohibitions in the book) to secure the Community's foremost ethical imperative: Sameness. From the elimination of color and difference to the regulation of the weather, homogeneity is the Community's most prominent organizing principle and the unconcealed object of Lowry's sustained critique.

This quest for sameness is perhaps most apparent in the obsessively monologic regulation of language in the novel. Jonas and his peers are routinely schooled in the necessity of being "careful about language," in the dangers inherent to hyperbolic, figurative, or ironic modes of expression that might admit space for dialogic innovation or imaginative imprecision (Lowry, 1993, p. 3). The verbal infelicities of the tragically clumsy Asher—

publicly humiliated for using "distraught" in place of the more precise "distracted" and, as a Three, having received "a series of painful lashes" for his willful conflation of "snack" and "smack"—serve as object lessons for Jonas in this regard, who takes great care to speak with precision, with one exception. After a particularly "warm" session with the Giver, Jonas asks his parents if they love him. Upon doing so "there was an awkward silence," before his parents chastise him for using a "very generalized word, so meaningless that it's become almost obsolete" (p. 127). Love is a concept that cannot be homogenized or standardized and has therefore been eliminated from the community's vocabulary. It thus marks the limits of thought itself within the community's enclosures, a crucial point to which we shall return.

Inasmuch as the representation of such state-mandated uniformity recalls Cold War caricatures of a hive-minded collective inhabiting dismally-uniform housing blocks, wearing identical clothes and driving identical cars, Lowry's (1993) criticism finds its mark, and the Community's repressive ethos of homogeneity may clearly be said to function as a foil for the novel's heroically untrammeled individual. Yet, as Herbert Marcuse recognized in 1964, the new "totalitarianism" of consumer capitalism operates precisely through its ability to manage social antagonism by absorbing and leveling cultural expression onto a one-dimensional plane in which radical differences are harmonized and neutralized through a superficially permissive "pluralism" that conceals the drab homogeneity and iron-clad material necessity that lie beneath. Thus, the suppression of history *as difference* is "not an academic but a political affair. It is the suppression of the society's own past—and of its future, inasmuch as this future invokes the qualitative change, the negation of the present," which is, as Adorno instructs, another word for Utopia (Marcuse, 1964/1991, p. 97).

For Marcuse (1964/1991), such policing of expression, inasmuch as it imposes sanctioned meanings and images and "militates against the development and expression of *concepts*," is nothing less than the suppression of history (p. 95). As he observes, "in its immediacy and directness," such meticulously abridged and functionalized language "impedes conceptual thinking; thus, it impedes thinking" as such, leading to an order of one-dimensional thought (p. 95). Marcuse writes:

> If the linguistic behavior blocks conceptual development, if it militates against abstraction and mediation, if it surrenders to the immediate facts, it repels recognition of the factors behind the facts, and thus repels recognition of the facts, and of their historical content. (p. 97)

Such a historyless world, he argues, in which,

> the categories of freedom have become interchangeable and even identical with their opposites is not only practicing Orwellian or Aesopian language,

> but is repulsing and forgetting the historical reality—the horror of fascism; the idea of socialism; the preconditions of democracy; the content of freedom. (pp. 97-98)

We argue that such totalitarian and anti-democratic impulses likewise inform the operational rationality of public schools today, specifically in regards to surveillance and standardization.

SURVEILLANCE SEEN AND UNSEEN

A standard feature of the contemporary dystopia from the ubiquitous telescreens of Orwell's (1949/1977) *1984* to the security cameras of Moore's (1982) *V for Vendetta*, omnipresent mass surveillance figures prominently in *The Giver* as well. In Lowry's (1993) dystopia, however, surveillance is, while pervasive, unobtrusive and almost totally unseen (save for the loudspeaker, which, significantly, no one except the Giver has the power to turn off). The unspectacular presence of the community's surveillance mechanisms may be said to trace the development within the dystopian genre of what Foucault (1977/1995) describes as the disciplinary transition from the culture of the *spectacle* to that of the *carceral* (pp. 298-299). While the former enacts public displays of bodily discipline, the latter is characterized by the naturalization and internalization of regulatory schemas; the mediating and mystifying presence of a byzantine bureaucracy; social and cognitive compartmentalization into discrete competencies; and the ceaseless surveillance that oversees the maintenance of the above.

The function of such stealth-surveillance is indicated in *The Giver* within the domains of the private—in the warning that Jonas receives after stealing the apple—as much as in that of the public—in the mechanical efficiency with which children are assigned professions and, as adults, given mates. In each case, judgments are determined with certainty based on information surreptitiously gathered by the community elders. "The community was so meticulously ordered, the choices so carefully made," notes Jonas as he waits for his assignment (Lowry, 1993, p. 48). When selected to become the Receiver of Memory, the Chief Elder's comment to Jonas serves the dual ideological functions of avuncular praise and reassurance as well as regulatory admonition: "Jonas was identified as a possible Receiver many years ago. We have observed him meticulously. There were no dreams of uncertainty" (p. 62).

Similarly, surveillance in our public schools, employed for both safety and examination, operates unquestioned. Schools require surveillance, we are told, for the sake of student and teacher safety. Video cameras, armed guards, and security checkpoint accesses are increasingly common in most public schools despite copious research demonstrating that children are safer inside of schools than out (Monahan & Torres, 2010). As Monahan and Torres (2010) remind us, both an armed guard and a closed-circuit surveillance system were in place at Columbine in 1999 and did nothing to deter the horrific events of April 20. Media coverage of the Columbine shooting has been pressed into service for a neoliberal ideological agenda, perpetuating irrational fears that public school violence is increasingly pervasive and that more restrictive and intrusive methods of subject management are required; captured on film, images of the shooting are strategically replayed to remind a fearful populace that public schools (like all unchecked *public* spaces) are inherently dangerous and require disciplinary instruments of social management that can be provided only by the unconstrained innovation of the profit-driven corporation. Ronnie Casella (2010), who researched 75 security businesses that court school districts, offers the following market-based analysis of "school fortification," and while we disagree with Casella's assertion that social control is not a motivator behind increased school surveillance, her larger argument is instructive:

> The fortification of schools is primarily a business response to safety. Safety has become a commodity that is sold by security professionals whose purpose, after all, is to make money and to create profit for the security companies for which they work … the installation of security equipment in schools is foremost a corporate transaction led not by people who can guarantee us safety, and not by tyrants imposing social control, but rather by business people who convince us that the products they have for sale will give us peace of mind. (p. 75)

A somewhat different (though certainly no less disciplinary or profitable) type of surveillance exists to monitor student and teacher performance. Standardized tests, ubiquitous in Grades 1-12 (and, for states accepting money from RTT, now in kindergarten) function to identify failing students, failing teachers, and failing schools, offering local, state, and federal educational agencies a proprietary view into public school classrooms, further ensuring that students are both subjected and regulated. The practical justification often voiced for these tests is that they protect our country's standing in the global economy as policymakers, in the absence of any empirical justification, have accepted the neoliberal article of faith that test scores measure economic competitiveness. Refusing to allow communities to democratically determine the means and ends of schooling, high-stakes standardized testing, coupled with national standards, is an efficient mechanism for guaranteeing that workers remain "on task."

Important to our reading of *The Giver*, surveillance by testing atomizes the educational process, transforming the student into an isolated data point and neglecting the importance of socioeconomic determinates. Failure to perform well on the test and in the system is clearly the fault of the student, or in the case of No Child Left Behind, the teacher. The society housing both and the macroeconomic conditions permeating it are left unexamined, unchallenged, and unchanged by a populace focused on data rather than existential realities. In classrooms where teacher pay is linked to student performance on these tests, students are little more than day laborers, who often leave school to complete hours of homework every night. The entire process, perpetuated in the name of economic competitiveness, is a renewed vindication of Marx (1848/1978), who lamented a society where children were "transformed into simple articles of commerce and instruments of labour" (p. 488). In the loveless classrooms of today, where the bottom line is market competitiveness, children are indeed instruments of labor, articles of commerce for teachers whose pay is increasingly linked to student output. The higher the children score, the bigger the teacher's bonus in a market not possible without this instrument of standardization. Lost in this individualist schooling for economy is any possibility of schooling for the other, for community beyond market, for democracy as space for transcendence and growth.

LOVE AS ONTOLOGICAL FORCE

Against popular readings to the contrary, therefore, we suggest that Jonas's revelation consists of precisely the obverse of the narrative's ostensibly individualist ethic. That is, Jonas's final decision to leave the Community is informed as much by his *love* for it as for his concern over his own future or that of the child (whose life he *selflessly* saves). By *love of community*, we do not mean to invoke here the spirit of *amor patriae*, the pieties of which serve only to stabilize the bureaucratic function of the state though compulsive rituals of submission, such as the daily "chanting of the morning anthem" found in any public classroom in the United States fully as much as in the totalitarian dystopia of *The Giver*. We do not intend the decadent forms of individualist or identitarian "*love of the same*" which, as Michael Hardt and Antonio Negri (2009) observe, "imagines people finding their match, like lost puzzle pieces, that now together make (or restore) a whole" (p. 183). Rather, the love that motivates Jonas's revolutionary act can be seen as what Hardt and Negri alternatively theorize as "an ontological event" that simultaneously "marks a rupture with what exists and the creation of the new" (p. 181).

Love, in this sense, is a kind of ontological force, an act transformative of being itself, a Whitmanesque "love of the farthest" or of the alterior that refuses the normative constraints of homogenizing, mechanical repetition. Love, therefore, always involves a deployment of force to the situation from which it emerges, transforming its coordinates and conditioning new and emergent situations from within. Initially bewildered and frightened by the Giver's revelations, which are altogether outside the comforting symbolic strictures of Jonas's former reality, Jonas soon comes to understand, *even to desire* the enlargement of his empathetic powers, even when those involve disorientation, uncertainty, doubt, even pain: the essential conditions, we submit, for effective and meaningful education. In other words, education, as the teacher already knows, is an agent of love, love unafraid of and even emboldened by *risk*, or the uncompromising wager on Elsewhere.

Such a conceptualization of love as an ontological forcing, as the spirit of risk that hazards beyond the enclosures of *certain* identity, informs our understanding of the novel's famously ambiguous conclusion. Against readings that posit an infinite return secured through asphyxiating formal closure, we read the final scene as the crystallization of the spirit of risk and of love: not the precarious self-regard of neoliberalism's chimerical individual, but the gestural figuration of the unfinished collective project of Utopia. We thus endeavor to complicate critical appraisals like those of Susan Louise Stewart (2007), who argues from a poststructuralist critique of humanism that "while it appears that Jonas's actions are quote radical, they are actually quite conservative," that "flight from the community is nothing less than a return to the humanist subject position many readers occupy, wherein the individual takes precedence over the community" (p. 25). Alternatively, and in accord with Latham (2004), who acknowledges the possibility that Jonas' departure may in fact return the community to one where feeling exists and is shared, we argue that in repudiating the "heuristic of fear" that Zygmunt Bauman (1993) privileges as the guiding principle of a pathologically cautious postmodern ethic, Jonas' final gambit exceeds the ideological and representational guarantees of Community bureaucracy and wagers on the uncertainty and vitality of Elsewhere.

Jonas' rejection of the Giver's mantle (as *subject supposed to know*) is therefore continuous with what Marcuse (1964/1991) terms "the great refusal" and is finally intelligible as an act of ontological becoming or of love. Risking the reintroduction of "unmediated" history into the hermetic enclosure of the Community, Jonas' departure is finally, then, the heroic rupturing of that outer boundary and the reaffirmation of the individual's role in *collective* possibility. The warmth and light toward which Jonas struggles is decidedly not the sanctuary of self-interested individualism—figured by the mortal threat of starvation and exposure—but is a community *not yet*, one that dialectically reconciles, mediates, or refuses the oppositional binary terms of totalitarian community and untrammeled individual and, for that reason, exceeds the representational limits of the novel itself. The novel thus achieves in its stubborn indeterminacy a formal expression of the prospective horizon that Ernst Bloch (1959/1986) holds as indispensable for utopian imagining. This imagined community, we suggest, is none other than true democracy, for which, in his one and only act as Giver, Jonas clears space by refusing the awful responsibility of the keeper of history and, in what is perhaps the greatest example of education in the novel, entrusting that responsibility to the community itself.

SCHOOLING FOR ELSEWHERE

Yet, one must ask, in the ebullient post-Cold War moment of the early nineties, *where* is Elsewhere? And given the book's subsequent installation as a perennial selection for secondary literary instruction, we might also inquire why today's young readers, for whom the political propaganda of 25 years ago is all but illegible, continue to identify with Jonas' search for alternatives to the Sameness? In short, we argue, Lowry invites us to ask, where is the Elsewhere of today's public classroom? Said differently, if public schools were spaces free of the authoritarian constraints of the market, what would they look like and how might they function? In keeping with the ambiguously utopian ending of the text, we would like to offer two opposing visions for Elsewhere's schools.

In *Beyond Learning: Democratic Education for a Human Future*, Gert Biesta (2006) argues that the educator in particular and education in general should focus on the task of bringing unique beings into existence. In his words: "The role of the educator ... has to be understood in terms of a responsibility for 'the coming into the world' of unique, singular beings, and a responsibility for the world as a world of plurality and difference" (p. 9). This requires the understanding that education is not merely a responsibility to the student; rather, "it is at the very same time a responsibility for the world. It is a responsibility to create and keep in existence a 'worldly space' through which new beginnings can come into presence" (p. 107). Biesta acknowledges that which market-driven educational reformers would have us ignore, that schools do not exist in a vacuum, that the means and ends of education transcend classroom walls, and that the issues that permeate our society permeate the schools tasked with either reproducing or re-imagining that society. While we acknowledge that asking teachers who are already overworked to take "responsibility for the world" is a tall order, especially in a world rife with issues outside of the control of teacher as individual, in Elsewhere's schools, we imagine a professional body of teachers capable of working together to realize change both in their classrooms and the communities housing them. This, arguably, has been the goal of Social Foundations programs across the country for the better part of 40 years.

Understood through Biesta, education for Elsewhere requires a partial rejection of or break with humanism as schooling's foundation. Biesta (2006) correctly argues that humanism "cannot grasp the uniqueness of each individual human being. It can only think of each newcomer as an instance of a human essence that has already been specified and is already known in advance" (p. 7). This is a part of humanism that has been pressed into service by neoliberal machinery with its requirements for docile, obedient bodies prepped for labor. Under neoliberal educational reforms, where Sameness permeates the curriculum, teachers are forced to compare students to the ideal human at grade level X, administering the proper curricula to produce a subject prepared to perform well at grade level Y. Truth, capital "T," and Beauty, capital "B," are pre-determined by market need and are not open for democratic debate or dissent. Recall the Common Core movement, which is in effect an operating manual to ensure quality control for factories. Following the manual will produce the ideal subject, or so the logic goes. This logic is certainly clear in Lowry's (1993) text, with the Community's carefully observed students following prescriptive curricula on their way to assured future employment. At the same time, this logic undergirds American public schools, where carefully observed students follow increasingly scripted curricula as they compete for selection into esteemed universities with no guarantee of future employment. We imagine schooling for Elsewhere to encourage disparate ends with children and adults co-creating the schools and the worlds housing them. This is not a far cry from what Dewey (1944) imagined in *Democracy and Education* or any of his major works regarding education for that matter.

Without being too prescriptive, a pedagogy respecting the uniqueness of beings would involve choice, the very choice eliminated in Lowry's dystopia and our own reality. In an English classroom a teacher might invite students to select a topic of some significance to who they were, are, or wish to be. A math teacher might ask students to explain the mathematics behind a topic of student choice. This could also take place in a history, geography or science classroom. What is important is not the subject per se but rather the exploration and mastery of said topic *with* a student driven by a very real desire to learn rather than *by* the compulsion of a teacher trying to make sure that every student absorbs every pre-determined, common-core fact.

Such an educative praxis would be determined by, and be inextricable from, the communities that it serves and sensitive to the dialectical interrelation of formerly isolated and specialized subjects. Thus, a group of students concerned about environmental issues might undertake a study of their local ecosystem. Extending beyond respecting the student as a unique being and recalling that Biesta (2006) argues that teachers have a responsibility towards the world housing those unique beings, the students might visit a local stream and run water quality tests to identify and quantify contaminants in the water supply as well as the soil lining the stream's banks. Working in conjunction with a history teacher, students might study the broad history of environmentalism as well as the history of local environmental practices including agriculture, livestock, factory farming, and so on. Interviews with local practitioners in these fields as well as with the corporate farming agencies that have colonized them would more deeply situate student learning within the worlds they emerge into.

Perhaps working in small groups, students might compare and contrast their findings with one another while at the same time using connections afforded by the web to reach out to larger communities of learners and scientists investigating similar phenomena. With the help of their language arts teacher(s), the students might work dialectically toward crafting a comprehensive diagnosis and plan of action for enacting change in their area of study. Contacting members of the media and approaching elected officials with compelling narratives, empirically-based research, and artistic representations of what the ecosystem of study could and arguably should be, students would learn that subjects are not ends unto themselves, but that math, science, English, history, and the arts can be used, dialectically, as part of a collective enterprise towards building a more humane world. This materialist pedagogy, both global and local, would restore a sense of place and of public that is missing from today's common core schooling.

In opposition to a negotiated schooling that respects the uniqueness of individual beings coming into existence in a world of plurality and difference, we wish to offer a vision of schooling for Elsewhere that has predetermined ends in mind for every student who walks into the classroom. Such students would be called "educated" when they prove to be able to identify, access, and utilize information from various knowledge systems in order to effect progressive change in a given space over a given amount of time. Nurturing the development of such individuals requires a much different type of teacher and teaching than what is articulated in *The Giver* (Lowry, 1993) or than exists in public schools today, especially in poor-minority schools where scripted lessons and teaching to the test have become ubiquitous (Perlstein, 2007; Ravitch, 2010). Elsewhere's teachers would cultivate intelligent behavior, promoting the creation of knowledge rather than its assimilation and regurgitation. They would help children develop skills and capacities such as impulse control and listening to others with understanding and empathy in opposition to the quick, reflexive answers and the indifference to others required by market-based schooling.

Elsewhere's teachers help nurture the development of critical, engaged doers as opposed to obedient, complacent consumers who are exhorted to shop in response to national crises. Teachers for Elsewhere help children synthesize ideas, evaluate and appraise work, discriminate results, critique and defend critiques. Such teachers encourage students to take calculated risks and engage passionately with work both chosen and assigned and ask them to employ creative curiosity, to think metacognitively, to act patiently as deconstructive-reconstructive thinkers who question, pose problems, imagine alternatives, and transfer ideas and artifacts from one realm of experience and expertise to another. And finally, teachers for Elsewhere encourage children to forgive and persevere, getting up after being knocked down, as the only thing any of us can guarantee is that you are either on your way up or on your way down, and there's no sense spending too much time carrying anger from the trip, or what Ralph Waldo Emerson (1847/2007) called dragging about the corpse of your memory. We imagine an Elsewhere populated by individuals who have learned both to forgive and to love, individuals capable of serious debate and engagement with others without resentment or intolerance for alternative points of views, individuals who pause, consider, and imagine futures that involve the synthesis of what at first appear to be impossibly incompatible ideas. Indeed, such traits are not far-removed from those possessed by Jonas as Receiver: intelligence, integrity, courage, endurance, perseverance, wisdom, and the capacity to see beyond. If we began our educational endeavors with such ends in mind, with special regard to asking students to see beyond, would we be imagining elsewhere or living it?

REFERENCES

Atwood, M. (1985). *The handmaid's tale.* Toronto, Ontario: McClelland and Stewart.

Adorno, T. (1997). *Aesthetic theory.* (R. Hullot-Kentnor, Trans.). Minneapolis, MN: University of Minnesota Press. (Original work published 1970)

Benjamin, W. (1968). Theses on the philosophy of history. (H. Zohn, Trans.). In H. Arendt (Ed.), *Illuminations: Essays and reflections* (pp. 253-264). New York, NY: Harcourt Brace.

Bauman, Z. (1993). *Postmodern ethics*. Malden, MA: Blackwell.

Biesta, G. (2006). *Beyond learning: Democratic education for a human future*. Boulder, CO: Paradigm Press.

Bloch, E. (1986). *The principle of hope* (Vol. 1). (N. Plaice, S. Plaice, P. Knight, Trans.). Cambridge, MA: MIT Press. (Original work published 1959)

Bradbury, R. (1953) *Fahrenheit 451*. New York, NY: Ballantine Books.

Casella, R. (2010). Safety or social control? The security fortification of schools in a capitalist society. In T. Monahan & R. Torres (Ed.), *Schools under surveillance: Cultures of control in public education* (pp. 73-86). Piscataway, NJ: Rutgers Universtiy Press.

The Common Core State Standards. (n.d.). Mission statement. Retrieved from http://www.corestandards.org.

Dewey, J. (1927) *The public and its problems*. Chicago, IL: The Swallow Press.

Dewey, J. (1944). *Democracy and education: An introduction to the philosophy of education*. New York, NY: The Free Press.

Emerson, R.W. (2007). *Essays: First series*. Stilwell, KS: Digireads.com. (Original work published 1847)

Foucault, M. (1995). *Discipline and punish*. (A. Sheridan, Trans.). New York, NY: Random House. (Original work published 1977)

Gingrich, N. (2002, May 22). We must expand our investment in science. Retrieved from http://www.aei.org/speech/education/we-must-expand-our-investment-in-science/

Hardt, M., & Negri, A. (2009). *Common wealth*. Cambridge, MA: The Belknap Press of Harvard University Press.

Jameson, F. (1981). *The Political unconscious: Narrative as socially symbolic act*. Ithaca, NY: Cornell University Press.

Kidd, K. (2005). "A" is for Auschwitz: psychoanalysis, trauma theory, and the "children's literature of atrocity." *Children's Literature, 33*, 120-149.

Lacan, J. (1967). The mistaking of the subject supposed to know. *Silicet, 1*, 31-41.

Latham, D. (2004). Discipline and its discontents: A foucauldian reading of the giver. *Children's Literature, 32*, 134-151.

Lowry, L. (1993). *The giver*. New York, NY: Random House.

Marcuse, H. (1991). *One-Dimensional man: Studies in the ideology of advanced industrial society*. Boston, MA: Beacon Press. (Original work published 1964)

Marx, K. (1978). Manifesto of the communist party. In R. Tucker, *The Marx-Engels reader* (2nd ed., pp. 469-500). New York, NY: W. W. Norton. (Original work published 1848).

Monahan, T. & Torres, R. (2010). Introduction. In T. Monahan & R. Torres, (Eds.), *Schools under surveillance: Cultures of control in public education* (pp. 1-18). Piscataway, NJ: Rutgers Universtiy Press.

Moore, A. (1982). *V for vendetta*. New York, NY: DC Comics.

Nichols, S., & Berliner, D. (2007). *Collateral damage: How high stakes testing corrupts America's schools*. Cambridge, MA: Harvard Education Press.

Obama, B. (2011, September 28). Remarks at Benjamin Banneker High School. Retrieved from http://m.whitehouse.gov/the-press-office/2011/09/28/remarks-president-back-school-speech.

Orwell, G. (1977). *1984*. NY: Penguin. (Original work published 1949)

Perlstein, L. (2007). *Tested: One American school struggles to make the grade*. New York, NY: Henry Holt.

Ravitch, D. (2010). *The death and life of the great American public school system*. New York, NY: Basic Books.

Ross, E. W. (2007). Social studies education. In D. Gabbard (Ed.), *Knowledge & power in the global economy: The effects of school reform in a neoliberal/neoconservative age* (2nd ed. pp. 367-365). New York, NY: Lawrence Erlbauum Associates.

Smith, J., & Kovacs, P. (2011). The impact of standards-based reform on teachers: The case of "No Child Left Behind." *Teachers and Teaching: Theory and Practice, 17*(2), 201-225.

Stuart, S. L. (2007). A return to normal: Lois Lowry's the giver. *The Lion and the Unicorn, 31*(1), 21-35.

Wegner, P. (2009). *Life between two deaths, 1989-2001: U.S. culture in the long nineties*. Durham, NC: Duke University Press.

Zamyatin, Y. (1960). *We* (B. G. Guerney, Trans.). New York, NY: Random House. (Original work published 1924)

CHAPTER 8

WHEN UNDERGRADUATE STUDENTS READ HUXLEY'S *BRAVE NEW WORLD* AND PLATO'S *THE REPUBLIC* IN AN EDUCATIONAL FOUNDATIONS COURSE

Steven P. Jones

INTRODUCTION

Borrowing from or being influenced by the great ideas of authors and philosophers who have gone before, and speaking directly or indirectly to the great texts those authors have produced—this is not just de rigueur for serious writers, but an essential act if they wish their own ideas to be taken seriously. As has been noted by a host of literary scholars, one of the great thinkers Aldous Huxley (1932/1998) speaks to in his dystopian novel *Brave New World* is Plato (1968), in particular the Plato (or, really, the Socrates) we encounter in *The Republic*.

But Huxley does much more than just borrow from or speak to Plato and his Socrates. In *Brave New World*, Huxley (1932/1998) takes on the

Dystopia and Education:
Insights Into Theory, Praxis, and Policy in an Age of Utopia-Gone-Wrong, pp. 117–136

ideas of Plato doggedly, point by point. He does this not as an antagonist of Socrates—not as, in *The Republic*, Thrasymachus would like to do to Socrates to embarrass him and prove him both wrong and naïve. Quite to the contrary, Huxley honors the knowledge and insight of Socrates, the great utopian idealist, even as he takes those ideas and fashions his dystopian masterpiece out of them. Socrates is, according to Huxley, right on every count—from the caste hierarchy, the passions that come with sexual relations and family, the importance of the noble lie, the philosopher/king, the passions aroused by music, and more.

The careful reader matches the arguments and explanations of Mustopha Mond in *Brave New World* to the arguments and explanations of Socrates in *The Republic*, and by doing so learns about some of the essential questions of political life—questions Huxley (1932/1998) embraces together with Socrates. Huxley often reverses Socratic dicta—Huxley and Socrates end up pursuing very different ideals and end up arguing for very different societies. Huxley's dystopia evinces an argument for personal freedom; Socrates' utopia evinces an argument for human perfection, the kind of rational human perfection realized by the philosopher-kings. And so we end up with a battle between the moderns and the ancients—Huxley favoring the murky, sometimes muddled and always problematic modern ideal of human freedom where characters like Helmholtz will energetically toil; and where Socrates favors the clear-sighted, managed world where a man like Socrates can realize the perfection of his nature. In a final ironic twist, the utopia argues for a controlled, stable, perfect hell in which not many moderns would want to live, and the dystopia argues for an unstable, imperfect but impassioned heaven where we will continue to labor.

Reading Huxley's (1932/1998) *Brave New World* as a conversation with Plato's (1968) *The Republic* deepens our understanding of the modern text, highlights the essential social and political questions that shape human life, and points to the tension between modernity and the ancient world. Reading this dystopia in terms of Plato's utopia also deepens how we read and understand this kind of literature. A dystopia starts by showing us what social life prevents; the utopia, by showing what is possible. But the best dystopias are really just like the best utopias—valuable for the picture of human possibilities that sooner or later emerge in the argument, but also as an argument for how to see the great issues and questions in the political and social world. A good dystopia and a good utopia give us tools to think with and ideas to think about.

The first part of this essay outlines some of the ways Huxley (1932/1998) takes up the ideas of Socrates as Socrates outlines the ideal city for his two chief interlocutors, Glaucon and Adeimantus in *The Republic of Plato* (1968). The second part of the essay discusses my experience teaching these texts in an undergraduate teacher education foundations course and includes excerpts from student papers produced in that course. The final section of the essay is really a special pleading on my part—a pleading for teacher education faculty to use dystopian literature not as a vehicle for a diatribe or harangue about the evils of modern society—especially modern capitalistic and technological societies—but as ways to take-up with students a more even-handed and respectful examination of complex educational and political ideas. For that is the chief outcome possible when students read both of these texts, even though, as we will see from the student essays, the kind of thinking that results is both gratifying and disappointing.

PARALLEL THEMES IN THE TWO TEXTS: THE CASTE SYSTEM AND NOBLE LIES

The use of the caste system in *Brave New World* is an example of something Huxley (1932/1998) "pulls inside-out," making this political feature a chief evil in his dystopia whereas it is one of Socrates' prize features in his idealized political scheme. Early in Book 2, Socrates decides that he, Glaucon, and Adeimantus need to "watch a city coming into being in speech" if they are to understand the nature of justice (Plato, 1968, 369a). A city "comes into being," Socrates says,

> because each of us isn't self-sufficient but is in need of much.... So, then, when one man takes on another for one need and another for another need, and, since many things are needed, many men gather in one settlement as partners and helpers, to this common settlement we give the name city, don't we? (369b)

The simple city needs people to do the work that satisfy a variety of needs. But what work is needed and who should do it? Would it be best if each separate man does all the tasks necessary to ensure his survival and the survival of his family—that is, should he hunt, and build shelter, and provide clothing, and do all the other necessary things? Or would it make more sense to divide up the tasks—that is, one man does the hunting for everyone, another builds the shelter, and another provides clothing? The three interlocutors quickly agree that this latter idea makes the most sense. But, then, how should they decide which man should hunt, which man should build, and which man provide clothing? This, too, they decide quickly: the one who is best at hunting should be the hunter, the one best at building should build shelter, and the one best at sewing should make the clothes. That is, they decide tasks based on the natural talents of the individual men.

This simple-minded plan masks profound political realities. If a city is to function properly, tasks need to be attended to faithfully and well. When Glaucon protests that Socrates' simple city "make[s] these men have their feast without relishes"—that is, that this simple city denies men the satisfaction of their appetites for food, luxury, and erotic pleasure—Socrates decides to build a second, more "feverish" city that would meet Glaucon's desires (Plato, 1968, 372c, 372e). But this new more luxurious city now needs both guardians of the city and those who would rule it. Now the interlocutors have a rule to follow in determining who should do each of these new tasks, in addition to the more basic ones they had discussed. The citizens who have a natural talent for war-making and defense should be the guardians—those with thymos, or a kind of prideful high-spiritedness; and those who have a natural talent for learning and acquiring wisdom and who have long had their loyalty and character tested in the public realm should be the philosopher/kings.

Thus, we have Plato's (1968) caste system: the artisans, on the bottom, who take care of the basic necessities of the city, from farming, to tool-making, to nursing, to doctoring; then the guardians, charged with defending the city and looking to preserve the common goods of the city; and the philosopher/kings who make the critical political, social, and educational decisions of the city.

Huxley's (1932/1998) caste society in *Brave New World* is, of course, horrifying, and the parallels and differences with Plato's caste scheme are critical to note. Certainly technology and nature are at odds with one another in Huxley's awful world—nothing like Plato's sense of "human nature" or talent will determine which human beings do what tasks—but Huxley joins with Plato's political wisdom in several key ways even as, again, he wishes to turn that wisdom inside-out. Social life demands certain things get done, and Socrates' feverish city has the same kind of complexities as Huxley's brave new world. As civil life demands hunting, shelter, and clothing in Socrates' city, so in Huxley's (1932/1998) dystopia

> The machine turns, turns and must keep on turning—forever. It is death if it stands still; wheels must turn steadily, but cannot turn untended. There must be men to tend them, men as steady as the wheels upon their axles, sane men, obedient men, stable in contentment. (p. 42)

Further, there must be someone in charge to ensure all of this happens: a World Controller.

The first job of a World Controller (or a philosopher/king) is not to see to the fulfillment of each individual human being—it is to make sure the city doesn't collapse, to make sure it isn't conquered, to make sure it keeps going. Huxley, of course, bemoans the dehumanizing that goes along with this while Socrates seems unperturbed. If the artisans do not get to realize their full humanity in Socrates' city, the philosopher/kings do. And the city will be better ruled because of this.

If we stopped here in our look at the texts, we would find much to talk about in an educational foundations class. Does it sound uncaring, unjust, or just plain wrong to say that a ruler, or set of rulers, ought to care more about the political unit than they care about the individuals in that unit—even full citizens in that city (or country)? Is it really more important to devise an educational system that intends to make "good citizens"—where "good" is understood as what is conducive to the continued strength of the city—than a system that worries about the personal welfare of its citizens? But, even as we might have these concerns, is not Mustapha Mond, in fact, right: that if the "wheels stop turning," we all die? And, so, shouldn't we worry about producing people willing to be "sane" and "stable" enough to keep the wheels turning? Can this be done without dehumanizing people?

But there is more to think about. Technology and hypnopaedia solve a political problem in Mustapha Mond's world that Socrates had to solve in different way: how to make sure everyone is relatively content with the task they have to do. Huxley takes care of that in his brave new world, first of all, through genetic engineering, then through the conditioning citizens receive—conditioning designed to make everyone glad they were in the particular caste for which they had been designed. An elaborate system of entertainment takes care of leisure time; "Solidarity" meetings and casual sexual relationships take care of erotic urges; and occasional technological tweaking of the human system—like pregnancy substitutes—take care of residua of human instincts. And if that doesn't work there is soma—that perfect drug that puts one "on holiday" whenever necessary.

Being "content" with the role one must play for the greater good of the society is a key political and educational issue. It certainly sounds, in Huxley's world, like it would be better to be an Alpha than a Delta or a Gamma—if one could only realize it. And it is just as likely in Socrates' ancient Athens that one might think it better to be a philosopher/king than someone who made tools all day or sews clothing—or someone who could die when sent on an excursion to defend the city. Socrates ensured that people would be content with their social roles by telling them a lie—albeit a "noble lie." The noble lie the rulers in Socrates' "perfect city" tell the ruled has two parts—first, that they are all brothers and sisters, all having been created under the earth before they were born from the earth. This part of the lie makes citizens fiercely loyal and determined: "And now, as though the land they are in were a mother and nurse, they must plan for and defend it, if anyone attacks, and they must think of the other citizens as brothers and born of the earth" (Plato, 1968, 414d). In

Socrates' world, a brotherhood is created from the motherland; in Huxley's (1932/1998) world, conditioning leads all to believe "Everyone belongs to everyone else" (p. 43 and elsewhere).

The second part of Socrates' lie has a very different function, however. This part of the lie explains why some people get to be rulers with all the power such a position brings; why others get to be guardians, with all the public honor and acclaim that comes with that position; and why the rest are artisans, given over to labor all their lives. In this part of the lie, the ruler makes the people believe that

> the god, in fashioning those of you who are competent to rule, mixed gold in at their birth; this is why they are most honored; in auxiliaries [guardians], silver; and iron and bronze in the farmers and the other craftsmen. (Plato, 1968, 415a)

This is a lie—there is, of course, no truth to it at all. Social roles would actually be decided by philosopher/kings who would examine the nature of each person carefully when he or she is young. This examination of natural gifts and propensities determines whether or not one is an artisan, a guardian, or a future ruler.

Here, in both texts, is great political wisdom: people need an explanation for why certain people seem to get the best goods society has to offer, and some do not. The people most in need of this explanation are those without the best goods. Why does a certain someone get fame, honor, acclaim and money, but not me? Lacking a good answer, revolution is not only possible, but inevitable. Lies told about why people get certain goods, and others do not, soothe pride and mitigate resentment. We can tell ourselves this story to assuage our pride: if the god(s) has put iron in my soul instead of gold, well, then, that's just the way it is. There is no human being to blame who is trying to get the best of me, and who am I to argue against the gods? There is no one to blame—I accept my place. It may seem as if Huxley's brave new world does not need a lie because it controls these instincts with genetic engineering, conditioning, and soma. But if it does not need a lie, it does need deception—a lie in different dress. The brave new world has secrets and a history only the World Controllers need to know about. It is usually best if very few people know the lies needing to be told or the history needing to be left out.

Socrates, ever insightful about human nature, adds one more aspect to this noble lie—something that cannot be added in Huxley's world. In Socrates' ideal city, all the men who have "gold" in their souls will mate with women who have gold in their souls; silver men mate with silver women; and bronze (or iron) men mate with bronze (or iron) women. One would expect with such mating arrangements that gold parents would have gold children, silver parents would have silver children, and bronze parents would have bronze children. But this is not always the case, and when gold parents have a silver or bronze baby, that child will be educated for a place in that new, more suitable caste—not the caste of the parents. Likewise for the silver and bronze parents who might give birth to a "gold" baby. So, while parents are locked in a particular caste, their children are not. This, too, mitigates the pride and resentment of citizens: their children may have better, happier, and more fulfilling lives than they are able to have.

The range of political, social and educational issues suggested by these caste societies and these noble lies are endless—and not simple. It is distasteful and entirely undemocratic to think about castes as being either necessary or desirable. And it's distasteful to think we are being "lied to" about who gets the goods of society and why—though we might be happier if we see what Socrates calls a lie as a "myth." But can we exist without castes, or lies, or myths? Or how do they get remade or re-presented so as to make them more palatable to us? What lies or myths about these sorts of things get told to us in our own country and time? If Huxley's technological and conditioning solutions are perfectly awful and unacceptable, do we want to argue for the entire dissolution of caste-like thinking? When we see manufactured Deltas and Gammas as something like horrifying machines, and when we encounter people like Lenina who seem to have some greater instincts that get no nurture or support, and people like Helmholtz who need to find words to describe the ideas they can't form in their minds—these make us recoil and want to go as far in the opposite direction as we can. We want to argue democratic and social justice ideals, and we want to argue for the best and highest education for all. But we risk political naïveté. After all, the wheels do need to keep turning. Not everyone can rule. Pride does need soothing, and satisfactory explanations need to be offered. And, just as in Huxley's horrifying world, we, too, in our own ways want to believe in "solidarity" or some sort of "we all belong to one another." And schools just might be instrumental in all this.

SEXUAL DESIRE, FAMILY, AND MUSIC

Huxley and Socrates agree on the nature of the family and on the importance of music, too. The family is the natural political unit, and from thinking about the nature of the family comes great political thinking. "Home, home," the Controller tells the new batch of Alpha males:

> a few small rooms, stiflingly over-inhabited by a man, by a periodically teeming woman, by a rabble of boys and girls of all ages. No air, no space;

> an understerilized prison; darkness, disease, and smells.... And home was as squalid psychically as physically. Psychically, it was a rabbit hole, a midden, hot with the frictions of tightly packed life, reeking with emotion. What suffocating intimacies, what dangerous, insane, obscene relationships between the members of the family group! Maniacally, the mother brooded over her children (*her* children) ... brooded over them like a cat over its kittens; but a cat that could talk, a cat that could say, "My baby, my baby," over and over again. "My baby, and oh, oh, at my breast, the little hands, the hunger, and that unspeakable agonizing pleasure! Till at last my baby sleeps, my baby sleeps with a bubble of white milk at the corner of his mouth. My little baby sleeps." (Huxley, 1932/1998, pp. 37, 38)

The history of this brave new world is told in the amazing third chapter of Huxley's book, and this history begins with the consideration of the home—it begins with these quotes. Considering the home first in the telling of social history is no accident—it must be considered first. Home is, first of all, a sexual consequence—a first social construct born of natural desire. If we consider the home carefully we confront the intersection of nature, sex, society, economy, politics, religion, purpose, and virtue. It is all there.

We may not want to assent to the description of the home as offered in Huxley's text, but that's just because we prefer to see our own homes and home life in more idyllic terms. Huxley's description, however, contains a great deal of truth. Home and family—wife, husband, and children—give us the strongest sense for "my" we will ever have in our lives—with all the madness that comes with it. And the home always points back to and reminds us of sexual desire, that most glorious and most awful longing we will ever feel. "Family, monogamy, romance. Everywhere exclusiveness, a narrow channeling of impulse and energy," the Controller tells his students (Huxley, 1932/1998, p. 40). The scene continues,

> "Think of water under pressure in a pipe." They thought of it. "I pierce it once," said the Controller. "What a jet!"
> He pierced it twenty times. There were twenty piddling little fountains.
> "My baby. My baby ...!"
> "Mother!" The madness is infectious.
> "My love, my one and only, precious, precious..."
>
> Mother, monogamy, romance. High spurts the fountain; fierce and foamy the wild jet. The urge has but a single outlet. My love, my baby. No wonder these poor premoderns were mad and wicked and miserable. Their world didn't allow them to take things easily, didn't allow them to be sane, virtuous, happy. (p. 41)

Here Huxley confronts the question of desire—especially sexual desire—as a political question. The home, being a sexual consequence, harbors all these sexual energies and brings them to the political, social sphere. Sexual desire is maddening; social life requires a certain sanity. Exclusive sexual energy is in every way at odds with social intercourse which demands cooperation and civility. The surest way to murder and mayhem is to deny a man possession of a woman and off-spring he has some reason to see as belonging to him.

What can political life do with (or to) sexual energies that seem to demand exclusivity? Can social life satisfy in a higher way all the desires men tend to want to feed in a private way? The answer is "yes" for both Socrates and Huxley, at least in these texts, and their solution is the same: do away with the family.[1] For Socrates, it matters not if artisans have private wives and families, homes, and private storehouses of worldly goods—it only matters that guardians and philosopher/kings have only the public good about which to worry. Marriage and the raising of their own children are denied them. At the level of the guardians and rulers, mating is too critical to be left to desire or chance. The rulers determine which men get to mate—the best men with the best women in hopes of producing the best off-spring—and "marriages" last only one night and are solely for the purposes of procreation. The best men and women mate as often as needed; lesser men can mate, but the off-spring is not to be kept. The men are told that the question of who gets to mate is determined by a lottery, but the lottery is fixed by the rulers so that only the best men and best women "win" the lottery—another of Socrates' lies told to keep people happy. Men would kill if they thought another man was keeping them from satisfying their erotic desires, but if it's just fate, well, then, who can complain?

Huxley, of course, solves the problem in a very different way: if the fountain spouts high, in foamy jets, when the pipe is pierced only once, then pierce it many times. Piddling little fountains cause no social instability. Exclusivity is the only thing not permitted in Huxley's new world, and children are conditioned from a very young age to engage widely in erotic play. A good "Orgy-porgy" or, at the very least, the biweekly solidarity service, tends to take care of sexual desire. The man regularly satisfied is not as dangerous as the man whose erotic desires are mounting.

Erotic desire is a theme not usually discussed in an educational foundations class, but the education of desire is *the* great theme among our greatest educational thinkers—especially Socrates and Rousseau (1762/1979) in *Emile*. If there is every reason to handle this theme cautiously and modestly in an undergraduate class, there is no good reason to leave it out, and these texts open-up this topic for discussion in clear and compelling ways. What do we do with man's worst (and best) passions? How does erotic desire become civilized? In our own society, where we have no desire to give up private goods and exclusivity—where we have people, families, and property we speak of as being "mine"—how possible is it to produce citizens who care as much or more about others or a "common good?" Aren't public schools being asked to serve two contrasting and competing ends—to prepare individuals to acquire as many private "goods" as possible while still preparing them to care about a public good?

Huxley (1932/1998) takes up Socrates' great theme of the power of music, though here Huxley offers but a nod in the direction of his great teacher, Socrates. Henry takes Lenina to the Westminster Abbey Cabaret featuring Calvin Stopes and his Sixteen Sexophonists. Four hundred couples dance on the floor, and the sexophones

> wailed like melodious cats under the moon, moaned in the alto and tenor registers as though the little death were upon them. Rich with a wealth of harmonics, their tremulous chorus mounted towards a climax, louder and ever louder—until at last, with a wave of his hand, the conductor let loose the final shattering note of ether-music and blew the sixteen merely human blowers clean out of existence. Thunder in A flat major. And then, in all but silence, in all but darkness, there followed a gradual deturgescence, a *diminuendo* sliding gradually, through quarter tones, down, down to a faintly whispered dominant chord that lingered on. (p. 76)

The connection between music and erotic desire—barely concealed in this description of the sexophones—is part of Socrates' teaching about music in Books Three and Four of *The Republic* (Plato, 1968). After considering, and severely censuring, the words (or lyrics) of the poems the young guardians are to hear as they are growing up, Socrates takes up the question of which scales are to be used in composing the music the young are to hear, and which rhythms. Some harmonies are best for wailing and lamentation, some for drinking, some for repose, and some for war-making—and it is only these last that the guardians are to hear (399a). And their war-making tempers, when it is time, are to be inflamed by just the right rhythm of the drums. These high-spirited young men need careful training—their souls need to be subdued or made malleable even while their spiritedness remains intact. Without music and gymnastic, the souls of these potentially noble youths will never be tamed. Their souls need to be "harmonized" (410d).

Music speaks, first and foremost, to what is "barbarous" in our souls (Bloom, 1987, p. 71.) Huxley's sexophones speak steamy sex, and the relentless, gradually building drum rhythms during the solidarity service can culminate only in Orgy-porgy. Man cannot help it. Music affects him that way—harmonies and rhythms much more than lyrics. The better, higher music respects the barbaric in man but lifts him beyond its baseness. The best music helps him praise the gods and realize higher potential. This was Socrates' teaching, attested to by Aristotle (who disagreed with Plato on many other points), and it is that which Huxley (1932/1998) uses and respects in *Brave New World*.

THE ALLEGORY OF THE CAVE

Finally, of course, Huxley (1932/1998) takes up Socrates' cave allegory. In every respect, the citizens of the brave new world are trapped in a cave, watching shadows on the wall and calling them truth. Helmholtz and John the Savage are the characters who struggle to get out of the cave. Barnard Marx is the interesting failure—his intuitions come more from his weaknesses rather than from strengths, unlike Helmoltz—but even Lenina has some sort of inkling that there is something more than what her society has given her to know, appreciate, and value. "Freedom" is what John believes he offers the Deltas when he throws their soma rations out the window, even as he has not become free himself. Freedom, and a genuine manhood, is at least part of what it means to be out of the cave for both John and Helmholtz. But it is also the ability to pursue the truth—just as it is for Socrates. When Helmholtz, Barnard, and John talk with Mond after the incident with the soma rations, Mond talks about "truth":

> "It's curious," he went on after a little pause, "to read what people in the time of Our Ford used to write about scientific progress. They seemed to have imagined that it could be allowed to go on indefinitely, regardless of everything else. Knowledge was the highest good, truth the supreme value; all the rest was secondary and subordinate. True, ideas were beginning to change even then. Our Ford himself did a great deal to shift the emphasis from truth and beauty to comfort and happiness. Mass production demanded the shift. Universal happiness keeps the wheels steadily turning; truth and beauty can't. And, of course, whenever the masses seized political power, then it was happiness rather than truth and beauty that mattered. Still, in spite of everything, unrestricted scientific research was still permitted. People still went on talking about truth and beauty as though they were the sovereign goods." (p. 228)

When Mustapha Mond reviews a scientific paper titled "A New Theory of Biology," he is sorry he needs to reject it. "It was a masterly piece of work," he says. Then,

> But once you began admitting explanations in terms of purpose—well, you didn't know what the result might be. It was the sort of idea that might easily decondition the more unsettled minds among the higher castes—make them lose their faith in happiness as the Sovereign Good and take to

> believing, instead, that the goal was somewhere beyond, somewhere outside the present human sphere; that the purpose of life was not the maintenance of well-being, but some intensification and refining of consciousness, some enlargement of knowledge. (Huxley, 1932/1998, p. 177)

Socrates would probably not disagree with Mustapha Mond that comfort and happiness are, in some sense, at odds with the pursuit of knowledge and truth, though he was much more worried about the corruption to knowledge and truth by pursuit of political power and false knowledge, or sophistry. Truth and beauty are the sovereign goods for Socrates—really, the good, the true, and the beautiful—though Socrates was less interested in the empirical truths of science than he was the absolute truths of philosophy uncovered only through the power of dialectic. Certainly he was concerned about "purpose," and purpose is exactly what gets controlled and limited when shadows are cast upon the wall of the cave or when books and ideas are limited and citizens are conditioned in certain ways.

Socrates is clearer than is Huxley about just who can and should escape the cave. The shadows on the wall are cast by leaders of the society for a reason. The mass of people need certain prejudices or myths or stories. These provide common thinking about important social concerns and bring order, stability, and, well—happiness. Most of us are lost without orienting understandings—we are rudderless, adrift, disoriented, and life lacks meaning and order. The best and brightest among us might feel these stories as a discomfort and be "compelled to stand up, to turn his [our] neck around, to walk and look up toward the light," but there is still some great distance from this initial move to the revealing of the true, the good, and the beautiful (Plato, 1968, 515c). Far more likely is it that those of us who feel the discomfiture of this social bondage will not make it out of the cave and reach true understanding; more likely we will become one of the false philosophers Socrates disdains so much (Plato, 1968, 489e-496a). We will be more dangerous, more of a social menace, and more unhappy than the lesser artisans content with the shadows on the wall.

The shadows on the wall of the cave are necessary for Socrates, and they shouldn't be done away with. Only the philosopher/kings can transcend them and attain true wisdom. The modern reader, caught in his or her own struggle to break away from false or limited social understandings, wants to celebrate Helmholtz's struggles in Huxley's (1932/1998) *Brave New World*, and he or she wants to remake a society that basically forces John to commit suicide at the end. Lenina and Fanny are denatured, Bernard is defective, and members of the lower castes lead such inhumane lives that it's almost impossible to defend the practice of subjugating citizens with shadows on the wall. Freedom—never the end in Socrates' world—becomes the only end in Huxley's world, and ours.

It is easy for us to want to liberate everyone from the shadows being cast on the wall of the cave—to lift all the oppressed from the lies and myths told by those who would subjugate the mass of us. But what are the lies and myths told to us—and who tells them? Do teachers tell them to their students? Would we be able to conduct school, or keep a stable society, without the fictions we tell people? Are lies always evil?

EXCERPTS FROM STUDENT ESSAYS

How much of all this students understand—and how they are able to put it together for themselves in thinking about education and themselves as teachers—is, of course, a bit up for grabs. I first had students read these texts and engage these ideas in 2001 in a "Capstone" class called *Education and the Seduction of Modern Culture*. This was a class intended for juniors, mostly, as a capstone to their general education classes, and it was open to students from across the university. We read a short essay by David Denby (1996) called "Buried alive: Our children and the avalanche of crud," a short story by Herbert Gold (1962) called "A Dog in Brooklyn, a Girl in Detroit: A Life Among the Humanities," followed by the first section of Allan Bloom's (1987) *The Closing of the American Mind*. These readings set up the idea some pretty serious thinkers were pretty certain that young people, such as the ones in my class, were utterly incapable of serious thought. Reading something serious like Plato's (1968) *The Republic*, I teased them, must be just for people living on the East coast and studying in places like Harvard—certainly not for undergraduates at Missouri State University. Then, of course, I offered them the challenge to prove these people wrong. Let's read *The Republic*, I told them—let's prove to ourselves that we can surmount the "seduction of modern culture" and be interested, vibrant, and intelligent readers. Then we started in on *The Republic*—usually taking about 8 weeks, meeting once a week for 2½ hours. Sometimes we made it all the way through the text, but more often we just read through Book Seven. Then it was off to Huxley's (1932/1998) *Brave New World* the last 2 or 3 weeks of the semester.

The Capstone course described above went away a few years ago, but I started teaching the same content in honors sections of Missouri State University's (MSU) educational foundations class titled "School and Society." I have not taught the version of the class described above in my "regular" School and Society classes. (The Capstone class in 2001 was a "regular" class, but in 2004 the honors college asked if I would teach it to honors students.) In the fall of 2011, however, I decided to try pieces of it in my "regular" foundations classes. We started the semester reading Huxley's (1932/1998) novel, interspersing four passages from Plato's (1968) *The Republic*, mostly as we were finishing our reading of the novel. We looked at the following passages: On the making of the two cities and the nature of the guardians (369b-376c); the noble lie (414d-417b); on marriage and the raising of children (457d-467d); and the cave allegory (514a-521a). Since then we have been off to some other material.

Students took an in-class exam after doing an initial reading, and then were given a take-home portion of the examination. They were to analyze and discuss one of the ideas taken up in both books—the caste system, the strange systems for sexual and family relationships, how to get out of the "cave" of social understandings, and so forth, in a five page paper.[2] Student essays (58 in two sections of the course) varied considerably in quality. I shall not burden the reader with the worst of them—worst because of technical writing difficulties, a failure to read carefully, or a failure to articulate a clear argument—and I have done some minor editing to what follows (though nothing which changes what I take to be the major points of the argument).

Most students chose to write about the caste systems and "cave" themes. One student wrote this about what gets taught in the two societies:

> I believe that the biggest difference in Socrates' allegory of the cave and Huxley's world is that the controllers in *Brave New World* are being very intentional in their choices of what they let citizens see, experience, think and feel. While their intentions are not necessarily malicious—they are only intended to perpetuate stability—they do come across as dangerous intentions. Mustapha Mond seems cold and calculating all the way until the end of the book where he speaks freely about his own journey out of the figurative cave, and, while his story is enlightening, it is also alarming in the fact that as the reader we are now fully aware that Mond has all the knowledge and understands the truth but has chosen to hide it from the world and become one of the men responsible for hiding truth from the masses.
>
> In Socrates' allegory, I believe the shadow teaching is more born out of casual neglect than malicious intent. I think this is a society in which people teach what they have been taught—they are not picking and choosing to hide the truth in the name of stability and are not claiming an "ignorance is bliss" stance or deciding what people can know. They are more settled into a complacency; they are more comfortable with the idea of only knowing what they need to know as opposed to examining more deeply. So while the ideas have a lot of parallels and the outcomes are similar, the motivation is entirely different, which I think is important to note.

A young woman who wants to teach high school mathematics wrote this in a paper that examined the struggle to get out of the cave, in both societies:

> The only problem with the society in *Brave New World* is truth and beauty are almost impossible to find. John the Savage comes from a different part of the world. He was forced out of the cave by his location. He was not conditioned in the way that most people are conditioned. He was able to explore truth and beauty, through the culture of Malpais and his book of Shakespeare's works. The Malpais culture taught John to search for answers to questions about the origin of the world and the purpose of life through religious mediums. John learns about expressions, emotions and beauty through Shakespeare. For example, John talks about his feelings of hatred towards Pope grow as he learns how to describe them. He says he, "never really hated him because he had never been able to say how much he hated him" (Huxley, 1932/1998, p. 132). Other people in the *Brave New World* are never given teachers, like Shakespeare, to teach them words to convey their ideas. Without the words, the individual ideas are too hard to manifest into reality. Therefore, most people ignore, or maybe do not even think of, the ideas that were not conditioned. The people are left with only the artificial shadows on the wall. The Malpais religion and Shakespeare were the teachers that dragged John out of the cave and taught him truths and values that are central to his being.

I did not want students to leave the worlds of Socrates' cave and Huxley's dystopia too quickly and begin speculating about what these ideas might mean to their teaching: it is too easy to leave texts behind or to try to use them without understanding them first. When they turned to thinking about how the lessons of Huxley's awful world and Socrates' cave might shape their teaching, however, most students tended to write something like this, written by a young man intending to be a high school English teacher:

> As a future educator, I plan on encouraging self-expression and individuality in my classroom. I will encourage the questioning of ideas. I understand the need for students to be realistic about their goals and aspirations, but as a teacher, I feel as though it will be my duty to encourage all of them to shoot for the highest level of achievement possible. A goal of my classroom will be to look beyond the shadows. What is upward and beyond? Where does the light come from? It is only by understanding and sympathizing with all areas of life that one can truly gain a proper perspective.

This is a natural reaction for an idealistic young person. Many of my students wrote about liberating their future students from any social conditioning or from imprisonment in a cave. There were fewer conclusions like this one where the writer confesses that these texts have created some real doubt and confusion. A young lady who is preparing to be a Family and Consumer Science teacher writes:

> These writings and questions make me question my position as a teacher. Everything that I thought I would share and practice with my students may not be exactly as cut and dry as I thought. I wonder if I, as a teacher, should be as blunt as to say that there is a caste system in our society today. I do not know if I should be so harsh as to say that not everyone here can be a doctor, lawyer or a millionaire. Maybe I should tell them that life is not that fair; and that not everyone has the skills to fit those roles. The real question is: should I keep this "noble lie" going? I feel I should tell my students that they need to reach for the stars and work hard. People do not just become successful overnight. They do have to work hard to move up. As a teacher I think I should be a source of guidance, but after reading this novel and these writings I feel that there is this harsh reality that has obliterated my childhood ideas.

This last passage is taken from a paper that had some glaring weaknesses, but I liked the paper because in it she admits her reading of the texts has left her a bit confused. The texts make her rethink "childhood ideas" and she decides that everything is not as "cut and dried" as she had thought. She has not, as many other students chose to do, read Huxley's dystopia and Plato's cave allegory as a simple call to arms. She has not thought enough about the noble lie and a caste society based on natural gifts—and perhaps she never will. But she recognizes, at least for a moment, that there is something like a caste system and a noble lie, even if she is not sure what to do with these "things." She is not likely to agree with Socrates' political insights and to see these things as ideal, but she has paused in her thinking of herself as a teacher.

One young woman—a future English teacher—did a tremendous job thinking through the ideas of Socrates and Huxley regarding the family. Near the end of the paper she writes:

> But are the common goods gained by the elimination of the family worth those things that are relinquished? Huxley is the one who provides us with our answer. While it seems clear to me that Socrates is speaking in earnest as he proposes methods of alienating children from their mothers so as to promote the common good, it seems as though Huxley is taking this idea to its furthest limits and demonstrating just how numbing the loss of the family would truly be for the human race. Every disadvantage brought about by familial notions is eradicated in their societies, but Huxley's dystopia emphasizes the tragic loss of all goodness generated by the family, as well. As Huxley's society moves in the singular direction of industrialization, particularly in regard to the formation of the next generations, all creativity and uniqueness is lost. When children are created on an assembly line rather than in the midst of passion between two individuals who are in love with each other, the essence of our humanity—our capacity for love and creativity—is lost. By strategically pairing the best with the best or altering genetics in hopes of creating the perfect offspring, humanity's greatest characteristics—

> our differences—are forfeited. These distinctions, or, as many in the brave new world would view them, our flaws, are what give us the creative abilities that allow humans to achieve individuality and create beautiful, unique, and meaningful works of art. When the souls of our children are created in the absence of passion, the resulting society, as Huxley demonstrates, is a monotone upholding of conventionality and conformity.

I cannot share other excellent essays with you here. Their excellence is not revealed in a paragraph or a sentence or two, but in their carefully worked out arguments throughout the paper. The best essay argued that in each of the four worlds in the two texts—Socrates' simple and luxurious cities, Huxley's brave new world and John the Savage's world in Malpais—man made the same mistake: he forfeited paradise in search of knowledge he could not attain, just like Adam and Eve in the Garden of Eden. Two other essays described the failures and successes of the major characters in *Brave New World* to escape the conditioning of their world in terms of Socrates' allegory—that is, just how far "out of the cave" each of them got. A music educator did a wonderful job discussing the kind of social worlds that urge comfort and happiness over a pursuit of truth and beauty.

Not all students found these readings valuable: some anonymous student end-of-course evaluations complained that these texts "didn't have anything to do with education." But in just the quick look I have offered here, I think most observers would agree that students got to do some good thinking about important educational matters.

THE TASK OF THE FOUNDATIONS OF EDUCATION CLASS

The teacher of a class in the foundations of education will surely be tempted to use dystopian literature, especially a book like Huxley's (1932/1998) *Brave New World*, as an outline of social ills and a list of horrors, usually inflicted on helpless people by power-grubbing, self-interested white men. This is not just a favorite theme of today's foundations professors—most of whom, these days, are trained in social foundations with a Marxist or critical theory bent; in many cases it is the *only* theme thought worthwhile. Huxley's work can lead to or support a long-lasting discussion of unfair and dehumanizing social conditions and practices that persist in today's world, especially those supported by corporate/capitalistic interests. And there are lots of things to rail about: racism, poverty, gender, sexuality, ethnic, and religious insensitivity, insistence on Protestant values, corporate intrusion, conservative politics, standardized tests, and so forth. The characters of Helmholtz and John the Savage, in particular, focus these issues as we see them struggling against their social constraints in order to realize something real, genuine, and wonderful—as we see them struggle to attain the full humanity that should have been theirs all along.

There is no need to teach Plato's (1968) *The Republic* in a foundations class—either excerpts from it or the whole text, as I have done in the past. Students won't miss it if it isn't there—though many decades ago, now, students used to read *The Republic* and texts like Rousseau's (1762/1979) *Emile* in philosophy of education classes. But as philosophy of education slid into sociology of education, and then became "foundations of education," before it slid out of the teacher education curriculum altogether (sometimes to be resurrected as a "multicultural education" class or, in some cases, an "introduction to teaching" class) serious reading of serious philosophy texts went out the window, too. And nobody seemed to mind. The only remaining territory undergraduate educational foundations faculty really want to preserve is the radically-minded critique of social and educational practices done in the name of social justice. And, of course, Socrates—being no democrat—doesn't fit in very well.

But a funny thing happens when you have students read and think about *The Republic*. They like it. And when you match *The Republic* (Plato, 1968) up with Huxley's (1932/1998) *Brave New World*, they like it even better. They not only have one weird society to try and figure out—and one strange brand of sexual politics, one brand of conditioning, one estrangement and limitation of human potential, and one vision of human possibilities—they have two. And the one, they are told, is a utopia—an ideal for which we would strive—and the other a dystopia—an absolute horror. And the same questions, issues, and politics get worried in both texts. This must signal that there are lasting issues at play here, issues that just might be at play in our own world—and just as confusingly.

Adding Plato's (1968) utopia to Huxley's (1932/1998) dystopia muddies up a foundations of education class. There is a lot of sorting out to do, and many questions to be asked. And both students and teacher sooner or later get the feeling that maybe these texts get us a little over our heads—that both Huxley and Plato have a depth of understanding that just is not available to us as readers and thinkers in a one semester course. We're missing something—maybe missing too much as we try to think about what this all might mean to us as teachers. But there is no denying, as we read and think about these texts, that we are on to *something* important—that some insight is just around the corner that might make a difference to us as a classroom teacher. Class discussions that search out this *something* are always lively.

I tell my students that there are three "characters" in Plato's (1968) allegory of the cave. There are, first of all, the cave dwellers—those "in it [the cave] from childhood with their legs and necks in bonds so that they are fixed, seeing only in front of them, unable because of the bond to turn their heads all the way around" (514a). And there are those people who carry the "artifacts" along the road above and behind the cave dwellers—those people (politicians, culture mongers, religious leaders, teachers, and foundations of education teachers?) who decide what shadows the people are to see. And there is the one who has been outside the cave and has returned—the one, presumably, who knows the truth and wants to rescue those who, like Helmholtz, seem to have something in them that wants to break free.

I ask them which of those three characters they think they are. Overwhelmingly, of course, they want to see themselves, as future teachers, as the one who knows the truth and comes to liberate those still stuck in bondage. In this, they are exactly like the foundations professor who knows the truth about social justice and wants to liberate his or her students, and everyone else, from their bondage. But, I ask them if it is not just as possible that they are one of the other characters—the one still stuck in the cave, calling the shadows "the truth," or, and worse, the one who is on the road casting shadows of artificial things? They are just young and unsure enough of themselves to be sobered by these questions. At this point, they begin to know that they do not know—which is, of course, all that Socrates would ask of them.

NOTES

1. Both Huxley and Socrates do away with the family, but, of course, neither would argue that this is really possible—no human being would allow it. It is, however, "ideal" in a theoretical way—it allows a discussion of the tension between private and public interests, ever at the heart of political theory.
2. The directions—save for some final instructions—were as follows:

> We have remarked in class that Aldous Huxley must have read Plato's Republic before he wrote his book. There are just too many parallels between them—a caste system, a strange system for sexual relationships, no natural family relationships, a struggle to get out of the "cave" of social understandings, etc. This section of the exam requires you to think about one of those themes.
>
> Your essay assignment is to think about one such theme emerging in both Brave New World and The Republic—from among the ones I just mentioned or some other you have noticed in your reading. Your task is, first of all, to establish why the theme is important to the overall meaning or understanding of each text. In doing so, you may discover that while the two texts address the same theme or idea, they do so with similar or very different viewpoints, intentions or understandings. Please explain the similarities and differences you uncover. The

reader should come away with a clear understanding of how these themes are important to any accurate understanding of the text.

You are also invited to reflect on how or why these themes are important to you, as you think about yourself as a classroom teacher—BUT THIS SHOULD NOT BE THE PRIMARY FOCUS OF YOUR REMARKS. Deal first with the texts, then conclude, if you'd like, with some limited reflections about how the texts reflect on current educational issues.

REFERENCES

Bloom, A. (1987). *The closing of the American mind*. New York, NY: Simon & Schuster.

Denby, D. (1996, July 15). Buried alive: our children and the avalanche of crud. *The New Yorker*, pp. 48-58.

Gold, H. (1962). A dog in Brooklyn, a girl in Detroit: A life among the humanities. In *The age of happy problems* (pp. 118-138). New York, NY: Dial Press.

Huxley, A. (1998). *Brave new world*. New York, NY: HarperCollins, Perennial Classics. (Original work published 1932)

Plato. (1968). *The republic of Plato*. (A. Bloom, Trans.). New York, NY: Basic Books.

Rousseau, J. (1979). *Emile, or on education*. (A. Bloom, Trans.). New York, NY: Basic Books. (Original work published 1762)

CHAPTER 9

"UNLEARNING" WITH THE DYSTOPIAN YOUTH

Sating Student Hunger With *The Hunger Games*

Becky L. Noel Smith

> *"Katniss, it's just hunting. You're the best hunter I know," says Gale. "It's not just hunting. They're armed. They think," I say. "So do you. And you've had more practice. Real practice," he says. "You know how to kill." The awful thing is that if I can forget they're people, it will be no different at all.*
>
> —Suzanne Collins (2008, p. 40)

CONSTRUCTING THE DYSTOPIAN YOUTH

I have often assumed that education policy has changed little since I entered the teaching profession in 2002. Perhaps this is something I can attribute to having only worked in this age of accountability. But, in justification of my naiveté, policymakers have maintained one constant over the last decade: their efforts have felt consistently and frustratingly illogical to someone who desires to take part in student learning.

Dystopia and Education:
Insights Into Theory, Praxis, and Policy in an Age of Utopia-Gone-Wrong, pp. 137–156

Shortly after the presidential changing of the guard, I disappointingly forced myself to conclude that the Obama administration's idea of education reform mimicked the tactics implemented by the Bush administration. It was as though the nation had simply followed bad policy with another version of equally bad policy. My mistake was in accepting that the two were virtually identical, though, because I failed to adequately examine their subtle differences. It is the subtleties in utopian education policies, however, which are worthy of our most intense scrutiny. If left unchecked, they burrow into us, our habits, and our institution where they thrive as some of the most insufferable contradictions.

The language and the targets of educational policy have gradually altered in the last decade, but the underlying measures have not. This has created a strange dynamic in terms of accountability. For example, the No Child Left Behind Act (NCLB) heavily emphasized "improving the academic achievement of the disadvantaged" (U.S. Department of Education, 2002, p. 15). The current reformative trend, Race to the Top (RTT), aims at "turning around the lowest-achieving schools" (U.S. Department of Education, 2009b, p. 10). On the surface, many would likely agree that providing extra attention to struggling schools and students sounds not only reasonable, but humane. The problem I wish to highlight here, however, lies within the linguistic shift from the disadvantaged students to the low-achieving schools. As Cusick (2008) explained, this transition in the language and focus of accountability suggests to the public that the nation's students are no longer held accountable for their own failure, and that the schools are perceived to instead be failing their students. This subtle change to the focus of education policy can certainly provide the appearance that there has been a shift in blame.

This appearance, however, is belied by one major factor which has remained unchanged by a decade of policy: the inordinate emphasis on high-stakes testing. Policymakers have continued to dictate that the only acceptable gauge of the educational effectiveness of a school is the statistical data derived from test scores. This means success or failure can still only be gleaned from the *students*, via *their* achievement scores. This effectively causes the prior linguistic shift of blame to be reversed so that all blame is ultimately redirected back onto the nation's youth. Meanwhile, the change in focus which appeared to divert blame away from the students actually expanded the target of blame to encompass not only the students, but their teachers, their administrators, and their schools as well. Therefore, by making no change to the emphasis on high-stakes testing, the progression from NCLB to RTT quite successfully allowed the federal government to widen the scope of its punitive target while simultaneously increasing the burden it places upon the youth.

The demands of grade-level promotion and graduation have long required that students produce scores to ensure their individual academic successes. However, school status, school-wide grades, adequate yearly progress, funding, and threats of school closure and charter conversion have been increasingly tied to student score production. Students have, therefore, progressively been burdened with the responsibility for securing the survivability of their schools as well. Since the sustainability or closure of a given school ultimately has a direct impact upon every pupil who attends that school, then the youth determine their fellow students' academic fates as well as their own. Finally, with growing realizations of performance-based pay under RTT and with the ironic creation of programs like *Recognizing Educational Success, Professional Excellence and Collaborative Teaching* (RESPECT), students are being forced to burden a new level of responsibility: their score production has come to directly impact the reputation, employment status, job security, and financial compensation for their teachers, school administrators, and superintendents.[1] Students no longer bear the weight of only their own individual academic well-being, because policymakers have effectively overcharged every testable child also with the well-being of their entire schooling community. Of course, this has happened in spite of growing concerns by states and educators regarding the corporate fetish of infinite growth and its application to learning gains, standards, and student expectations under the current policy (Banjo, 2011; Oregon Department of Education, 2011; Tatter, 2011).

The moral issue here, of course, is that the burden upon the students has definitively changed due to the merge of financial and punitive threats. However, the glaring side effect of this progression is that an exorbitant amount of attention has been drawn to those students who are perceived to be preventing the nation from meeting the prescribed goal of "increased productivity and effectiveness" (U.S. Department of Education, 2009b, p. 2). The competitive nature of education policies has caused the potentially utopian question, "Who are *we* leaving behind?" to be fully distorted into its dystopian version, "*Who* is holding *us* back?" (Apple, 2001). Under these circumstances, the youth most responsible for securing the survivability of the schooling communities are those same students whom educators and policymakers claim typically struggle to succeed, and remain, in the schooling institution (Ravitch, 2010). So, through the subtleties of a prolonged political metamorphosis, the children have come to bear the responsibility for the successes or failures of the adults whom society has charged with tending to the students. In an even more inhumane twist, educational policy has evolved so that the greatest burden of responsibility is placed upon those children it recognizes as being the neediest.

The U.S. Department of Education (2009b) refers to these children as "high-need students." They are such a large and diverse group of students that it might be easier to name the race and socioeconomic status of those who do *not* fit into this category of concern. These students are:

> at risk of educational failure or otherwise in need of special assistance and support, such as students who are living in poverty, who attend high-minority schools … who are far below grade level, who have left school before receiving a regular high school diploma, who are at risk of not graduating with a diploma on time, who are homeless, who are in foster care, who have been incarcerated, who have disabilities, or who are English language learners. (p. 12)

Nichols and Berliner (2007) also referred to this group of students as "score suppressors," and they warned, "A new form of discrimination is apparently creeping into our schools, and it is against ... those children who keep the school from looking good on high-stakes tests" (p. 11). It is disheartening to admit that the nation has indeed lived down to these authors' expectations. By gradually assigning the burden of accountability to high-need students, educational policy has manufactured and promoted the notion that these individuals negatively impact their schooling communities. Through this process, children have been converted into financial and occupational risks by the fabricated correlations between student score production, job security, and school funding (Apple, 2001; Nichols & Berliner, 2007).

The age of accountability has, therefore, definitely succeeded in providing extra attention for the students who struggle to survive in the nation's schools. However, the attention directed *at* them has burdened them to the point that they are now grossly and inaccurately projected to be "too risky to be teachable," "too far behind to catch up," and "the worst of the worst." The crushing weight of our attention has shaped them into dystopian youth. As rising numbers of lawsuits and claims of discrimination by high-need students demonstrate, the type of attention we have aimed at them has encouraged people and schools to find creative ways to avoid teaching and enrolling them altogether (Abramson, 2011; Frankenberg, Siegel-Hawley, & Wang, 2010; McGrory & Hiaasen, 2011; Ravitch, 2010; Vaznis, 2009; Winerip, 2011). The dystopian youth, then, are the vast numbers of school children who suffer the immense challenge of surviving the burden and the attention forced upon them by policies and mandates. I take the stance that such results constitute the epitome of utopian policy turned dystopian.

The construction of the dystopian youth, though, is not a new phenomenon. Educational historians have demonstrated that the creation of an inferior cultural group by the dominant cultural group has been a continual theme in the struggles over America's education system (Kaestle, 1983; Spring, 2005; Tyack, 1974). The construction of the dystopian youth as laid out here is simply another swell in that tragic trend, and it has been exacerbated by the financial and occupational hazards created by current education policy.

The following portion of this chapter stems from a semester of volunteering in a remedial high school reading class. The students and their mentor permitted me to share with them the experience of reading the novel *The Hunger Games*. In what follows, I interweave the narrative from my classroom experience with that of the novel. The intent of this approach is twofold: I strive to draw into sharp relief the various dystopian themes I have observed in the schooling experience, and describe what happens when one reads dystopian literature with dystopian youth. Finally, I conclude the chapter with an interpretation of how the nation's policies relate to the experience I describe.

"UNLEARNING" IN *THE HUNGER GAMES*

> *Thought can more easily traverse an unexplored region than it can undo what has been so thoroughly done as to be ingrained in unconscious habit.*
>
> —John Dewey (1910/1997, p. 121).

The responsibilities of motherhood and graduate school ensured that it had been several years since I had been in the K-12 classroom on a regular basis. I approached the end of my course work at the university, and it seemed fitting to resituate myself in the classroom setting once again, even if only to peer through the adjustments achieved in my own perspective via graduate school studies.

One can easily forget the poignancy of life until she is reacquainted with the social and emotional density of a high school campus. But rest assured, tragedy and hope are both alive and well in and around Grace's classroom. She is a reading teacher. The students with whom she shares her days range from those who have been in and out of remedial courses since elementary school to those who are enrolled in the school's advanced placement and international baccalaureate (IB) courses. They are a diverse group of kids; but their commonality is that each is preparing to make a second or third attempt to pass the state's standardized test. The test is the last major hoop for the students of this district, and the failure to pass jeopardizes their chances to receive standard diplomas at graduation. This one criterion qualifies every one of Grace's students as "high-need" by the state and federal government, although a majority of them qualify on various levels.[2]

Grace was very frank that her primary educative aim is to get her students to become life-long readers. However, she also admits that the resources which trickle down to her through the bureaucratic chain often do little, if anything, to help her realize that goal. In a time when scripted curricula, research-based programs, computer-based drill, and data-driven instructional methods are often the panacea for the dystopian youth, her prescription for struggling readers seems profoundly basic: put books in their hands. Despite the integrity of Grace's personal aim, her job, financial security, and success rest only upon her ability to get her students to pass the test. Fortunately, she is quite good at both. It does not take a keen observer to see, though, that her effectiveness in meeting the state's expectation is little more than a side effect of loving her students and giving top priority to her personal teaching goal.

The first book Grace placed in the hands of her students' that semester was *The Hunger Games*, a dystopian youth novel by Suzanne Collins (2008). The story takes place in Panem: a post-American, postapocalyptic country that sprawls across the remnants of North America. Residing in what is referred to as "the Capitol," the ruling class guarantees peace by maintaining state control over the military and police, the media, education, the workforce, and the food supply. Panem originally consisted of thirteen districts; but as the citizens are unceasingly reminded, District 13 was annihilated many years ago in the people's failed revolt against the Capitol. The districts have since been forced into segregation with no communication or travel among the remaining 12.

The comforts afforded to the residents of each district are proportional to the benefits their industries offer to the Capitol. The buildings, streets, and bodies in District 12 are perpetually enshrouded in a layer of coal dust, the by-product of its mines. It is not surprising that this place, once known as Appalachia, is ranked lowest in favorability by an elite class which privileges superficiality, materialism, and gluttonous indulgence. Katniss, the 16-year-old heroine, resides in the poorest section of District 12—"the Seam"; and although the Capitol would have citizens believe otherwise, the most common cause of death among her people is starvation.

It is out of pure necessity, therefore, that Katniss has become a skilled hunter. She forages in the woods beyond the electrified chain-link fence that she has been taught was designed to protect her district. Katniss knowingly risks "the severest of penalties" every time she squeezes under the fence to seek sustenance, but watching her sister and mother waste away is not an option for her (Collins, 2008, p. 5). She further supplements her family's meager living by selling and trading the excesses of her illegal harvests among a network of people at the black market, called the Hob. Of course, the mayor and the "Peacekeepers" are willing to overlook the illegalities of her poaching and trading as long as she allows them to reap some of the delicious benefits from her efforts.

Exploring Our District

We began the unit with a class set of books: exactly 26. Since Grace's six classes had to share this one set, she decided there would be no homework or outside reading. Grace and I were excited to see what types of questions and discussions would arise as everyone became acquainted with the plot and characters, so she and I eagerly dived into reading aloud with the students. Grace also used this time to interject commentary and model various reading strategies, but many of the students were exceptionally quiet. In response to their silence, Grace and I attempted to bring the reading process outside of our heads so they could hear our individual questions and thought processes as we read. We juxtaposed our thoughts and perspectives against one another, and our debate seemed to assist in drawing some of the students out of their torpor. However, the difficulty of eliciting responses from them was far more exhausting and challenging than I remembered from my days in the classroom.

Many students were initially too blinded by the contrasts between America and Panem to make out the subtle similarities between life and the book. Students across all Grace's classes reiterated that, aside from the burden of taxes and being forced to go to school, they were all pretty much free to do whatever they wished. (In hindsight, we should have asked what they were reading in social studies.) Grace and I encouraged them to look deeper, and we raised questions about the purposes, pros, and cons of school uniforms and about the fences and gates surrounding school campuses and neighborhoods. Issues of class and segregation worked their way into the conversations. We talked about the ways the merchants of District 12 viewed people from the Seam, how those from the Capitol treated the people of the districts, and how these perceptions and actions both worked to shape Katniss' self-conception. One student was quick to offer her insight on the topic: "That's like how the IB kids see us." Sadly, the "us" to whom she referred was everyone sitting in Grace's class; and to my surprise, not a single student contested or even seemed the slightest bit stirred by her statement regarding the school's academic hierarchy.

We had been reading for about two and a half weeks when the execution of Troy Davis wound its way into a conversation.[3] At the mention of Davis' name, the room became flooded with the reaction of one young man. This student's abruptness startled everyone, and his friends ribbed him for his outburst and the fact that he had never yet opened his book, much less contributed to any of the conversations. Issues related to race became part of our conversations as this student shared with his classmates Davis' story and his own frustrations about the execution. One young woman was overwhelmed, unable to comprehend the inhumanity of persisting with the execution of a human being when the emergence of so much doubt suggested possible innocence: Grace and I felt ill-equipped to provide her with answers. A theme had emerged from this conversation, though, and we explored it with the students throughout the rest of the semester. "How can they live with themselves?" Grace's student had pleaded through her tears, "How can they just kill him?"

Fabricating the Arena

The Capitol educates the people of Panem with an annual celebration of peace, prosperity, and power. The Hunger Games is a Foucauldian spectacle of the scaffold that serves as a symbolic reenactment of the Capitol's glorious defeat of the people in the revolution of the Dark Days.[4] The children of the Capitol are exempt from the honors of participation, of course, but each of the remaining twelve districts uses a lottery to choose one boy and one girl to compete in the games. These 24 children, known as tributes, spend weeks fighting one another to the death in a high-tech arena that is manufactured and continuously manipulated by the Capitol. The ceremonial festivities and games are not only nationally broadcast for everyone's entertainment; they are *required* viewing for every citizen of Panem.

Some tributes spend the entirety of their young lives preparing for the honor to compete in the games, even though this is technically forbidden. Their bodies, however, always bear the unmistakable evidence of nourishment and physical training. Katniss refers to these tributes as "the Careers." They never fail to come from the three districts of greatest wealth and highest favor by the Capitol, and there is a heavy contrast between the Careers and the youth from other districts.

The children of the poor districts always approach the arena gaunt and weakened from lifelong malnourishment. Unlike those in the favored districts, the poor families' lack of resources forces them to make horrific gambles. During periods of exceptional hunger, the children may request additional rations of grain and oil for their starving loved ones. This comes at a cost, of course. Restitution is paid to the Capitol by multiplying the number of times each emaciated child's name is added to the annual lottery for the games. The hungrier the child, the greater the probability she will be chosen to compete. Thereby, the Capitol virtually ensures that the children who represent the poorest districts are also the districts' neediest. The Capitol further incentivizes the children to fight by promising to reward the victor's entire district with the necessities to sustain life for one whole year.

Midgame Rule Changes

I arrived at school one morning to a significantly distraught-looking Grace. She informed me that, according to state policy, her classes were too large. In an effort to avoid the state penalties for noncompliance, the administration had to withdraw several students from each of her classes and reassign them to a substitute until another teacher could be hired. Period after period, I watched Grace tearfully announce the names of the students who were required to leave her class. The students, Grace, and I had spent a couple of weeks investing in one another and in the book by this point, and we had just begun to develop a decent rhythm to our discussions. The displeasure was apparent among all the classes that day, and in protest, one student outright refused to leave Grace's class.

On another occasion Grace received news that the format for the state reading test had changed from paper to a computerized version. The students were only 2 weeks away from their scheduled test date, and the results from the exam would determine their promotion and graduation. With so much resting on this one test, the change came as quite a shock to some of them. One student blurted out in frustration, "What happens if I refuse to take it on the computer? What happens if I demand to take it on paper?" She argued that all their prior experiences, and ultimately their comfort, revolved around the tangibility of a paper test. They would no longer be able to mark clues and notate their thoughts and ideas in the text. Their concerns were met by the explanation that the computer would allow them to highlight portions of the test, but this seemed to do little to appease those who were visibly angered by the change. The state had changed the game, and the switch had eliminated the ability to use one of their greatest strategies.

It was about this same time when things seemed to accelerate in the classroom. The storyline had picked up and so had the participation. Some of the students who had been virtually silent finally began expressing some of their insights. Several conversations circulated around student perspectives on corruption and the law. They brought up parallels between the police force and Panem's Peacekeepers, and we debated the boundaries between brutality and keeping the peace. We discussed the place of the people and the governments involved in the Arab Spring. Some students were shocked by their lack of knowledge regarding the

Occupy Wall Street movement and claimed they had heard nothing of it in the news. These reactions segued into discussions on both the freedom of assembly and the functions of technology and the media. We talked about the similarities between "reality TV" and the Hunger Games, and we questioned the place of the viewer in such forms of entertainment. We examined our perceptions on femininity and power through the character traits of Katniss and the paternalistic relationship with her mentor. Students who had witnessed the effects of posttraumatic stress disorder likened the Hunger Games to war, and the psychologically- and emotionally-altered victors of the games to the veterans in their own families. Connections between life and the text flowed freely among all of us. Finally, in the midst of chatter that always swelled toward the end of class, I unexpectedly caught the amused look of one student as he muttered his own revelation to himself: "I'll be damned ... books *are* like life." Although it was likely for very different reasons, our eyes met with equal surprise.

Sustenance as Resistance

The Capitol enjoys broadcasting the notion that Katniss volunteered to fight for District 12, but she had no choice when they drew her sister Prim's name in the lottery. If she had not sacrificed herself, they would have thrown 12-year-old Prim into the Hunger Games' arena for slaughter instead. It was simply a desperate attempt to spare the life of the only person she really loves. Katniss is small in comparison to the other tributes, but she has an advantage no previous tribute from District 12 has ever had: the struggle to survive and her strategic disobedience of the Capitol's rules on poaching and trading have combined to reward Katniss not only with nourishment, but also with skills and knowledge.

The "docile bodies" finally began to wake, and when they did, they were surprisingly ravenous.[5] The students not only resisted closing their books, but some became voraciously possessive over the time allotted for reading as well. At least two students regularly attempted to skip other classes so they could attend additional reading periods. When one student was called to the guidance office during class, he retorted that he would gladly accept a disciplinary referral instead for his refusal to leave the classroom while we were reading. The students were insatiable, but it was also the week before their state assessment. Grace had to take them to the computer lab to prepare, yet they had already been bucking against anything related to the test. Someone even threatened to stay home "sick" on the days the class would be doing test preparations. A compromise was struck, though, when Grace allowed them to take the books to the lab. They were further placated by the lag of the new computer system; the system was so slow they could squeeze in some reading between screen updates.

The end of another school day arrived, and as Grace gathered the books off the vacant desks, she told me the class set had dwindled from 26 to only 19. No one had asked to borrow any. Of course, she did not have enough books to spare even if she wanted to loan them out. However, no one had complained of a book shortage during class either. We both laughed as we realized her students were actually taking the books from the shelves. Grace was absolutely thrilled, and in response to her students' desires, she bought six more copies to place on the shelf the following morning.

Grace waited until the end of the unit before she made a joke to one class about the disappearing and reappearing books. Silence was followed by one student sheepishly admitting that she had borrowed a book. Grace and I could only chuckle at the absurdity that a child would feel guilty for taking, of all things, a book. Our response must have eased the tension, however, because the classroom suddenly assumed the atmosphere of a confessional. A second student admitted that she had also borrowed a copy, and then slowly, the students began sharing with us the creative ways they sought to read the story outside class. One young man chimed in with a hilarious anecdote about his first trip to the public library. Another two classmates explained how they had gathered for nightly phone conferences in which one young lady sifted through an unpunctuated, pirated text on the internet so she could read aloud to her friend who was without computer access. As if on cue, the classroom confessional was interrupted by a student who knocked on the door to return the copy that he had also taken from the class. The irony in timing and circumstance was affirmed by everyone's laughter.

The other classes had similar stories, of course. Many kids told us they had purchased books or downloaded copies to phones and reading devices. These students did not surprise me, though, because we typically knew as soon as someone bought a copy. Most of them had approached us to ask that we share in their pride: they were reading on their own, and it was the first time many of them liked a book enough to acquire their very own copies. In fact, these students often triggered the frequent damage-control drills Grace and I had to run in order to keep those who had read ahead of us on their own time from spoiling the story for their classmates.

There was one young lady who had read only 10 pages of the story with us before she bought a copy and devoted one entire night to reading the remaining 364 pages. Another student returned from a forced, 2-week-long absence bursting with excitement because he had completed *The Hunger Games* and its sequel on his own. Several students shared stories about parents who were so shocked and elated by their child's request to actually purchase a book that they gave the child the entire trilogy. One student spoke so incessantly about the book at home that three members of her family finally agreed to read it with her. In the end, all 32 books found their way back to the bookshelf. Quite a few even came back in the hands of students who had been plucked from the class earlier in the semester. These children had absolutely no obligation to finish the story, but upon returning their borrowed copies to Grace, they often asked if they could get in line to read the sequel.

It was the last day of *The Hunger Games* unit, and we all participated in a gallery walk to view the students' final projects. The atmosphere was casual, but the conversations and critiques energized the room with a sense of pride and satisfaction. One student talked with me a while amid the buzz of the classroom. We exchanged our thoughts on various student projects and certain aspects of the book. I expressed how much I valued her contributions to our class discussions throughout the semester and that I thought she had some truly insightful things to share. I encouraged her to keep speaking. Her questioning of my sincerity suggested that she was shocked by my compliments, and she said she often failed to share her thoughts because she did not believe she was smart. She then proceeded to tell me what I can only assume were portions to the story of how she came to find her way into Grace's class.

She said her family taught her to read at an early age. She had a great love for books and the library as a young child, but her years in school had done little to feed her love for reading. She finished her story by telling me, "They just kept forcing, and forcing, and forcing me to read stuff I didn't want to. So I finally just gave up. I thought I was bad at reading, but I'm trying to unlearn that now."

SATING HUNGER IN GRACE'S CLASS

Film production for *The Hunger Games* (Jacobsen, Kilik, & Ross, 2012) was in progress while we were reading the book with the students, so I would be short-sighted if I failed to question the influence of commercialism upon the students' motivations to read. Of the six classes that read with us, only a handful of students had read the book prior to the unit, and only a few seemed aware that there was to be a film adaptation. The students' lack of awareness of the movie and the indifference many initially had to the book suggest that the hype which often accompanies such a production may have had little to do with hooking their interest.

Another point to note is that our conversations became more student-guided as we progressed through the book; yet the film never developed into a dominant theme in any of our discussions. This is not to say that the movie did not occasionally fuel our curiosity as we got further into the story, however. We all questioned how the characters and the arena would be portrayed, but these questions often spurred critical debate. A few students brought up racial stereotyping in the media when they perceived that the actors who played the two tributes from Panem's agricultural district appeared to be African American. This was a point Grace, many students, and I had completely overlooked; so in the end, I felt we successfully reaped benefits from our few film-related discussions.

I have since contacted Grace to see if the students' enthusiasm for reading was sustained beyond *The Hunger Games*. She said large numbers of students have been patiently waiting their turns to read her few copies of the remaining books in the trilogy. She also informed me that they followed our unit with *A Long Way Gone: Memoirs of a Boy Soldier*, a book that is also thematically rich in struggle and hope (Beah, 2007). It is about a young man's survival through the terrors of war-torn Sierra Leone; to my knowledge, Hollywood has neglected to grasp it. When I inquired about the students' reception of it, Grace replied, "Oh, they devoured it!" I cannot be entirely certain, but the fact that their interest in reading has not only survived but flourished does lead me to believe that the Hollywood hype may not have been a major motivating factor in their eagerness to read.

As an educator, I found the students' enthusiasm for reading to be exhilarating. I was thrilled to witness so many students grow to express varying degrees of self-confidence, engrossment, or faith in their own abilities to read, think, and speak. As amazing as this was to experience, however, the overwhelming intensity of their actions and their interest in reading suggested something deeply tragic about their schooling scenarios.

The angles of emaciation are only gradually carved into the face of a child. Shadows on the skin, like the scrapes of the rasp, indicate the depth of hunger; but the reality of how truly starved the child is becomes most evident once you place before her something of nutritive value. When Grace initially set this book before her students, quite a few reacted with a complete lack of interest or even aversion. Their prevalent interjections about hating reading, not being good at it, or not understanding the relevance of reading in their lives required Grace and me to first treat the damage caused by years of being misdiagnosed and mistreated as dystopian youth. We struggled immensely to get many of the students simply to begin talking with us about the book. However, we broke from the habits of the commonly prescribed treatment and enticed them with only three things: the content of the story, connections to real life, and our persistent support. The more we encouraged them to try reading, the more their passion for it surged. The strength of their desire became most pronounced when their ability to read something of value was threatened by another round of the dystopian, standardized, accountability panacea.

That is, as Grace was required to resort to the deficiency of isolated skills and test preparation that is so common to remediation (Ede, 2006; Gillborn & Youdell, 2000; Kozol, 2005), the students reacted with complete repulsion and outright resistance. Upon returning to the substance of books, though, their interest in reading was sustained.

The actions, reactions, enthusiasm, and even resistance by Grace's students indicate the severity of both the misdiagnosis by the state and federal governments and the dearth of substance within the commonly prescribed treatment. However, once the dystrophic symptoms caused by the misdiagnosis were on the mend, most students seemed to develop and maintain a desire to read. Throughout the entire process, however, the students did consistently display a complete aversion to choking down the nutritionally devoid curriculum that is often the standardized fare of remediation. This persistent reaction emphasized the ineffectiveness of the standardized panacea as well as the potency of the treatment Grace provides.

"CHALLENGING" OUR YOUTH

In the first year of his appointment as secretary of education, Arne Duncan shared an anecdote about speaking with some dystopian youth. He claimed,

> I talked to the ninth-graders and they begged to be challenged. They think everyone's given up on them. No one expects them to succeed. Yet, despite bleak conditions, they still believe in the redeeming power of education ... I won't play the blame game, but I also won't make excuses for failure. I am much more interested in finding ways to fix these schools than in analyzing who's at fault. (U.S. Department of Education, 2009a, para. 7 & 9)

Duncan acknowledged the detrimental side-effects of the nation's education policy in the first half of this quote; but the remainder illuminates an unwillingness to further inquire about possible sources of the damage. Of course, the irony of his statement should be obvious if both my argument and my narrative have been sufficiently expressed: the nation is currently engaged in an enormous blame game which aims directly at the dystopian youth, and the rules for the game are maintained and continually redefined through our usually misguided policies. The most disturbing point, however, is that the secretary of education chose to follow his irony with this moral claim:

> States and districts have a legal obligation to hold administrators and teachers accountable, demand change and, where necessary, compel it. They have a moral obligation to do the right thing for those children—*no matter how painful and unpleasant.* (para. 10, emphasis mine)

Despite numerous re-readings of this statement, I am unable to discern if Duncan intended that it be the children, the educators, or both, who should create and endure the pain and unpleasantries of the schooling experience. Regardless of the target, though, we must ask whether such a prescription is moral in any scenario. Is this really what the citizenry desires for the education of our youth?

My experience with Grace's students, although admittedly limited and preliminary, demonstrates two things: (1) there is a significant amount of truth in Duncan's description of student perspectives, and (2) the arena for those disturbing perspectives is constructed by adults whenever we allow these policies to force any child into this horrifying game. These conclusions, then, require that I contend with the secretary's idea that our nation's children are begging "to be challenged."

The word "challenge" means "produce difficulty, test, try, make demands, tax" or to "provoke, dare, give an ultimatum, throw down the gauntlet, threaten, gage, defy, summon, beard, make a stand, face off, cross, stare down" (McCutcheon, 2010, p. 102). It most often carries the tone of confrontation or battle, especially when it is used to indicate a competition or a *race* to the top. The last decade of education policy has evolved to ensure that the dystopian youth are significantly challenged by the discrimination, the burden, and the stigma that have been created for them. They are challenged further by the unreasonable lengths they must go to scavenge for bits of literary or intellectual substance. Most tragically, their greatest challenge may be the act of "unlearning": the failure they have to overcome was never truly their own. So contrary to Duncan's claim, I think he has severely misinterpreted the cries of the dystopian youth. My years of experience in this field have taught me that these students are not only begging to be emancipated from the "challenge," but they are pleading for something meaningful.

A SUGGESTION: SUPPORT STUDENTS THROUGH MEANINGFUL STRUGGLE

The process of learning, especially in the most profound and meaningful sense, can undoubtedly be an exhausting struggle. In fact, John Dewey's (1910/1997) description of the thought process can initially project a somewhat cautionary tone to the learner: "Reflective thinking is always more or less troublesome because ... it involves willingness to endure a condition of mental unrest and disturbance" (p. 13). Dewey also referred to the suspension of judgement as a "condition of mental uneasiness" which "is likely to be somewhat painful" (p. 13). That being said, Dewey's (1920) words also serve as a reminder that "This close connection between doing and suffering or undergoing forms what we call experience" (p. 86).

Therefore, Dewey's sentiments regarding the frustrations of the thought process are not meant to cause hesitation. They instead overlay the necessary strains which are part of many of life's worthwhile experiences: the physical exertion of scaling an ascent; the exhaustion from nursing a sick child to health; the trial and failure of assistive approaches in helping another human being rediscover self-confidence; and, even, the pain of "unlearning" those things we have been taught so unjustly. Despite the discomforting phases, experience remains intrinsically meaningful because the struggle invests in its own resolution. But when we fail to experience the necessary and restorative powers of resolution, then we are left spent and unfulfilled by our efforts.

As both a student and a teacher, I find that learning typically assumes this unfulfilling feeling as the direction or process is needlessly dictated and imposed from outside and above. That is, when those far removed from the struggle create enough dissonance that it not only dominates our efforts, but it becomes the very interference that renders indiscernible the resolution to our struggle. In the absence of resolution, then, one fails to be recharged:

> Disconnected doing and disconnected suffering are neither of them experiences.... The movements amount to nothing; they have no consequences for life. Or, if they have, these consequences are not connected with prior doing. There is no experience, no learning, no cumulative process. (Dewey, 1920, p. 86)

This is often the point where struggle succumbs to misery.

Meaningful growth, however, is conceived in one's internal fight to understand. There are times when it certainly can be accompanied by a disorienting reorganization of schematic structures, or the tentative adjustment to an evolved perspective. However, the fact that some crisis-induced or consciousness-altering experiences can occasionally yield this type of physical and emotional drain does not mean that this was what Dewey envisioned for the education of our children. Nor does it mean learning and teaching experiences need ever be made into the increasingly torturous processes they have become. The struggle for growth can be taken in stride and with a great deal of enjoyment and will; but the community of learners must be allowed to take part in defining the direction for their efforts (Freire, 1970/2000). Only then can the learning process be saturated with *their* sense of meaningfulness.

The beauty of supporting our students through their meaningful struggles is that the energy surges from within *them*. It pushes them through to the resolution of their own efforts, which replenishes them while setting them up for their next endeavors. This approach to learning and teaching fuels a cycle by which meaningful resolutions and the liberation from the miseries of coercion can mutually reinforce one another. This continuity of growth works to the benefit of the students and the educator: with enough support, Grace's students grew to willingly struggle through words and meaningful concepts with absolutely no punitive assaults or burdens offered on our part. The most amazing thing to witness, though, was how they were fuelled by their own sense of purpose and curiosity.

The Hunger Games struck different chords among all the students, but the most emotional and sustained reactions undoubtedly arose when the social injustices in the story reflected the life experience of the students. An articulation of the exact reasons that specific students identified with this story is beyond the scope of this chapter, but I can say the students generally appeared to be drawn toward tales of tragedy. In fact, many of the books on Grace's shelves were laden with struggles to overcome social injustice; and fascinatingly, both current and former students showed up before school and between classes to ask that Grace suggest more titles and lend these tragically hopeful books to them. On occasion, even students unknown to Grace would appear and say with cautious curiosity, "So, I've heard you read good books in here." She indulged every student interest with a book talk prior to handing over her suggestion. The brevity of the transactions and the reciprocal payments of sincere gratitude played out like a scene from the Hob in District 12.

When Grace gave her students dystopian literature, the youth revealed in both subtlety and outburst exactly how guilty our society is of not loving them and how starved they are for intellectual content and meaningful learning experiences. Students who are drawn to tales of tragedy suggest much about their own experiences, questions, aspirations, and determination. The meanings they make and share from their literary transactions hint at where they have been and where they desire to go next (Dewey, 1910/1997; Rosenblatt, 1986). This is also the very place where hope rises out of dystopia. Student reactions hold the potential for their expansion in understanding, and therefore it is the task of the educator to listen intently for those suggestions that the students often and unconsciously reveal. Upon extracting the hints from conversation and writing, the teacher is then enabled to provide meaningful suggestions to the students. I do not claim that this is easy or exact, especially at the onset; the fact that every human brings an entirely different history and experience means that it is a process which certainly cannot be standardized or scripted. However, once it is underway, the process is far more therapeutic than plodding through the standardized and remedial labors that are the source of most classroom miseries.

Observing the inner workings of Grace's school only seemed to emphasize how easy it is for educators to feel powerless against the illogicality of standardization, remediation, and bureaucracy which plagues our schools.

Trudging through the desolate landscape that has been ravaged by the nation's dystopian educational policies is by no means a pleasant existence; but the prospects to emerge are quite promising if we rely upon our students for guidance and rejuvenation. I offer my thoughts and the narrative of this experience to Grace and any other educator dedicated to lovingly helping our youth navigate beyond the failures they have absorbed from years of slogging through an environment which has been largely inhospitable toward them. As for where to begin, I suggest a book from the dystopian genre. It may be presumptuous to expect a class full of students to connect instantly with books that explore the conflicts related to class, race, gender, or sexuality. However, it is fair to conclude that by classifying our students as "high-need," we have taught the youth of our nation far more about oppression than many of us might care to admit. Allowing the students, and ourselves, to explore these oppressive experiences is the only way to begin kindling hope out of the dystopian state in which we find ourselves.

NOTES

1. "teachers find themselves in schools with cultures where inflexible work rules discourage innovation and restrict their opportunities to work together and take on leadership responsibilities" (U.S. Department of Education, 2012, p. 1). The RESPECT Program, one created by the U.S. Department of Education, fails to address how the policies of standardization and top-down management have created the very symptoms (systematic inflexibility and defamation those who teach high-needs students) the program aims to ameliorate.
2. The names of students and teacher have been changed to protect the identities of those with whom I shared this experience.
3. Troy Anthony Davis was convicted of killing a Georgia police officer. He was executed despite public protest, appeals to the Supreme Court, and growing questions about the validity of the evidence used to convict him (Severson, 2011).
4. Those in power define and measure the licentious activities of others. By virtue of this "right," they possess the power to accuse and sentence those who fall outside their defined parameters. Those responsible for sentencing are also responsible for seeing to the terms and means of punishment. The spectacle of punishment allows the remainder of the public to see the strength of the punishing class, while simultaneously lending clout to that class' ability to accurately define such undesirable behaviors. The viewing public begins to accept the strength of those in power, and this acceptance works to reinforce and glorify those in power while further vilifying the "guilty" (Foucault, 1977, Part 1, Section 2).
5. Like the spectacle of the scaffold, the schooling institution utilizes examination and documentation as surveillance. This allows for and reinforces

the ability of those in power to define the types of knowledge that are valuable. Examinations then function as the mechanism for those in power to "prove" the capacity and value of each individual. This bolsters both positions of power and subordination, while disciplining the subordinated into "docile bodies" (Foucault, 1977, Section 3).

REFERENCES

Abramson, L. (2011, November 15). Does New Orleans welcome disabled students? *All Things Considered Podcast.* Podcast retrieved from http://www.npr.org/2011/11/15/142138523/does-new-orleans-welcome-disabled-students

Apple, M. W. (2001). *Educating the "right" way: Markets, standards, and inequality.* New York, NY: Routledge.

Banjo, S. (2011, September 19). Half of Conn. schools don't meet federal education standards. *The Wall Street Journal.* Retrieved from http://blogs.wsj.com/metropolis/2011/09/19/half-of-conn-schools-dont-meet-federal-education-standards.

Beah, I. (2007). *A long way gone: Memoirs of a boy soldier.* New York, NY: Sarah Crichton Books.

Collins, S. (2008). *The hunger games.* New York, NY: Scholastic.

Cusick, P. A. (2008). Why do kids hate school? Why do we care? In S. Jones, E. Sheffield, & C. Pearman (Eds.), *Why kids hate school* (pp. 3-9). Dubuque, IA: Kendall Hunt.

Dewey, J. (1997). *How we think.* Mineola, NY: Dover. (Original work published 1910)

Dewey, J. (1920). *Reconstruction in philosophy.* New York, NY: Henry Holt.

Ede, A. (2006). Scripted curriculum: Is it a prescription for success? *Childhood Education, 83*(1), 29-32.

Frankenberg, E., Siegel-Hawley, G., & Wang, J. (2010). *Choice without equity: Charter school segregation and the need for civil rights standards.* Los Angeles, CA: The Civil Rights Project/Proyecto Derechos Civiles at UCLA. Retrieved from http://civilrightsproject.ucla.edu/research/k-12-education/integration-and-diversity/choice-without-equity-2009-report/frankenberg-choices-without-equity-2010.pdf

Freire, P. (2000). *Pedagogy of the oppressed.* New York, NY: The Continuum International Publishing Group. (Original work published 1970)

Foucault, M. (1977). *Discipline & punish: The birth of the prison* (A. Sheridan, Trans.). New York, NY: Random House.

Gillborn, D., & Youdell, D. (2000). *Rationing education: Policy, practice, reform, and equity.* Buckingham, England: Open University Press.

Jacobson, N., Kilik, J. (Producers), & Ross, G. (Director). (2012). *The Hunger Games* [Motion picture]. United States of America: Lionsgate.

Kaestle, C. F. (1983). *Pillars of the republic: Common schools and American society, 1780-1860.* New York, NY: Hill and Wang.

Kozol, J. (2005). *The shame of the nation: The restoration of apartheid schooling in America.* New York, NY: Crown.

McCutcheon, M. (Ed.). (2010). *Roget's super thesaurus* (4th ed.). Cincinnati, OH: Reader's Digest Books.

McGrory, K., & Hiaasen, S. (2011, December 16). Charter schools enrolling low number of poor students. *The Miami Herald*. Retrieved from http://www.miamiherald.com/2011/12/16/2548465/charters-schools-enrolling-low.html.

Nichols, S. L. & Berliner, D. C. (2007). *Collateral damage: How high-stakes testing corrupts America's schools*. Cambridge, MA: Harvard Education Press.

Oregon Department of Education. (2011, August 2). *Student achievement increases but fewer Oregon schools meet federal standards under new adequate yearly progress targets*. Salem, Oregon: Author. Retrieved from http://www.ode.state.or.us/news/announcements/announcement.aspx?ID= 7494&TypeID=5.

Ravitch, D. (2010). *The death and life of the great American school system: How testing and choice are undermining education*. New York, NY: Basic Books.

Rosenblatt, L. M. (1986). The aesthetic transaction. *Journal of Aesthetic Education, 20*(4), 122-128.

Severson, K. (2011, September 21). Davis is executed in Georgia. *The New York Times*. Retrieved from http://www.nytimes.com/2011/09/22/us/final-pleas-and-vigils-in-troy-davis-execution.html?pagewanted=all.

Spring, J. (2005). *The American school, 1642-2000*. New York, NY: McGraw-Hill.

Tatter, G. (2011, September 1). Increase in federal education standards leaves local schools behind. *The Daily Tar Heel*. Retrieved from http://www.dailytarheel.com/index.php/ article/2011/08/abc_v._nclb_0824

Tyack, D. B. (1974). *The one best system: A history of American urban education*. Cambridge, MA: Harvard University Press.

U.S. Department of Education. (2002). *Public Law print of PL 107-110, the No Child Left Behind Act of 2001*. Washington, DC: Author. Retrieved from http://www2.ed.gov/policy/ elsec/leg/esea02/107-110.pdf

U.S. Department of Education. (2009a). *Turning around the bottom five percent: Secretary Arne Duncan's remarks at the National Alliance for Public Charter Schools Conference*. Washington, DC: Author. Retrieved from http://www2.ed.gov/news/speeches/ 2009/06/06222009.html.

U.S. Department of Education. (2009b). *Race to the top program executive summary*, Washington, DC: Author. Retrieved from http://www2.ed.gov/programs/racetothetop/ executive-summary.pdf.

U.S. Department of Education. (2012). *RESPECT Program*. Washington, DC: Author. Retrieved from http://www.ed.gov/blog/wp-content/uploads/2012/02/RESPECT_Program.pdf

Vaznis, J. (2009, August 12). Charter schools lag in serving the neediest. *Boston Globe*. Retrieved from http://www.boston.com/news/education/k_12/articles/2009/08/12/ charter_schools_lag_in_serving_students_with_special_needs

Winerip, M. (2011, July 10). Message from a charter school: Thrive or transfer. *The New York Times*. Retrieved from http://www.nytimes.com/2011/07/11/nyregion/charter-school-sends-message-thrive-or-transfer.html?_r=1

CHAPTER 10

GAMING AS VIRTUAL EDUCATION

Insights From Dystopian Art

Stefan J. Sheffield

> *I'm Andrew Ryan and I'm here to ask you a question: Is a man not entitled to the sweat of his brow?" 'No.' Says the man in Washington. 'It belongs to the poor.' 'No.' Says the man in the Vatican. 'It belongs to god.' 'No.' Says the man in Moscow. 'It belongs to everyone.' I rejected these answers. Instead I chose something different. I chose Rapture. A city where the artist would not fear the censor. Where the scientist would not be bound by petty morality? Where the great would not be constrained by the small? And with the sweat of your brow rapture can become your city as well.*
>
> —Levine, 2007

INTRODUCTION

Video games, much like music and movies before them, have come under scrutiny since their inception for their interactive portrayal of violence. Video games have been cited as one of the causes for many acts of violence in the past 20 years:

Dystopia and Education:
Insights Into Theory, Praxis, and Policy in an Age of Utopia-Gone-Wrong, pp. 157–165

> Exposure to violence in media, including television, movies, music, and video games, represents a significant risk to the health of children and adolescents. Extensive research evidence indicates that media violence can contribute to aggressive behavior, desensitization to violence, nightmares, and fear of being harmed. (American Academy of Pediatrics, 2009, para. 1)

Florida Attorney Jack Thompson is one of the loudest voices in this demonization of violent videogames (see Benedetti, 2007). Thompson has most recently blamed Bill Gates and the game *Counter Strike* for training Seung-Hui Cho for the tragic Virginia tech massacre: "This is not rocket science. When a kid who has never killed anyone in his life goes on a rampage and looks like the Terminator, he's a video gamer" (Cliffe, 2000, para. 20). My claim in this chapter is that it is not the violent actions and images of video games that influence people to commit violent acts themselves, but the lack of discussion surrounding these actions that contributes to the real life violent acts. Additionally, I will argue that understanding particular video games as important forms of dystopian art can aid in seeing their value in educational contexts. With this in mind, I conclude that videogames of the dystopian genre might be used as a tool to spark discussions about the way violence makes us feel and about why gratuitous violence is not a realistic way to solve problems.

As an example of how I have been personally affected by such dystopian video games, I present the *Call of Duty* (COD) series by Activision. COD is not a game series typically thought of as one that pushes intellectual boundaries; most of the millions who play COD do so with a competitive mindset only. However, in its seventh iteration, *Call of Duty Modern Warfare 2* (MW2) (McCandlish, 2009), the single player campaign takes players through a war story—the standard shoot-the-bad-guys type of story—but its presentation is such that it haunts players long after it is played. The game takes place in a first person perspective and opens with one of the most memorable scenes in gaming: the player is thrust into complete control of a terrorist. As the first level begins, the player has no idea that he/she will be playing the role of a terrorist. A few other men stand around the player's character in an elevator waiting for the mission objective. One of the men pulls a mask over his face and says "No Russian," and as the elevator doors open your comrades begin to gun down everyone in the airport and you, the player, are asked to join in the melee.

Many people I have talked to about this scene have said that they froze—unable to shoot a single person. Certainly everyone I know will agree that killing is wrong; and, my claim here is that putting the player in the shoes of a murderous antagonist as they commit this most heinous act is something that no other medium can achieve—and it totally works. As the player, you can feel the emotional repercussions of this action and these emotions force you to question your own morality (just as any other dystopian work would do), but in a more engaging and interactive fashion than, say, a dystopian novel.

For me, when the war in MW2 moved back to the United States and the scenes were of tanks rolling through the very suburbs that I drive by every day, and the fire fights were taking place on top of restaurants and shops I see every day, it did not *desensitize* me to violence, it made me more sensitive to the impact of violence. I have never had a piece of literature force me to experience the terror of war as much as the MW2 suburb scene. Once again, I am not discounting the value of literature or film in any way, but I would argue that there is a significant qualitative difference between the passive experience of reading a book or watching a film and the active experience of playing a video game.

Adam Biessener (2009) writes that the "No Russian" level "makes the player a part of truly heinous acts." He also notes that the "mission draws the morality of war and espionage into sharp focus in a way that simply shooting the bad guys cannot." Biessener concludes that this level is one of the more emotional moments in the game and he is "proud that our medium can address such weighty issues without resorting to adolescent black-and-white absolutes" (para. 10). I am not suggesting that COD/MW2 should be taught in school along side *Of Mice and Men* or *Lord of the Flies,* but I am suggesting that video games that accomplish this kind of emotional engagement have great potential as teaching tools (Golding, 1959; Steinbeck, 1937).

VIDEO GAMES AS DYSTOPIAN ART

Art itself is extremely difficult to define. Video games are a very young art form, no more than 60 years old. Well known film critic, Roger Ebert (2010), claims that video games are not art and can never be:

> One obvious difference between art and games is that you can win a game. It has rules, points, objectives, and an outcome. Santiago might cite an immersive game without points or rules, but I would say then it ceases to be a game and becomes a representation of a story, a novel, a play, dance, a film. Those are things you cannot win; you can only experience them. (para. 11)

These comments sparked much debate within the gaming community and Ebert continued to facilitate that debate. He created an online poll asking what people valued more, Mark Twain's (1885) *Huckleberry Finn* or a great videogame; 12,000 clicks later, videogames were ahead with 55% of the vote.

The issue with comparing video games with other works of art is clearly a generational matter. Of course video games do not have as many intellectually stimulating works as that found in literature—works that have been around for literally thousands of years compared to the several decade history of video games. In the above quote Ebert suggests that video games can never be art because they have rules and are competitive, and that is true about most traditional games, but not video games. When one plays any of the dystopian games I mention (and several I don't) the player comes to realize that "beating" the game doesn't just mean getting a high score; it means that the player has fully experienced the story and world that was laid out for him or her. I have been trying to take the phrase "beating" a game out of my vocabulary because it gives a misconception about the medium. Finishing a game is very akin to finishing a book or a film. Struggle does not take away from art and, in fact, only adds to the act of experiencing the piece of art in question. The fact that some sections of a videogame have tasks that take some semblance of skill to complete should not take away its potential as art. That is why reading difficult books can be so rewarding—the journey is only a journey because of the struggle.

Another common belief about art is that a person can reexperience that art by returning to it, and get something different out of it with each new experience. I feel this experiential quality rings especially true for dystopian themed art. I have, for example, played and replayed *Bioshock* and *Mass Effect* several times and I am not attempting to finish the game faster than I did the time before or get a better score (Hudson, 2007; Levine, 2007). I am playing it to see what I missed the previous time. Each time I have replayed these games I have learned a little more—much like Dystopian literature such as *1984* or *A Clockwork Orange* (Burgess, 1962/1986; Orwell, 1949/2001). On this count I agree with John Dewey's (1934) suggestion that "any practical activity will, provided that it is integrated and moves by its own urge to fulfillment, have esthetic quality" (p. 41). And certainly in my experience, video games provide the gamer with exactly this kind of emotional, aesthetic, experience. Also, I would argue that video games meet the expectation that art consist of a dialogue between the medium and the person experiencing that medium (Burgess, 1962/1986, p. xiv). On these counts, video games are art.

BIOSHOCK, ATLAS SHRUGGED AND DYSTOPIAN ART

Bioshock, a first person shooter game loosely based on Ayn Rand's (1957) novel *Atlas Shrugged,* was released in August of 2007, garnering much critical acclaim. *Atlas Shrugged* is the story of John Galt, a man who used his new electric motor to power his utopia in the Colorado mountains. They called this utopia "Galts Gulch." He then began inviting all of the world's greatest minds, inventors, artists, doctors, philosophers and, scientists, all those who keep society running, to come live in Galt's utopia free from the struggles of classism and all the other hardships that come with living in a typical capitalistic society. *Bioshock* is a sequel of sorts to *Atlas Shrugged* as it tells the tale of what may happen to that perfect society in a few years time through the eyes of a gamer-turned-game-character.

In *Bioshock*, Rapture is a city meant to have no constraints upon the creators. A secret hide out under the Atlantic Ocean for the world's greatest and most revered minds and those members of society trying to escape the common ideologies and philosophies from around the globe. After some time, the biologists of Rapture find a new chemical compound called "ADAM" that can be harvested from the stem cells of a specific species of sea slug that live on the ocean floor surrounding the city. However, after harvesting those stem cells they must be surgically implanted into young girls deemed "little sisters" turning them into a breeder of ADAM. ADAM is a DNA altering substance that not only strengthens the user's physical prowess, but can also rewrite genetic coding when injected giving the user incredible powers to create fire, ice, and a host of other telekinetic abilities. ADAM, however, is not an endlessly renewable resource.

As the supply of ADAM begins to deplete, divides are formed—the kind of social divides that Andrew Ryan meant to avoid. Classism becomes more and more apparent as the poor begin to attack the little sisters for their precious ADAM, and the rich begin to wall themselves up behind high tech locks and protect themselves with genetically enhanced bodyguards and security drones. ADAM is the catalyst for the civil war that takes place between Rapture's elite and the disenfranchised poor that fled to Rapture to get away from this very problem.

The beginning of the game thrusts the players into a Rapture torn apart by the civil war. Very few citizens are left, most have gone mad from ADAM abuse, and those who have not gone insane from ADAM addiction are trying to survive as best as they can. As an outsider you are first greeted by a man by the name of Atlas whose disembodied voice crackles through a walkie-talkie found in the bathysphere the player rode down in, and he proposes to help you as long as you can reach him and save his family from Andrew Ryan. Atlas knows of a way out of the city, he is the player's tour guide through Rapture providing you with each succeeding objective and always urging you to complete those objectives with a "would you kindly?" And of course, this being a video game, you go from one objective to the next as each plan of escape falls apart until the player reaches the climax where your objective is "Would you kindly kill Andrew Ryan." Ryan begs for his life and tries to explain himself, but the player no longer has a choice in the matter as the protagonist picks up a golf club and beats Andrew Ryan to death.

Bioshock is considered one of the best first person shooter games to have ever been released, and will surely keep that reputation for many years to come. Game reviewer Sean Malloy (2007) of the 1UPnetwork said that he had "never been so emotionally involved in an escort mission before. Games don't normally warrant the kind of discussions I have had about *Bioshock*. This is something special" (para. 5). Given *Bioshock's* level of emotional engagement and potential as a source of discussion, it meets the criteria of art suggested above.

Bioshock has all the great game play one would expect from one of this genre of video games. The player takes control of a virtual character seeing the world through his eyes while participating in strategic combat featuring a variety of weapons. The aspect that makes *Bioshock* stand out among what is fast becoming one of the most overpopulated and watered down genres in video gaming is the nature of the philosophical and moral questions with which it forces the player to engage concerning rational self-interest and the illusion of choice. Each Character in the game is a portrait of failed objectivism—whether it's the ADAM crazed lower class or the hidden elite—no one in rapture is able to escape their own human flaws. The world becomes a perfect example of why an objectivist theory, one based solely on rational self-interest, never works.[1] Throughout the game the player is given the choice to harvest and kill the Little Sisters for their ADAM or help them escape Rapture; either option allows the player's character to gain more power, but harvesting them yields immediate results, while saving the little sisters grants more power later in the game. The little sister's choice becomes allegorical for many different ethical dilemmas, from veganism to abortion. Dystopian themed art, such as *Bioshock*, seems to be one of the best ways to raise these important philosophical and ethical questions and the video game genre is one that is unfortunately overlooked as a tool for discussing such issues, particularly in schools.

Freedom of choice, though constrained in similar ways to traditional dystopian art and literature by the parameters of the particular game, is a leading trend in game development; it allows the user to feel as if he or she can do whatever he or she wants in that particular game world. Open world games are usually not bound by sequences of obligatory missions leading the player through a tightly constructed roller coaster ride of a story where the player is led down a fatalistic path. Open world games are more organic, more artful, and allow the user to choose what to do and when to do it.

The *Grand Theft Auto* and *Elder Scrolls* serials are prime examples of this open world type of game (Benzies, 2008; Howard, 2011). *Bioshock* is another one of those games that is widely considered "open world." It thrusts the players into Rapture and lets them walk around the city; the player is allowed and, in fact, encouraged to explore every inch of Rapture. When Atlas asks a player to kindly go somewhere or do something, the player has the option to explore other choices before continuing the main mission. In *Bioshock* this sense of freedom and choice is shattered when the player finds out that his character was being controlled by hypnosis during his whole stay in Rapture by the very man who was promising to help the player escape. The player then finds out Atlas's true intentions of using an outsider to further gain power in Rapture. The idea of a false sense of freedom is a classic theme of dystopian art. It is oftentimes the main theme. The government is the controlling force censoring and using subliminal messages to implement that control.

VIDEO GAMES AS EDUCATIONAL TOOLS

Many schools have adopted the use of educational games (i.e., math and typing games) on the computer to help students become more interested in class work. However, the excitement of playing a game quickly vanishes after you realize that the monotony of doing a math problem over and over again cannot be cloaked by the fact that you are doing it on a computer screen with bland cartoon characters bossing you around rather than your real teacher. I do not mean gaming in that sense. I mean using big budget games like the ones I mentioned above in the classroom and teaching them as you might teach the *Lord of the Flies* or one of Shakespeare's plays (Golding, 1959). Many games feature the same themes as many of our classic novels. Video games, in particular, often represent a dystopian society because stories of dystopian societies often provide the best opportunity to raise important philosophical and ethical questions. If *Bioshock* were to be taught in an upper level high school class, students' interest in dystopian art would be sparked. As kids become less and less interested in reading, it is important to use these games and new technologies as a launching pad for exploring dystopia in all aspects of education. *Bioshock* stresses the importance of choice and whether or not freedom of choice actually exists, as well as exploring ideas of classism and objectivism. Each inhabitant in Rapture has their own personal story and each of those stories can be as powerfully educating as the character that the player controls. As such, video Games are a practice in activism and have been creating a generation of problem solvers and critical thinkers since their inception. In each game world there is a problem to be solved, a difference to be made. The activity might be saving the galaxy from an evil galactic empire or it could be something as small as getting across the road as a frog; but, all of the puzzles and struggles that gamers face within the digital world can be used as tools to prepare them for a future life of thoughtful activism.

COD does not have the same educational potential as *Bioshock*, but the aforementioned "No Russian" level might be used to discuss the feelings that come from being involved in emotionally intense situations without having to experience the real world tragedy associated with violence. COD should be used as a way to discuss the repercussions of violence and war with students. Every time a tragic act of violence occurs, like the Columbine massacre or the Aurora, Colorado theater shooting, there exists an opportunity not to demonize the shooters or their habits, but a time to reconsider our society's values and ask what we can do to prevent these atrocities from happening in the future. It is quite obvious that getting more locks on our doors and putting cameras on every street corner is not a successful preventative reaction. I believe that having students experience these acts in a virtual setting where no lives are lost can create a lasting and positive impact on them and allow youth an opportunity to make mindful decisions about how to react to these situations rather than mindlessly locking ourselves away until we all live in our own private prisons. If we don't start to change the way we react to violence, our society might easily become the next Rapture.

Using these types of games in education as a teaching tool can open up many new possibilities for keeping students engaged and classroom experiences reflective of the actual lives of young people. Games should no longer be looked at as just a source of entertainment. The games I have mentioned and many other games out now have as much intellectual and educational merit as the classic texts taught in school; they just come in a different, more interactive, package. Video games are not going away. We have an amazing opportunity to use these games not only as a tool for entertainment but as a very flexible teaching tool. It is high time that these tools be incorporated into our curriculum so our educational system can change and evolve with the students struggling to operate within it.

NOTE

1. "Objectivism" here and throughout this chapter refers to the philosophical system developed by Ayn Rand and born from her beliefs in rational self-interest, the independence of reality, laissez faire capitalism, among others.

REFERENCES

American Academy of Pediatrics. (2009, October). Policy statement—Media violence. Retrieved from http://www.ncbi.nlm.nih.gov/pubmed/19841118

Biessner, A. (2009). Call of duty: Modern warfare 2. *Gameinformer.* Retrieved from http://www.gameinformer.com/games/call_of_duty_modern_warfare_2 /b/xbox360/archive/2009/11/09/review-call-of-duty-modern-warfare-2.aspx

Benedetti, W. (2007, April 20). *Were videogames to blame for the massacre? MSNBC.* Retrieved from http://www.msnbc.msn.com/id/18220228/ns/technology_and_science-games/t/were-video-games-blame-massacre/#.UG8x-VHrSSo

Benzies, L. (2008). *Grand theft auto.* Toronto, Ontario: Rockstar Toronto.

Burgess, A. (1986). *A clockwork orange.* New York, NY: W.W. Norton. (Original work published 1962)

Cliffe, J. (2000). *Counter-strike.* Kirkland, WA: Valve.

Dewey, J. (1934). *Art as experience.* New York, NY: Perigree.

Ebert, R. (2010, April 16). Video Games Can Never be Art. In *Chicago Sun Times.* Retrieved from http://blogs.suntimes.com/ebert/2010/04/video_games_can_never_be_art.html

Golding, W. (1959). *Lord of the flies.* New York, NY: Penguin Books.

Howard, T. (2011). *Elder scrolls.* Rockville, MD: Bethesda.

Hudson, C. (2007). *Mass effect.* Edmonton, Alberta, Canada: Bioware.

Levine, K. (2007). *Bioshock.* Boston, MA: 2K Boston.

Malloy, S. (2007, September 20). BioShock Review for PC. *1UP.* Retrieved from http://www.1up.com/reviews/bioshock_2

McCandlish, M. (2009). *Call of duty.* Santa Monica, CA: Activision.

Orwell, G. (2001). *1984.* New York, NY: Harcourt. (Original work published 1949)

Rand, A. (1957). *Atlas shrugged.* New York, NY: Random House.

Steinbeck, J. (1937). *Of mice and men.* New York, NY: Covici-Friedd.

Twain, M. (Samuel Clemons) (1885). *Adventures of Huckleberry Finn* (Tom Sawyer's Comrade). New York, NY: Charles L. Webster and Company.

SECTION III: POLICY

ARE UTOPIAN EDUCATIONAL POLICIES INHERENTLY DYSTOPIAN?

Jessica A. Heybach and Eric C. Sheffield

As was mentioned in the Preface, this project grew out of a concern that educational policy mandates, those expected to produce universal outcomes and dictated from afar, were fundamentally reflective of utopias-gone-wrong. "All children can learn" and "100% proficiency in math and reading by 2014"—phrases, cloaked in utopian thinking, have led to the enactment of policies that truly terrorize teachers and students alike. Although American educational policies have always been ripe with utopian fantasies, today's policies have taken a literal technocratic turn into an educational policy crazy-land. In this third section, our authors examine current policy mandates themselves and describe their frighteningly dystopian character.

It seems that mass education cannot easily avoid mechanization, dehumanization, and the distortion of individual identities. Schools are inhabited by our most vulnerable citizens, the young, who are often the victims of oppressive—yet deeply pedagogical—institutional policies. In 1933, John Dewey wrote a brief editorial where he argued, "The most utopian thing in Utopia is that there are no schools at all." "No schools at all" seems an absurdity, utterly impossible, given the insidious nature of schools and educational policy meant to shape every aspect of a child's life today. Rather, today, "all we have is school" has become an ideological hysteria and the means to bring about a perfect society at all costs. In the face of Dewey's warning, that in Utopia there are "no schools," possibly, the most dystopian thing in Dystopia is that there are schools?

CHAPTER 11

IN SEARCH OF EQUAL EDUCATIONAL OPPORTUNITY FOR HARRISON BERGERON

John E. Petrovic

> *Your Honor, years ago I recognized my kinship with all living beings, and I made up my mind then that I was not one bit better than the meanest on earth. I said then, and I say now, that while there is a lower class, I am in it; and while there is a criminal element, I am of it; and while there is a soul in prison, I am not free.*
>
> —Eugene V. Debbs (1918, para. 1)

INTRODUCTION

Dystopian literature and other media typically present stories dealing, at first blush, with utopian societies. But these societies are revealed to be the result of repression, coercion, and controlled states. This is certainly the case with Kurt Vonnegut's (1968) short story, *Harrison Bergeron,* a story of brutally enforced state-egalitarianism. A brief anecdote explains why this particular story stood out for me and foreshadows my interpretation: A bipartisan group was watching a football game

Dystopia and Education:
Insights Into Theory, Praxis, and Policy in an Age of Utopia-Gone-Wrong, pp. 169–184

in the fall of 2010. After a great 70 yard pass play, which resulted in a touchdown, the defensive player could be seen berating the referee, clearly shouting, arms flailing. At that point, one of my friends began to mock the player. "C'mon ref! It's not fair! He's too good!" While we all thought it quite funny, I also recognized the strong critique of liberals in the seemingly light-hearted banter. The latter was intended by the speaker, the former hidden to him in the power and opaqueness of ideology. I also recognized *Harrison Bergeron*.

Harrison Bergeron presents a society of equals (Vonnegut, 1968). Or, more accurately, a society of equalization in which those with naturally advantageous qualities—physical prowess, beauty, intelligence, and so forth—are handicapped so that no one is better off. *Harrison Bergeron*[1] has a number of such qualities and must, therefore, carry weights to hamper his physical prowess, put black caps on his teeth to disguise his beauty, and wear headphones producing distracting noise to counter his intelligence. Vonnegut's (1968) short story has been cited in important court cases in the same way invoked, unknowingly, by my football fanatic friend. For example, Casey Martin, who has a painful congenital defect in his right leg, sued the Professional Golf Association (PGA) for the accommodation of a golf cart, riding in golf carts being prohibited by PGA rule. Invoking the Americans With Disabilities Act, Casey won his suit by a 7-2 decision in the Supreme Court of the United States. In his dissent, Justice Antonin Scalia wrote that the majority's

> Alice in Wonderland determination that there are such things as judicially determinable "essential" and "nonessential" rules of a made-up game; and its Animal Farm determination that fairness and the ADA mean that everyone gets to play by individualized rules which will assure that no one's lack of ability (or at least no one's lack of ability so pronounced that it amounts to a disability) will be a handicap. The year was 2001, and "everybody was finally equal." (*PGA Tour, Inc. v. Casey Martin,* para. 3)

Scalia cites several dystopian sources in his dissent; but the final quote is taken from *Harrison Bergeron*.

In this chapter, I first consider these and other conservative interpretations of *Harrison Bergeron* arguing that the story is, in fact, a satire of conservative renderings of what equality might require and of socialist thought generally. Drawing on both liberal and radical egalitarian political philosophy, I employ this satirical reading to explore what equality is and entails, including the key concept of equality of condition. This discussion is important to informing a philosophy of education, especially as concerns conceptualizations of equal educational opportunity.

FORMALIST VERSUS ACTUALIST RENDERINGS OF EQUALITY

In his dissent, Scalia supports a formalist account of equality. Once the game is set, "made-up," everyone is equally permitted to play. The rules do not discriminate by one's race, color, creed, ability, and so forth. In education, the 1954 *Brown* decision ushered in a similar mindset. The chains were removed for Black students from the schoolhouse door and equal educational opportunity was achieved. Those who do not accept this conclusion likely reject a formalist conception of equality, at least in certain contexts or under certain circumstances, and most likely cleave, instead, to an actualist conception. The latter are what the likes of Scalia and most other right-thinkers miscast as *Harrison Bergeron*. But these two conceptions require further delineation before proceeding. In this section, I critique conservative readings of *Harrison Bergeron* to distinguish between formalist and actualist assumptions regarding equality.

Formal equality builds on the Aristotelian proviso to treat like cases alike. The difficult matter is to determine in what normatively relevant respect persons share equal status. In our system of jurisprudence, this is determined by personhood. Any two persons will be treated equally, that is, the same, before the eyes of the law. If you grab a face mask as a football player, you will be penalized regardless of your race or religion. You will also be penalized, conservative interpreters of *Harrison Bergeron* would quickly point out, regardless of your ability. This, recall, was Scalia's logic. To his mind, Casey Martin has the same opportunity as anyone else to play the game of golf.

Of course, a key assumption that undergirds this logic of formal opportunity extends from the notion of "fair play." However, I find it problematic to argue that Casey Martin is involved in a "fair" competition, even as the rules are the same. In fact, it is not fair *because* the rules are the same. Scalia would hold, however, that it may be unfortunate, but it is not unfair. We cannot possibly level the playing field in all areas of human conduct that will account for all natural contingencies. On the one hand, if Martin's condition affects his ability to play golf, this does not mean that the opportunity does not exist. On the other hand, if the rules state that people with such conditions may not play, then the opportunity is taken away. If it were this simple, conservatives and I might agree on this basic point. But it is not quite this simple.

Formal accounts of opportunity become crude and inhumane once they extend beyond the literal playing field into social contexts. This is because we cannot carry the assumptions of a meritocratic order into social contexts. There is a difference between natural and social effects on opportunity, even though the distinction may not be easily teased apart. Despite my examples, I am not particularly interested in whether or not everyone has a fair or even unfair opportunity to play golf or football. I am interested in whether or not everyone has a fair chance at realizing a rewarding life. This requires actual, not formal, accounts of equality, especially as regards equality of educational opportunity. Such accounts "sanction intervening in the social system to minimize fortuitousness in individuals' lives" (Howe, 1997, p. 20).

The distinction between actualist and formalist accounts of equality is fruitfully illustrated in a commentary on Vice President Biden by John Stossel. In a segment titled "Must We all be Equal?," Stossel (2010) observes that at the Democratic National Convention Vice President Joe Biden said that "Equality is the American creed." Stossel goes on to point out that "[He is] not saying that the VP has become our 'Handicapper General' [a character and office in *Harrison Bergeron*], but at the convention he [Biden] did claim the American dream, where anyone can make it, is slipping away. So it is the job of government to fix that." Biden, Stossel would contend, is an actualist. Thusly, Stossel sets up his interview with Thor Halvorssen and Chandler Tuttle, who produced and directed, respectively, a 2009 film adaptation of *Harrison Bergeron* titled *2081*.

In the interview, Stossel (2010) points out that Halvorssen and Tuttle disagree with the Vice President. This leads into Halvorssen's formalist explanation of equality: "people misunderstand the issue of 'we are equal.' We're all equal inasmuch as you, and Chandler, and I should not be treated by a court differently ... equality of conditions is different from equality before the law." He goes on to explain that equality of conditions is when "they want to *make* us equal." In fact, in a 1995 screen version, Harrison Bergeron exclaims, "You haven't made everyone equal. You've made them the same and there's a big difference" (Nadler, Glascoe, Hackett, & Pierson 1995). After all, the story begins,

> The year was 2081, and everybody was finally equal. They weren't only equal before God and the law. They were equal every which way. Nobody was smarter than anybody else. Nobody was better looking than anybody else. Nobody was stronger or quicker than anybody else. (Vonnegut, 1968, p. 7)

This equation of egalitarianism with sameness is a typical and effective rhetorical device of the right. Thus, Halvorssen's interpretation may be understandable. It is, however, from a philosophical perspective, a complete misreading of progressive egalitarian thought. There are no progressive egalitarians who argue for the level of equality (equality as sameness) that conservatives claim. It is, in fact, quite the contrary. Take, for example, the work of the radical egalitarian, Kai Nielsen. Nielsen (1985) pointedly argues that the purpose of his principles of egalitarianism is not to "reduce people to a uniform sameness of condition, such that they all get the same things, do the same things, have the same interests and in general behave in the same way" (p. 59). Indeed, the leap in logic that expands some level of equality of wealth or condition to a sameness of every other aspect of the human condition is telling evidence of the single-mindedly and sadly pecuniary view of human nature typical of conservative thought.

Given this, from a literary perspective (a perspective that would seem relevant if one is producing a film adaptation of a literary piece), the equation of progressive (and/or radical) egalitarianism with sameness is to take great artistic license and present a complete misreading of Vonnegut. Taken from Vonnegut's standpoint, as a humanist deeply influenced by socialist leaders including Eugene V. Debbs, *Harrison Bergeron* "gives not a possible egalitarianism of the future ... but rather an enactment of how absurd society would be if egalitarianism were what America's dominant culture [read: conservative] thinks it is" (Hattenhauer, 1998, p. 389).

Stossel's (2010) critique of Vice President Biden for intimating that "it is the job of government to fix" diminishing access to the American dream is similarly contrary to Vonnegut's views: Vonnegut would agree with the Vice President. As Marvin (2002) points out, Orwell is the only writer that Vonnegut would admit to imitating, "not because of Orwell's satirizing of communism (usually miscast as a synonym of socialism by the right), but, as Vonnegut declared, because 'I like [Orwell's] concern for the poor, I like his socialism, I like his simplicity'" (p. 19). Vonnegut believed that wealth must be shared and that government must play a role in ensuring that happens.[2] Thus, *Harrison Bergeron* is a satire, not of the left and progressive egalitarians, but of Halvorssen, Stossel, and Scalia, among the many others who wrongly believe that formal equality and capitalism are synonymous with democracy. Thus, when Stossel opines, based on *his* reading of *Harrison Bergeron*, that "Kurt Vonnegut understood the threat of government-imposed equality," Stossel has not really read Vonnegut.

CAPITALISM, DEMOCRACY, AND SAMENESS

The confused conflation of capitalism with democracy is, perhaps, an aside, but an important one. For it is this confusion that allows, or perhaps requires, Halvorssen and Stossel to focus on the beginning and miss the ending of *Bergeron*. This is ideologically telling. In his culminating protest, Harrison Bergeron enters a television studio where a live broadcast of the ballet is taking place. On stage, having broken free from his various handicapping devices, he declares, "I am the Emperor!" "Do you hear? I am the Emperor! Everybody must do what I say at once!" (Vonnegut, 1968, p. 11).

Could it be that Vonnegut is suggesting that a society that is not more egalitarian becomes a fascist state? But then Harrison looks to the musicians and commands, "Play your best, and I will make you barons and dukes and earls" (Vonnegut, 1968, p. 12). So, instead of a fascist state, perhaps Vonnegut is suggesting a feudal society. Today, when 74% of wealth is controlled by 10% of the population, nearly a quarter of all children live in poverty, and the 400 wealthiest people in the nation own more than the bottom 155 million combined,[3] Vonnegut seems prescient: the Lords are few, the serfs many. This is precisely why Vonnegut points out that, "left unchecked, capitalism will erode the democratic foundations of the United States" (as cited in Marvin, 2002, p. 19). Of course, in their remake of *Harrison Bergeron*, Halvorssen and Tuttle (2009) are careful to occlude this interpretation, conveniently deleting Harrison's lines naming emperors, barons, dukes, and earls.[4] But such artistic license, perhaps deceit, does not change the clear relationship Vonnegut recognized between capitalism and democracy: it is a parasitic one and the two, therefore, must not be conflated.

Vonnegut did not see sameness as an outcome of socialism or egalitarianism,[5] but simple economic fairness. This fairness (and, yes, I unapologetically defend the redistribution of wealth as fairness) is required for robust democracies to obtain. As Atilio Boron (2006) points out, while the right may claim a "capitalist democracy," this description is a sort of Hegelian inversion of the real relationship: democratic capitalism. This, Boron explains, recovers the true meaning of democracy in capitalist societies

> by underlining the fact that its structural features and defining aspects—"free" and periodic elections, individual rights and freedoms, etc.— are ... only political forms whose operation and specific efficacy are unable to neutralize, let alone dissolve, the intrinsically and hopelessly anti-democratic structure of capitalist society. (p. 32)

The gross income gaps between rich and poor already cited and the gross poverty that are unavoidable by-products (that is to say, they are structural) of unfettered capitalism are anathematic to democracy since they create power and privilege for a relative few, including the very basic material welfare necessary to any robust ideal of freedom, supposedly at the heart of democracy. So, yes, a certain degree of sameness, equality of condition, is required for democracy. But, as noted previously, the right takes their critique of the left much further, intimating (as evidenced by their misinterpretations of *Harrison Bergeron*) that progressive egalitarianism (actualism) demands some sort of absolute sameness in terms of ability, appearance, intelligence, and so forth. The most radical egalitarians reject this and the degree of equality of condition, in terms of material and social welfare, varies among egalitarians.[6]

Another criticism of egalitarianism is the accusation of "group-think." This, of course, comes from Orwell (1949/1977). Obviously, there are, in any political system, groups of people who share certain values and ideological perspectives. This is why political parties exist. The wars waged by the dominant voices in the United States (rhetorical and military[7]) against the left over the past 40 years have led to the misbelief that so-called group think is proprietary to the left. Nevertheless, the recent debacle over the debt ceiling, Tea Party madness, and Grover Norquist pledge signers are quintessential examples of group-think. So is it leftist or rightist politics that lead to this kind of sameness? Vonnegut provides some insight here pointing out that the United States was hated around the world long before the election of George W. Bush, which Vonnegut (2003) refers to as "the Mickey Mouse coup d'état." He goes on to explain that "we weren't hated, as Bush would have it, because of our liberty and justice for all. We are hated because our corporations have been the principal deliverers and imposers of new technologies and economic schemes which have wrecked cultures" (as cited in Barsamian, 2004, p. 11). In other words, it is corporate America and their conservative, free-market, political lackeys who, by wrecking cultures, produce sameness even as or because they promote grossly unjust economic difference. Think strip malls, McDonalds, Wal-Mart. What did they replace? Whom did they displace? This sameness is a result of the so-called "free" market with its emphasis on efficiency, productivity, calculability, control, and profit at the expense of humanity while free-marketeers seek trade restrictions and limits on, not expansion of, choice.

FORMAL AND ACTUAL EQUAL EDUCATIONAL OPPORTUNITY

In the previous sections, I first argued that there is an important distinction to be made between formalist and actualist renderings of opportunity. I then observed how capitalism, the preferred foundation of formalism, results in economic difference anathematic to the democracy that proponents of formalism pretend to defend while leading to the very cultural and ideological sameness they are supposed to abhor. In this section, I turn to a discussion of how the formalist/actualist distinction has informed conceptualizations of equal educational opportunity (EEO). For surely EEO is an essential prerequisite to equal opportunity more generally. Working through an historical overview of the development of EEO as a philosophical construct, I argue that the most robust actualist conceptualizations rightly disallow the gross economic differences accepted by free-marketeers and are perfectly contrary to the sameness depicted in *Harrison Bergeron*.

Interpretations of and debates around EEO were especially invigorated by James Coleman's landmark study in 1966 and his subsequent interpretations of EEO. Coleman (1968) argues that the evolution of the concept of EEO has gone through several stages. The first stage consisted of the idea that all children must be exposed to the same curriculum in the same school. Here "equal" meant "same." The second stage assumed different interests and abilities and therefore equality required providing different curricular choices. The third stage inserted "separate but equal" into the concept. In the United States, this stage ended in 1954 with the decision handed down by the Supreme Court in *Brown vs. Board of Education*.

Until the Brown decision, the concept of EEO largely assumed a natural passivity upon the part of the school. That is to say that the institution provided an opportunity of which children and their parents should take advantage. This is what Nicholas Burbules and Ann Sherman (1979) later referred to as a "formalist" interpretation of EEO. Following the discussion of formalism above, formalist interpretations of EEO view it as obtaining once the conditions of access have been equalized. The de jure end of segregation, for example, could be argued to meet this standard of EEO, despite any other conditions. "Formalist interpretations are minimalist, requiring only absence of formal barriers to access"; therefore, it is arguable that equal opportunity is even available through such a conception (Howe, 1997, p. 20).

Formalism is fatally flawed in application to EEO for the same reason it is flawed more generally: it assumes, as I alluded to earlier, that we live in a meritocracy. We, in fact, live in a society of full social stratification wherein, on the one hand, the wealthy can ensure the success (in terms of wealth and general welfare) of their children regardless of ability. Where, on the other hand, hard work by those living in or on the edge of poverty is much more akin to treading water than swimming the channel. Some might find that acceptable; it's just the way things are. As problematic as such a position is generally, formalism must be seen as morally repugnant (if it shouldn't be already) when applied as an interpretation of EEO. Shouldn't a degree of equality of condition, rejected by formalists, apply, at least, to schools? Without considering equality of condition, what might children be left with at school?

In his many stinging exposés, Jonathan Kozol (1992) describes the *Savage Inequalities* manifest in underfunded, understaffed schools that children attend across the country: rat-infested, unheated, uncooled, unsanitary sites of "education" wherein students lack basic educational necessities (e.g., books). Formally speaking, children in these neighborhoods have educational opportunity. Thus, for example, was *Harrison Bergeron* invoked in a Kansas Supreme Court case involving the equalization of school funding. In this case, attorneys argued that the lesson of

Harrison Bergeron was that "forced equality would be a nightmare, so unequal funding of public schools is ok" (Rothschild, 2005). Here *Harrison Bergeron* is used in a way that would make Vonnegut (1968) cringe. Equalization of school funding seems to be perfectly consistent with Vonnegut's contention that "It's perfectly normal to be a socialist. It's perfectly normal to be in favor of fire departments." Further, toward the end of his life, Vonnegut (2003) lamented the lack of progressive political leaders. "There was a time," he noted, "when I could vote for economic justice, and I can't anymore" (as cited in Barsamian, 2004, p. 15).

Such economic justice would include, for Vonnegut, not just funding for fire departments but for schools (among other important public services) to promote equal educational opportunity. In 2005, Vonnegut expressed a fairly straightforward philosophy of equal educational opportunity:

> My dream for America was great public schools. I thought we should be the envy of the world with our public schools. And I went to such a public school. So I knew such a school was possible.... We had a daily paper. We had a debating team. We had a fencing team. We had a chorus, a jazz band, a serious orchestra. And all of this with the great depression going on and I wanted everybody to have such a school. We could afford it if we didn't spend all the money on weaponry. (A Tribute)

In short, funding matters and not everything should be funded equally. To provide EEO, funding clearly matters in schools. But, it also matters beyond school (cf. Berliner, 2009). Poverty matters, as Vonnegut clearly understood, and its consideration brings into clarity why the distinction between natural and social contingencies cannot be viewed as severable—as is the tendency among formalists. This is to say that poverty matters since it affects not only the overall schooling experience but also achievement. First, children living in poverty tend to go to the savagely unequal schools Kozol (1992) describes. Second, underachievement (typically credited to natural ability by formalists) has social causes: poverty, malnutrition, dangerous living conditions, and so forth.

The simple fact of social causation of underachievement requires, at minimum, an actualist interpretation of EEO. (I should observe that even if underachievement did not have social causes and even if there were no achievement gap, actualist interpretations must prevail simply because it is immoral to keep children trapped in such conditions of schooling. This is, in EEO, equality of material condition.) This is why the Brown decision to undo "separate but equal" schools went somewhat further than the brand of formalism described. It introduced the idea that "the *effects* of [segregated] schools were, or were likely to be, different" (Coleman, 1968, p. 15, emphasis in original). Even though the decision did not use effects of schooling as a criterion of inequality but only as justification for a criterion of racial integration (making integration the key to EEO), such effects must be taken into consideration in order to determine the extent to which EEO obtains. As Coleman (1968) observes,

> the concept implied effective equality of opportunity ... the crucial point [being] that effects of inputs have come to constitute the basis for assessment of school quality (and thus equality of opportunity) in place of using certain inputs by definition as measures of quality. (pp. 18-19)

Furthermore, this requires looking, as Coleman did in his study, at the myriad ways that schools (through facilities, resources, teachers, practices, etc.) affect the effects. In other words, the Coleman (1968) report pushed the concept of EEO into another stage, one in which inputs must be taken into consideration and one which no longer assumed that schools could or should be passive institutions that somehow provided EEO merely by keeping the doors unlocked.

This actualist interpretation of EEO leads to the critique that the initial practice of providing free education with a common curriculum ignores facts relating to effective opportunity by not considering what barriers, beyond formal, legal barriers, might actually restrict access to education (socioeconomic status, prior experiences, motivation, poor facilities, etc). A la Coleman (1968), Nicholas Burbules and Ann Sherman (1979) point out that an actualist interpretation will find "equal" to mean "fitting or fair opportunities" and the responsibility of "making use of the opportunities" should not lie solely on individuals but on the institutions as well "to provide compensations that will make the exercising of opportunities more likely" (p. 107). While actualism may be flawed by the indeterminacy of the myriad, morally relevant factors that affect either ability or willingness to act upon one's formal opportunities, it is not fatally so. For teachers are trained to take into account the backgrounds and experiences of their students in order to identify, whenever possible, the morally relevant factors impacting learning and the overall schooling experience of students. Indeterminate, yes, but not unidentifiable.

It is important to note, however, that not all actualist interpretations of EEO are progressive. We can see a conservative actualism, for example, in the work of someone like E. D. Hirsch. Hirsch (1988) recognizes that certain groups are at a disadvantage by virtue of things such as their cultural, linguistic, and economic status and that restrains them from taking advantage of opportunity. Hirsch argues that "at the heart of modern nationhood is the teaching of literacy and a common culture through a national system of education" (p. 73). In creating this culture, Hirsch sees the cultural backgrounds of minority students as "cultural deprivations"

(p. 114). Their experiences are not to be built on but replaced. These deprivations provide Hirsch with the reason to promote what he calls the acculturative responsibility of the schools. For teaching "the ways of one's community has always been and still remains the essence of the education of our children" (p. 18). In order to have equal opportunity, Hirsch believes that the culture of dominant society must be instilled in historically disadvantaged groups. I suspect that this is a brand of actualism to which many conservative readers might cleave. But notice that Hirsch's actualism is different not merely because it is unexpectedly conservative, but also because it speaks to an equality of outcome as opposed to the equality of material condition to which Kozol's (1992) critiques speak so clearly. Also, notice that Hirsch's conservative EEO leads to an outcome of sameness—the very thing that *Harrison Bergeron* (Vonnegut, 1968) is invoked against in conservative interpretations.

Nevertheless, equality of outcome, that is to say learning outcomes, is a brand of equality of condition that must be factored in alongside equality of material condition for EEO. Vonnegut recognized the connection between material condition and outcomes. Commenting on the Kansas case, he noted, "Kansas is apparently handicapping schoolchildren, no matter how gifted and talented, with lousy educations if their parents are poor" (Rothschild, 2005). Tracing back to Coleman's argument that the effects of inputs must be considered, Howe (1989, 1997) argues that actualist conceptions collapse into effects or outcomes-oriented ones, and that this is a legitimate interpretation of EEO. This is so since education represents an opportunity chain, such that future links are dependent upon previous ones. One cannot proceed on to studying great literature without learning how to read first. One, of course, might choose not to read great literature, but the opportunity cannot exist without the prior link. Thus, some level of equality of outcome (here Howe defers to Amy Gutmann's, 1987, "democratic threshold") is required for EEO.

It is here that conservative critics tend to attack progressive egalitarianism with cries of sameness and "dumbing down" and holding back the talented through equality of condition as sameness. But the sameness that progressives are speaking to here refers to a sameness in the level of equality of condition as learning outcomes necessary for democratic participation and, as Gutmann (1987) puts it, "rational deliberation of competing conceptions of the good life and the good society" (p. 44). I have already shown how conservative renderings of EEO lead to a far deeper level of sameness. Furthermore, Howe (1997) addresses this problem by noting that EEO must call into question dominant values that preserve the status quo and sameness. Here Howe uses Hirsch as his point of departure.

Drawing on Dewey, Howe (1997) argues that experiences are continuous and are shaped by prior experiences. "Each experience is determined by the interaction between an individual's state and the conditions in the environment that prompt it" (p. 57). Children arrive in school with their different linguistic and cultural understandings already in place and they are continuously reinforced while interacting with their family and community members. Thus, the interpretation of EEO that comes from Hirsch's thinking would mean "abandoning the fundamental [educational] principle of connection with life experiences" (Dewey, 1938/2004 p. 78). Hirsch takes a quintessentially conservative position to the extent that (1) it assumes educators and/or policymakers know best, need not consider the learners' experiences and mental makeup, and may instill in students whatever someone other than the child or parent considers valuable; (2) it sends the message to disadvantaged groups that their cultures or languages are inferior; and, (3) it preserves the inequitable status quo and power relations. This position is "a proposal worse than ineffectual. It constitutes an obstacle to equality of educational opportunity for those groups historically excluded from participation" (Howe, 1997, pp. 2-3). Thus, Howe's (1997) interpretation of EEO includes "the needs, interests, and perspectives of all groups—especially groups that have been historically excluded" (pp. 2-3). It provides space for people to have a voice in determining what Howe calls "opportunities worth wanting." To be worth wanting, taking advantage of these opportunities must not require anyone to give up his or her identity. As Iris Marion Young (1990) puts it from the ideal of participatory democratic theory,

> Groups with different circumstances or forms of life should be able to participate together in public institutions without shedding their distinct identities or suffering disadvantage because of them. The goal is not to give special compensation to the deviant until they achieve normality, but rather to denormalize the way institutions formulate their rules by revealing the plural circumstances and needs that exist, or ought to exist, within them. (p. 134)

In this sense, participatory democratic theory seeks to overcome the deficiency of majoritarian democracy which, supported by the minimal ideal of formal equality, is "notoriously susceptible to having the [cultural] majority capture the state and its economic and political powers" (Fakuda-Parr, 2004).

CONCLUSION: WHAT IS EEO FOR HARRISON BERGERON?

Harrison Bergeron (Vonnegut, 1968), first and foremost, satirizes the shrill rightist critiques of progressive ideals about equality of condition. Indeed, the kind of sameness that one finds in some dystopian literature such as *Harrison Bergeron* is more likely to be the result of rightist thinking, as I have argued. But we tend not to see this clearly as Stossel, Fox News Corp, and corporate media generally serve the same purpose as the mental-handicapping radios in *Harrison Bergeron*. Neil Postman (1985) captures the claptrap that passes as news today and its effect:

> This ensemble of electronic techniques called into being a new world—a peek-a-boo world, where now this event, now that, pops into view for a moment, then vanishes again. It is a world without much coherence or sense; a world that does not permit us to do anything; a world that is, like the child's game of peek-a-boo, entirely self-contained. But like peek-a-boo, it is also endlessly entertaining. (p. 77)

In other words, the "news" today serves much the same purpose as, say, the National Football League (NFL) and other corporate entertainment: distraction. Having occupied our minds away from important issues of the day with the NFL, *American Idol* (2002-2012), *Jersey Shore* (2009-2012), ad nauseum, the corporate news media can simply then tell us what the important issues are. The bewildered herd has been tamed and consent manufactured (cf. Herman & Chomsky, 2002). Thus, corporate media can simply and effectively tell the herd that equality is socialism and the "logical" extension of socialism is *Harrison Bergeron*. The fact that *Bergeron* is a critique of these interpretations is irrelevant, lost in entertainment. Also lost, then, is the meaning of equality from the left and its reasonableness. For, when the left speaks of any degree of sameness, it is the sameness required to yield *effective* opportunity; that is, opportunities that can be effectively acted upon. This requires a certain degree of equality of material condition and welfare. The income gap between rich and poor in the United States, the largest gap in the industrialized world, undermines such equality.

Those who invoke Vonnegut against the promotion of progressive equality do so in error. Throughout this chapter, I have provided examples by Vonnegut himself to substantiate this claim. Here we might consider two further examples. First, one of Vonnegut's heroes was New Deal President Franklin Roosevelt. As Vonnegut (2003) passionately pointed out, "You have never seen greatness in a presidency; I have. It was a rich kid who you would think had every reason to be a horse's ass—Franklin Roosevelt. He was humane and wise and resourceful. He was called a traitor to his class. With George Bush, that charge would never stick" (as cited in Barsamian, 2004, p. 14). Second, I began this chapter with the opening line of Eugene V. Debbs' statement before the federal court in Cleveland upon being convicted of violating the Sedition Act. Of this passage, Vonnegut opined "What is wrong with that? Of course, Jesus got crucified for saying the same thing.... Socialism is, in fact, a form of Christianity, people wishing to imitate Christ" (as cited in Barsamian, 2004, pp. 15-16). Kai Nielsen (1985), arguing for radical egalitarianism (socialism), contends that:

> there is ... a plain and evident disparity in terms of the whole life prospects of the child of a doctor and the child of a dishwasher, even when these children are equally intelligent, hard-working, and the like. We feel that it is wrong—unfair—that their whole life prospects should be so very different. (p. 208)

I referred to this earlier as a full system of social stratification; a system in which the success of children of the wealthy is all but guaranteed, regardless of their ability. This is why EEO is such an important concept: it is to serve the purpose of education as the great equalizer. While intertwined with other forms of opportunity and affected by broader social conditions (e.g., poverty), equal educational opportunity is an important tool in resolving the radically different life prospects among different groups of children. Under conservative conceptions, EEO would provide Harrison Bergeron the opportunity to pursue his greatness. He would probably be in a segregated class, segregated ostensibly along the lines of ability that will just happen to result in segregation along the lines of class and race as well. He would be rewarded for his physical and mental superiority (merit) and his achievements would owe only to that. All children would rise or fall accordingly.

But we do not live in a society where social causation can so easily be dismissed. Under progressive conceptions, EEO would provide Harrison Bergeron the opportunity to pursue his greatness *and* his humanity. Unlike the fascist he became, he would recognize the different starting places of his classmates, he would be among them, and he would care. This is because EEO requires teachers to know each of their students' backgrounds, experiences, needs, and interests, including Harrison Bergeron's. It requires them to provide students opportunities to see both themselves and their peers in the curriculum. It requires them to ask students to interpret the world through different lenses, not just their own or the lenses forced upon them. This cannot occur in segregated or tracked classrooms. As I mentioned earlier, conservatives would attack this view of EEO with cries of sameness and "dumbing down." But, as I argued against Hirsch, the progressive ideal of EEO is completely contrary to this. Furthermore, the overarching purpose of schools should be to educate for democracy, not stratification, and we all benefit from this, including Harrison Bergeron.

NOTES

1. Italics indicates referral to the short story and nonitalics referral to the character in the story.
2. Here one might consider as further evidence Vonnegut's (1965) novel *God Bless You, Mr. Rosewater,* a defense of redistribution and a sustained critique of capitalism.
3. Sources, respectively, (1) Center on Budget and Policy Priorities, http://www.cbpp.org/cms/?fa=view&id=3629; (2) U.S. Bureau of the Census, Income, Poverty, and Health Insurance Coverage in the United States: 2010, Report P60, n. 238, Table B-2, pp. 68-73; (3) Politifact, http://www.politifact.com/wisconsin/statements/2011/mar/10/michael-moore/michael-moore-says-400-americans-have-more-wealth-/
4. In their remake, all of the lines quoted are replaced with one word: "Music!"
5. Note that socialism and radical egalitarianism can, arguably, be used interchangeably. However, there are various strands of egalitarianism that are certainly not socialist.
6. Here we might consider the liberal egalitarianism of John Rawls against the radical egalitarianism of Kai Nielsen. Rawls' difference principle guiding distribution is, arguably, quite minimal.
7. I note Reagan's illegal war in Nicaragua, the overthrow of the democratically elected Salvador Allende in Chile, and similar U.S. backed military incursions (including the CIA) in Haiti, El Salvador, Brazil, and so forth

REFERENCES

A tribute to Kurt Vonnegut. (2005, October 7). *NOW* [Television News Program]. Retrieved from http://www.dailymotion.com/video/x1pjlw_now-a-tribute-to-kurt-vonnegut-pbs_creation

Barsamian, D. (2004). *Louder than bombs: Interviews from The Progressive magazine*. Cambridge, MA: South End Press.

Berliner, D. C. (2009). *Poverty and potential: Out-of-school factors and school success.* Boulder and Tempe: Education and the Public Interest Center & Education Policy Research Unit. Retrieved from http://epicpolicy.org/publication/poverty-and-potential

Boron, A. (2006). The truth about capitalist democracy. *Socialist Register,* 28-58.

Burbules, N., & Sherman, A. (1979). Equal educational opportunity: Ideal or ideology. *Philosophy of Education 1979*, 105-114.

Coleman, J. (1968). The concept of equality of educational opportunity. *Harvard Educational Review, 38*, 7-22.

Debbs, E. V. (1918). Statement to the Court upon being convicted of violating the Sedition Act. Retrieved from http://www.marxists.org/archive/debs/works/1918/court.htm

Dewey, J. (1933, April 23). [Editorial] Dewey outlines utopian schools. *New York Times*, Education section, p. 7.

Dewey, J. (2004). *Experience and education*. New York, NY: Macmillan. (Original work published 1938)

Fakuda-Parr, S. (2004, July). *Human development report 2004: Cultural liberty in today's diverse world* [Audio recording]. London, England: Overseas Development Institute. Retrieved from http://www.odi.org.uk/events/undpjuly04/meetingrepR.html

Gutmann, A. (1987). *Democratic education*. Princeton, NJ: Princeton University Press.

Halvorseen, T. (Producer), & Tuttle, C. (Director). (2009). *2081* [Motion picture]. United States: Independent.

Hattenhauer, D. (1998). The politics of Kurt Vonnegut's "Harrison Bergeron." *Studies in Short Fiction, 35*, 387-392.

Herman E. S., & Chomsky, N. (2002). *Manufacturing consent: The political economy of the mass media*. New York, NY: Pantheon.

Hirsch, E. D. (1988). *Cultural literacy: What every American needs to know*. New York, NY: Random House.

Howe, K. R. (1989). In defense of outcomes-based conceptions of equal educational opportunity. *Educational Theory, 39*, 317-336.

Howe, K. R. (1997). *Understanding equal educational opportunity: Social justice, democracy, and schooling*. New York, NY: Teachers College Press.

Kozol, J. (1992). *Savage inequalities: Children in America's schools*. New York, NY: Harper Perennial.

Marvin, T. F. (2002). *Kurt Vonnegut: A critical companion*. Westport, CT: Greenwood Press.

Nadler, J. Glascoe, J., Hackett, J., Pierson, J. (Producers) & Pittman, B. (Director). (1995). *Harrison Bergeron* [Motion Picture]. United States: Republic Pictures.

Nielsen, K. (1985). *Equality and liberty: A defense of radical egalitarianism*. Totowa, NJ: Rowman and Allanheld.

Orwell, G. (1977) *1984*. New York, NY: Penguin. (Original work published 1949)

PGA Tour, Inc. v. Casey Martin, 532 U.S. 661 (2001). Retrieved from http://www.law.cornell.edu /supct/ html/ 00-24.ZD.html

Postman, N. (1985). *Amusing ourselves to death: Public discourse in the age of show business*. New York, NY: Viking.

Rothschild, S. (2005, May 5). Vonnegut: Lawyers could use literary lesson. Retrieved from http://www2.ljworld.com/news/2005/may/05/vonnegut_lawyers_could/

Salsano, S., Jeffress, S., French, J. (Producers). (2009-2012). *Jersey shore* [Television series]. New York: 495 Productions.

Stossel, J. (2010, February 11). Fox News. Retrieved from http://www.youtube.com/watch?v=kFMR1o0OTTM &feature=related

Vonnegut, K. (1965). *God bless you, Mr. Rosewater.* New York, NY: Dell.

Vonnegut, K. (1968). Harrison Bergeron. In *Welcome to the monkey house* (pp. 7-13). New York, NY: Delacorte Press.

Warwick, K., Frot-Coutaz, C., Fuller, S., & Lythgoe, N. (Producers). (2002-2012). *American idol* [Television series]. London, England: Fremantle Media.

Young, I. M. (1990). *Justice and the politics of difference*. Princeton, NJ: Princeton University Press.

CHAPTER 12

AN EDUCATIONAL DYSTOPIA

Mary Shelley's *Frankenstein* and Race To The Top

Bradley D. Rowe and Taylor Lacy Klassman

INTRODUCTION

Mary Shelley's *Frankenstein* (1831/2003) is conventionally read as a work of gothic literature—and for good reason—but it can also be interpreted as a text of educational thought (McWhir, 1990). In this chapter, we extend our reading of the novel to encompass dystopia and educational policy. Shelley's romantic narrative offers much to think about concerning the role and purpose of education in contemporary times. In questioning the guiding assumptions and central aims of the Obama Administration's educational reform program, Race to the Top (RTT), we do not simply take issue with the initiative as a flawed policy *in* education. We take issue with the larger problem that RTT exemplifies, and that is the problem *of* education today; namely, that it increasingly resembles the education of Victor Frankenstein—narrow, technical, scientific, and reduced to the status of training.

Dystopia and Education:
Insights Into Theory, Praxis, and Policy in an Age of Utopia-Gone-Wrong, pp. 185–199

Similar to Victor's tale, too many actors in education are guided—or, more accurately *mis*guided—by unrealistic utopian ideals that are more and more unraveling into dystopian realities. We believe that there is more than merely the potential for dystopia; we feel that dystopia is very real and felt in our lives, even though it is a dystopia not fully realized as in the fictional films and novels examined in this collection. It is more likely the case that nations, and certainly this is the case with the United States, hold degrees and qualities of dystopia without overtly reflecting the state-sponsored, systematic repression and terror depicted in the genre. We agree with the editors in their introduction to this volume that there is "growing evidence" that "utopia is devolving into a dystopia." Our chapter attempts to further make sense of this point. Like evolution, devolution is a process of multifaceted, gradual transformation. If it comes, dystopia will not be brought about by a single stroke but through ongoing processes of cultural change. For better or worse, education—as the transmission of culture through the socialization of generations—has and will continue to play an integral part in this transformation.

An absolute dystopian educational system, operating within an absolute dystopian society, would command, indoctrinate, and coerce youth to conform to its dehumanizing totalitarian government. RTT does not perform this function. RTT is linked to dystopia in a different but more complex way: its mandates add force to an educational milieu that teeters on some features of dystopia. These features include, but are not limited to: degeneration of individuality and autonomy; loss of love and devaluing of human emotion; hegemony of the technological and scientific agenda for the purpose of profit and consolidated power; commodification of human relationships via the swelling of "dysfunctional cyber relationships;" and an escalating "insensitivity and indifference to critical sociocultural problems" (Dreyer & Lebeko, 2009, para. 3). It is impossible to know whether or not these features will ever fully devolve into an Orwellian despotic and oppressive surveillance state. What we do know, and what we hope to show in this chapter, is that we are presently living out *some* realities and attributes of dystopia that manifest in both educational institutions and in society at large.

Frankenstein is appealing and helpful as a means to better understand our simultaneous moment of utopia and dystopia, for we exist in both (Shelley, 1831/2003). Balancing both perfectionist visions and nightmarish possibilities, we find ourselves at a critical junction in discussing and debating the role and purposes of education. So many students in the midst of living out RTT are prepared, tested, molded, and quelled into pseudo-functioning robots. Passionate, talented, and inquisitive children are being siphoned into prepackaged ideals of success—programmed to remain loyal to the bureaucratic and technological powers they can hardly detect as destructive. Students, at all levels of schooling, are being narrowly educated like Victor Frankenstein. Just as she unsettled the Enlightenment landscape of her day, Shelley also destabilizes our contemporary education landscape, generating good reason to be skeptical of discourse and policy undergirded by an ideology of scientific-economic-technological utopianism.

The education of Victor Frankenstein is fraught with utopian ideals—ideals that very much inspire him in his work but that also, in time, transpire into out-of-control terror and violence. With high hopes of breaking through what were once believed to be insurmountable barriers of human knowledge, Victor brazenly claims, "I will pioneer a new way, explore unknown powers, and unfold to the world the deepest mysteries of creation" (Shelley, 1831/2003, p. 49). Victor's primary goal of inventing life represents perfection, the ultimate scientific experiment that holds larger social significance that we identify as fundamental to utopia. Defying Nature's limits and God's will, Victor attempts to create the perfect man, bringing science one step closer in manufacturing an idyllic world wherein all disease would be, in the doctor's words, banished "from the human frame and render man invulnerable to any but a violent death" (p. 42). The boundless visionary continues:

> Life and death appeared to me ideal bounds, which I should first break through, and pour a torrent of light into our dark world. A new species would bless me as its creator and source; many happy and excellent natures would owe their being to me. No father could claim the gratitude of his child so completely as I should deserve theirs. (p. 55)

Of course, this is only the beginning of the dystopian fright Shelley pens for her readers.

Immediately after Victor succeeds where all others before him have failed, we see that his experiment goes wrong in the worst sort of way. The possibilities of utopia disappear in an instant, as he admits, "the beauty of the dream vanished, and breathless horror and disgust filled my heart" (Shelley, 1831/2003, p. 58). Freshly introduced into the world and immediately misunderstood by his maker, the monster—the product of Victor unearthing the "deepest mysteries of creation"—would proceed to induce fear and horror in the hearts and minds of the very people Victor saw himself saving. By killing off his creator's loved ones, one by one, the monster signifies "utopia-gone-wrong" (Dreyer & Lebeko, 2009, para. 3). In *Frankenstein*, we find a nexus of utopia and dystopia, two seemingly contradictory worlds coalescing around the question: what happens when unattainable utopianism goes awry?

ROMANTICISM AND EDUCATION

During the 2008 presidential campaign, cable-news pundits often described then-candidate Barack Obama, in a pejorative tone, as a "hopeful romantic." Outside of literary and philosophical circles, to be called a "romantic" is to be slandered as an overly-sentimental idealist, someone out of touch with the world. This popular view is a perversion and twisting of a once nuanced intellectual movement. John Willinsky (1990) writes that the term "romanticism" has slipped to the "maledictive level because its roots have been obscured; we have lost sight of the wealth of ideas and inspiration that first launched the original array of romantic visions" (p. 2). We will argue that the forgotten roots of the romantics—the late-18th to mid-19th century European novelists, poets, philosophers, and artists who rebelled against the more insidious, overstretched values of the Enlightenment—comprise a vision of education that we need now more than ever. The most useful thing to do is not attempt to define the Romantic Movement as a whole, but to take *Frankenstein*, one of the seminal works of the movement, and relate it to our topic.

Before we move on, it is important to retrace and expose some of the historical and ideological underpinnings of the sort of narrow education that is championed in RTT. In doing so, we revisit why, on the heels of the Enlightenment, education was so central to the romantics, and why the romantics are so central to education. The romantics did more than just criticize the Enlightenment. With their wild imaginations, with their dynamic artistic and literary expression, the romantics wanted to imaginatively augment what the Enlightenment thinkers missed in their thin and superficial representations of human beings, education, and the world. A particularly troubling misconception is that the romantics did not understand the "real" world. Many of them tried to capture, on a descriptive level, the reality of nature and culture, while demonstrating "the conviction that new and powerful ways of making sense of reality were combining with new ways of truly expressing that sense" (Egan, 1990, p. 288). If the Enlightenment wanted to understand and explain the world mainly through science and philosophy, the romantics wanted to understand and illustrate the world mainly through art and literature.

The arts, not education, are typically associated with Romanticism, but education was also an important and creative avenue through which the romantics wanted to hone and express their visions. Frederick Beiser (2003) sees education as the most important question for the German romantic movement. He suggests we have "inherited many beliefs about education that are the legacy of the romantics," such as:

> the value of individuality, the negative role of sexual stereotypes, the rights of both sexes to an education, the importance of educating the senses as well as the intellect, the central role of the experience of love in the development of the personality, and the fundamental importance of love in marriage: we virtually take all of these ideas for granted today, but the romantics were among the very first to defend them. (p. 131)

In looking at the romantic ideal of *Bildung*, we see how vital education was to the movement. While the "notoriously rich and ambiguous" German term is difficult to translate, *Bildung* refers to the holistic education of the human person; and the growth, formation, and "self-realization of the individual," with the source of this realization in the human heart (Beiser, 2003, pp. 131, 133). *Bildung* requires education in the broadest sense, and balance is crucial. Romantics didn't outright shun reason and rationality; they attempted to make human experience more nuanced by enriching and expanding the human mind, by synthesizing the binaries of reason/ emotion and mind/body. Yes, education should advance and train the rational mind, but it also should nourish the body and soul: we should be educated with passion and heart. And while emotion usually takes center stage in romantic works, sensibility does not entirely depose of reason. Sensibility and feelings coincide and interact with rational intellect in order to cultivate human imagination, perhaps the most central theme that resurfaces throughout romantic literature. If the Enlightenment exalted human rationality, Romanticism exalted human imagination.

Bildung resisted the narrow utilitarian education reforms of the Enlightenment. As the romantics saw it, these reforms threatened the development of a well-rounded person and the broad understanding of the human condition by focusing on the applicable, technical, and instrumental, and these required a highly-professionalized education that was implemented to serve new economies and new technologies (Beiser, 2003, p. 137). Beiser (2003) explains:

> The romantics were the first to protest against some of the more negative consequences of modernity, especially the technological domination of society and nature.... As part of their rebellion against the hegemony of technology the romantics criticized the growing professionalization and vocationalization of education, which would reduce education down to learning technical skills. The romantics were among the first rebels against these trends, and their objections against them remain as valid today as they were in the late eighteenth century. (pp. 131-132)

It could be argued that the romantics' objections are *even more* valid today. The romantic opposition to the Enlightenment reforms—and their reasons for this resistance—provide a framework through which we can better understand and resist current policies that drive the presumption that education is mainly about technical training for employment. Rather than education aimed at cultivating a well-rounded human person who sees work as only one aspect of living a meaningful and fulfilling life, RTT conceptualizes education as predominantly a means to become an employee to help American dominate the world economic and political order. We find this purpose of education, which goes largely unquestioned by the consenting majority, deeply disturbing and dangerous.

Before we continue, it is important to point out that *Bildung* was the German romantics' utopian vision, their own perfectionist model in developing the "ideal human being" (Beiser, 2003, p. 132). Just as Victor wanted to perfect humanity through science, the romantics wanted to perfect humanity through a holistic education. That is why we are not saying that a romantic education is the answer to our societal and educational problems; and we certainly are not arguing to prescribe *Bildung* as education policy (critiquing dystopia is not the same thing as calling for utopia). What we are calling for is a more robust and broad conception of education and its purposes to challenge the status quo of education-as-job-training. We offer Romanticism and the sort of education central to it as a way to critically analyze contemporary educational policy and practice. We see the intellectual movement as key in complicating and complementing education today; for one need not spend much time in schools or academia to see that STEM (science, technology, engineering, mathematics) is overshadowing, and sometimes completely uprooting, long-standing modes of human education. As we move forward, Shelley will present a cultural critique of the Enlightenment as it relates to what the romantics feared regarding education: A culture of technicians socialized through highly specialized training.

FRANKENSTEIN

In addition to furnishing a narrative of utopia-turned-dystopia, *Frankenstein* serves as a way to examine the zeitgeist of professional and specialized education that belies *Bildung* through belittling or ignoring the moral, philosophical, and aesthetic questions of the humanities. Victor's education embodies not only the instrumentality of the Enlightenment but also the results-driven, standardization of education today. With her extraordinary literary talent and provocative prose, Shelley ponders many questions germane to education today: what is education for? What does it mean to be an educated human being? What is the role of humility in education? What happens when ethical questions are separate from scientific and technical ones? Taking readers' imaginations to the absolute brink with her eerie depictions and tragic storyline, Shelley dramatizes these questions that speak to the nature, purposes, and dangers of education.

Most of us are familiar with the story, but we ought to point out that Victor Frankenstein has been portrayed through popular films as a "mad scientist" who irresponsibly uses science to do God's work of creating life. Now, Victor did border on insane but this was not until later in the story after he was successful in inventing life. Victor's work was the logical outcome of the pursuit of knowledge and scientific discovery. He was not crazy during his experiments and Shelley wants us to see this: "I am not recording the vision of a madman" (Shelley, 1831/2003, p. 53). But for the sake of argument, let us allow the popular stereotype and work from the premise that he was doing the work of a mad scientist. As such, rarely do we inquire into what made Victor so mad or why he was so irresponsible. We believe we need to look at this scientist's education to do so.

Shelley devises two very different educations: one for Frankenstein and another for his scientific invention, the Creature. While the Creature's education is also insufficient, we'll focus on Victor's education because it is the direction that education is increasingly taking, the direction of narrow technical training aimed toward an idealistic aim that could never be achieved without tragic consequences (McWhir, 1990). Victor was educated in some of the finest European institutions, where he studied the sciences, mainly chemistry, anatomy, and physiology. His education is in the Enlightenment vein: scientific, rational, mechanistic pursuit of knowledge. Committed to the Enlightenment ambition of understanding and controlling nature, Victor maintained "a fervent longing to penetrate the secrets of nature," desperately wanting to break away from tradition and the old ways of doing science (Shelley, 1831/2003, p. 41). For Victor, the arts, literature, ethics, and politics were dismissed as irrelevant or altogether ignored.

Victor was predominantly concerned with *what works* and was never really challenged to contemplate the broader moral questions concerning value and meaning, the deeper philosophical and humanistic questions of *why*. Frankenstein's education did not afford him enough exposure to the humanities to balance and complement the sciences; science was his "sole occupation" (Shelley, 1831/2003, p. 51). The danger in this type of funneled knowledge is losing all that lies outside the view of the scientist's microscopic lens. His educational experience mirrored what we consider training for a technical profession. As philosopher *and* scientist Bernard Rollin (1995) writes, "We do not educate scientists or physicians to be virtuous citizens, we train them in a technocratic way" (p. 31). Practical and technical, Victor's training was overwhelmingly about *how* to achieve the end of bestowing "animation upon lifeless matter" (Shelley, 1831/2003, p. 53). And when he cashed-in on his education and began to invent life, moral reflection, critical thinking, or forethought on the possible unintended and dangerous consequences of science, could not be drawn on, only an obsession with the functional *how*. As a result, Dr. Frankenstein gives birth to his un-named, desolate creation who eventually emulates the ugliness and marginalization of the silenced dystopian community.

The pivotal scene in *Frankenstein* is when the Creature first opens his eyes in Victor's laboratory and is immediately misjudged as a threat, as a demonic other. Seeing his invention as an ugly wretch, Victor is disgusted, panics, and flees for no good reason, forsaking and marginalizing his creation with a superficial frail reaction. When the doctor's utopian dream goes awry, he neglects and abandons the dystopian actuality. The Creature had only been living for seconds and had done nothing wrong; he was just not pleasant to look at. Frankenstein's reaction was unscientific and irresponsible because his education never allowed him to respond as a well-rounded (but surely not perfect) human person should: with an open mind and welcoming heart.

For some, the story is antiscience, but the book is much more rich, presenting an argument for an education comprehensive enough to bring the powers of knowledge, science, and technology under human control—or at least the opportunity to try. Yes, Dr. Frankenstein infused life into an inanimate body, but what was it that turned this creature into a monster? It would be short-sighted to blame "science" for the disastrous result of Victor's work, which is an uncontrollable monster wreaking havoc and terror by murdering innocents. *Science alone does not invent rampaging monsters; uneducated humans who lack understanding do*. Responsibility, then, should be placed on the narrow, overly-technical education of Dr. Frankenstein, which closely resembles the procedural specialists and technocrats trained in dismissing the social, political, and moral dimensions of their work.

As we learn from Shelley, the Creature was at first innocent, even yearning to be embraced and loved by humanity. But Victor never knew just how convivial his creation was until it was too late because his education insufficiently prepared him to cope with his invention and ill-prepared him to relate with the Creature humanely and intelligently. Dr. Frankenstein created a deformed creature, and nothing more. It was human social norms (the Creature was rejected by other human beings in the story), coupled with miseducation and misunderstanding of Victor, that transformed the Creature into a murdering monster.

Education is essential because, as Shelley teaches us, we should not be so narrow-minded in what we think qualifies as learning and we should not run away from our obligations like Victor Frankenstein. Only through an education that involves serious exposure to the disciplines that have critical reflection at their core—philosophy, literature, art, the classics—

can we learn how not to be servile to these technological and scientific monsters of our making. The hubristic Victor never acquired a disposition thoughtful or humble enough to give him the predisposition to reflect over the acutely relevant question Peyton Richter (1975) poses: "If nature must be ruthlessly mutilated and man and society completely manipulated in order to reach utopia, is it really worth attaining?" (p. 14). In the next section, we see how educational policy is engendering a culture of technicians who, like Victor Frankenstein, are predominantly (if not entirely) concerned with the functional *how,* neglecting our moral and social obligations to ask *why.*

RACING TO THE TOP, CREATING MONSTERS

In this section, we offer a critical analysis of the current administration's plan for improving education. RTT is President Obama's signature contribution in education reform. It is a massive federal grant program instituted as part of the American Recovery and Reinvestment Act of 2009, a historic piece of legislation engineered to "stimulate the economy, support job creation, and invest in critical sectors, including education" (Department of Education [DOE], 2009, p. 2). The Administration honors this abstract goal through more concrete means. RTT rewards the states that propose and carry out effective educational reform plans, as defined and prioritized by the U.S. Department of Education and the White House. The economic goals of RTT eclipse all other purposes of education. For example, the first of four "core education reform areas" is "adopting standards and assessments that prepare students to succeed in college and the workplace and to compete in the global economy" (p. 2). As such, state officials and policy reformers are in a frenzy to implement new standards, raise test scores, and institute rigorous accountability measures and more assessments in order to meet the DOE's demands for funding. Consequently, in meeting the Department's demands for funding, states must meet the Administration's education goals. Since states had to clearly lay out exactly how their policies would honor the core aim of employment and competition, and since education-as-job-training is so widely taken for granted as the chief purpose of education, policies are being put in place throughout the country that even further reinforce and inflate this economic utopian idealism. As clearly stated, successful states "will offer models for others to follow and will spread the best reform ideas across their States, and across the country" (p. 2).

Criticisms are needed for at least two reasons. First, President Obama—arguably the most prominent national political figure within the past 40 years for social change—does not challenge the same old story of education and schools serving primarily economic purposes (as we are learning, he is challenging very few same old stories). Second, and more importantly, there are very real dangers to the education of the human self, and to the education of citizens in a democratic society, when education is packaged as specialized job training. As Henry Giroux (2009) explains:

> Reducing the purpose of schooling to the teaching of work-related skills not only opens the door to defining education as a private rather than a public good; such a view also limits the horizon of what a critical education might be by confusing training with education while offering reforms that are both narrowly instrumental and ideologically suspect. (p. 258)

When *public* education, as a purchasable good, is conceived and carried out chiefly as preparation for the *private* job sector, it predominantly serves the interests of the marketplace and corporations, not the interests of the public. Now it is possible to reconcile the interests of the public with the private, but it's becoming less clear that this is happening with escalating corporatization and commercialization of traditional public spaces. The consequence of this privatization trend is that market values, such as competition, materialism, efficiency, and consumerism, hold authority over public values, such as citizenship, community activism, equality, and the general civic good. Anyone who believes that becoming a good citizen is something that needs to be learned in schools—and that civic learning and critical thinking necessitate a deep understanding and appreciation of democratic processes and values—has very good reason to turn a skeptic's eye toward the reform plans of RTT.

RTT brings with it disastrous implications for civic, moral, and aesthetic education. Sympathetic to the romantic project, we are heartbroken that education is more and more functioning as the main servant to the "god of Economic Utility"—what Neil Postman (1996) calls that "passionless god, cold and severe" (p. 27). Youth are increasingly interpreting not only their educational experience, but sense of self, others, and the world in chiefly economic and technological terms, around this deity's main commandments: efficiency, profit, competition, and consuming. The dreadful result: *living a human life becomes the very same thing as earning a living.*

At the beginning of the chapter, we mentioned that RTT is emblematic of the larger problem of education. Let us now look beyond RTT to further support this claim. The introductory paragraph to the White House's "Guiding Principles" for K-12 education states:

> Providing a high-quality education for all children is critical to America's economic future. Our nation's economic competitiveness and the path to

> the American Dream depend on providing every child with an education that will enable them to succeed in a global economy that is predicated on knowledge and innovation. President Obama is committed to providing every child access to a complete and competitive education, from cradle through career. (White House, 2012, para. 1)

The inseparability of education and the economy takes on even more authority in Obama's vision of higher education, as the *main* purpose of education is to train students for employment in the global economy. Any hope that President Obama would propose a more humane, democratic, or liberal sort of higher education, perhaps different from his conservative predecessors, now seems asinine. In depressive economic times, during a speech to students at the University of Texas, the President made it clear why he was taking the time out of his schedule to give a speech on education, using the justification that "Education is *the* economic issue of our time." The President's remarks on education were dominated with the following phrases: "lead the world," "out-compete," "out-educate," "growth sectors of our economy," "prepare our graduates to succeed in this economy," "lead the global economy in this century," "workers compete," and "make sure America remains number one" (White House, 2010a, para. 11, emphasis ours). Of course, there were his usual warm and optimistic overtones, but on a campus to the youth that elected him for political and social change, nothing meaningful was said about education cultivating an engaged citizenry, justice, or democracy, which are the substances that would lead to the change he advocates. This speech is indicative of Obama's policies in general, as he routinely and passionately advocates for market conceptions of education, unabashed reverence for careers and capital, all under the umbrella of a nation dominating the global stage.

To be fair, on rare occasions Obama uses language that affords education a more substantial purpose. In fact, the President's occasional bold and humane ideas regarding education can be found in his talks to younger school-age children. In a back-to-school speech to students in Philadelphia, the President affirmed that education is about more than just "getting a good job" and should give "each and every one of us the chance to fulfill our promise, and to be the best version of ourselves we can be" (White House, 2010b, para. 29). He goes on to discuss the role education plays in building mutual respect and character, and the importance of children embracing the wonders and diversity of life. While the President may feel in his heart that education is about more than getting a job, his rhetoric (and the policies match) almost always returns to the utopian, market-based conception of education. Earlier in the same talk, he says,

> The farther you go in school, the farther you go in life. And at a time when other countries are competing with us like never before, when students around the world … are working harder than ever, and doing better than ever, your success in school is not just going to determine your success, it's going to determine America's success in the 21st century. (White House, 2010b, para. 13)

We have now returned to the land of educational utopia, and it is clear that the competitive, global, capitalistic, and economic goals of education are by far the most celebrated and valued, and thus occupy the prevailing role in both rhetoric and formal programs in virtually every level of education today.

While universities, schools, think-tanks, and "evidence-based" research organizations may be getting more stimulus money from this Administration, it is education that is suffering a devastating blow. Obama routinely conflates education and labor force training. "Folks need a college degree." Then, in the very next line in his University of Texas speech, he says, "They need workforce training" (White House, 2010a, para. 21). As if education is synonymous with workforce training! There is an important distinction to be made between *education* and *training*. Training is particular preparation and instruction, mechanistic and highly controlled; it requires less critical reflection, and is more about doing than about knowing and understanding, just like Victor Frankenstein's training. While beneficial for mastering a specific skill-set—like how to re-animate a patchwork of corpses—training is antithetical to a more holistic way to self-realization, to interdisciplinary dialogue and synthesis incumbent upon liberal learning. Unlike training, education involves cultivating the human faculties of reason, reflection, imagination, and for a nurturing enrichment and self-actualization, which do not have to be pursued as utopian ideals. Certainly the training that is so zealously endorsed in the leading reform areas of STEM cannot produce the open-minded, warm-hearted educated human beings who, unlike Victor Frankenstein, would not abandon but try to understand hideous creatures.

These criticisms do not mean that education should not help youth acquire meaningful and gainful work, for education does and should do this. On the other hand, we do not want readers to take from these criticisms that we must yield to the perfectionist aims of *Bildung*. However, some form of a romantic education is needed in order to cultivate the human faculties of intellect and sensibility for a more well-rounded human being, even if this education falls short of utopian holism. In taking insights from Shelley and the Romantics, we learn that to reduce human lives (especially children) to mere cogs in the engine of global capitalism; to reduce learners to trainees, employees, and competitors; to assume such shallow conceptions of the human person, is to go down the path of inventing havoc-wreaking monsters. In an age when education is economics and economics is education, when "education is *the* economic issue of our time," how many Victor Frankensteins will be trained in the laboratories that are present-day schools and universities? And what sort of new, terrifying monsters might they manufacture?

CONCLUDING REMARKS: CHALLENGING DYSTOPIA WITH LOVE

To end, we both ardently believe that romantic love needs to reassume a role in our discussions of the nature and purposes of education. We intentionally use the word "reassume" because we are not calling for anything new; long before the onset of the romantic era, love once occupied an indispensible role in human education. The ancient Greeks, the first philosophers of education in the West, recognized the intimate relationship between learning, knowledge, and love. Philosophy—*philo-sophia*—translates to "love of wisdom," and the Greek concept of *eros* demonstrates how love and desire were fused into the very fabric of teaching and learning. Like the romantics, the Greeks believed in a richness, complexity, and longing for wisdom that transcended the acquisition of practical skills and information. But sadly today, education encourages us to honor the immediacy and convenience of fact and information over the profundity of the human heart.

Schools are filled with teachers and administrates, who mostly have the best of intentions, but who are functionaries, reduced to serving the prespecified policies and confines of authorities outside of their control. Thus, as a strategy of survival, those working in schools too often operate under notions of distance and coldness, guised as "professionalism," where there is little love or desire. And yet teachers and learners—from all walks of life, in and outside the concrete walls of the schoolhouse—need not take academic courses on Romanticism or read Plato's *Republic* to know how important it is to love and be loved. We intuitively know how vital love is for the human condition; without it, like Shelley's monster, we whither; without love, we become violent, alone, miserable, and unloved monsters.

Given the extent of ignorance, hatred, bigotry, and ruthless bullying, schools and other educational institutions would do well to make a concerted effort to draw upon love and emotion for meaning and direction. A sad loss in the land of dystopia is that of love and individuality. "We realize our common humanity," writes Beiser (2003) "only through love.... It is also through love that I fulfill my individuality because love derives from my innermost self, from my unique passions and desires, and it consists in a unique bond between myself and another" (p. 133). This is the way of the Romantics, who want humanity to learn to love others—not just the beautiful but also to love the silence, the dark, the sublime, to love even the insane, weird, and ugly. How can youth be *educated* to love when they are *trained* to believe that they have to go to school to become not caring and contemplative, but to become competitive and consumptive, to get to the promise land of winners that awaits at "the top"?

Right before our eyes, a world of romance, depth of personality, and humanistic insight becomes a world of well-schooled drones that see it as right and good to slavishly appease the god of economic utility, because they cannot envision a flourishing life without "success" defined by the all-mighty dollar. RTT reforms might help America achieve further global supremacy as an economic and technological power. Reforms might make us better employees, higher skilled and trained technicians, more efficient information seekers and consumers. But all the while, we fear that we'll become more materialistic, self-interested, and one-dimensional. We fear we are losing imagination, becoming inferior educators and learners, bad artists, worse thinkers and writers. But what we fear the most about an educational dystopia is that youth will be so mesmerized by the technological-scientific-business utopianism they will never learn to love misunderstood, deformed creatures.

REFERENCES

Beiser, F. (2003). Romanticism. In R. Curren (Ed.), *A companion to the philosophy of education* (pp. 130-142). Malden, MA: Blackwell.

Department of Education. (2009, November). Race to the top program executive summary. Retrieved from http://www2.ed.gov/programs/racetothetop/executive-summary.pdf

Dreyer, E., & Lebeko, J. (2009). Dystopia. Introduction to exhibition. Retrieved from http://web.up.ac.za/sitefiles/file/46/1584/Dystopia%20Unisa.pdf

Egan, K. (1990). Recapitulating romanticism in education. In J. Willinsky (Ed.) *The educational legacy of romanticism* (pp. 287-305). Waterloo, Canada: Wilfrid Laurier University.

Giroux, H. (2009). Obama's dilemma: Postpartisan politics and the crisis of American education. *Harvard Educational Review, 79*(2), 250-266.

McWhir, A. (1990). Teaching the monster to read: Mary Shelley, education, and *Frankenstein*. In J. Willinksy (Ed.), *The educational legacy of romanticism* (pp. 73-92). Waterloo, Canada: Wilfrid Laurier University.

Postman, N. (1996). *The end of education: Redefining the value of school*. New York, NY: Vintage.

Richter, P. E. (1975). *Utopia/Dystopia?* Cambridge, MA: Schenkman.

Rollin, B. (1995). *The Frankenstein syndrome: Ethical and social issues in the genetic engineering of animals*. Cambridge, England: Cambridge University Press.

Shelley, M. (2003). *Frankenstein: Or, the modern Prometheus*. London, England: Penguin. (Original work published 1831)

White House. (2010, August 9). Remarks by the President on higher education and the economy at the University of Texas at Austin. Speech delivered to students at the University of Texas. Retrieved from http://www.whitehouse.gov/the-press-office/ 2010/08/09/remarks-president-higher-education-and-economy-university-texas-austin

White House. (2010a, September 14). Remarks by the President in back to school speech in Philadelphia, Pennsylvania. Retrieved from http://www.whitehouse.gov/the-press-office/2010/09/14/remarks-president-back-school-speech-philadelphia-pennsylvania

White House. (2010b, November 3). Press conference by the President. Retrieved from http://www.whitehouse.gov/the-press-office/2010/11/03/press-conference-president

White House. (2012). Education. Retrieved from http://www.whitehouse.gov/issues/education

Willinsky, J. (Ed.). (1990). *The educational legacy of romanticism*. Waterloo, Canada: Wilfrid Laurier University.

CHAPTER 13

ORWELL'S *1984* AND EDUCATION AS COMMODITY SPECTACLE

Dennis Attick

INTRODUCTION

In his book, *Why Orwell Matters*, Christopher Hitchens (2002) argues that *Nineteen Eighty-Four* (referred to as *1984* hereafter) is a novel that

> created physical and mental fear in the first people to read it. Into these noir pages Orwell poured everything he had learned, heaping agony on misery on defeat, and synthesizing much of his study of literature as well as his condensed and concentrated experience as a journalist. (p. 188)

It is *1984* that represents George Orwell at his darkest and most pessimistic. This dystopia is, at once, a reflection on Orwell's lived experiences with fascism in the early 20th century, and a warning to future generations about the dehumanization that can be wrought by repressive tyranny and fascist governments. Having written about the plight of the working class as a journalist in England during the early 20th century, as well as chronicling a tyrannical dictatorship in Spain years later, Orwell became one of the 20th century's most vocal critics of imperialism and totalitarianism.

Dystopia and Education:
Insights Into Theory, Praxis, and Policy in an Age of Utopia-Gone-Wrong, pp. 201–212

Writing nearly 20 years after Orwell published *1984*, Guy Debord (1967/1983), in his book, *Society of the Spectacle*, furthers Hegelian and Marxist notions of alienation in arguing for a new understanding of alienation in modern capitalist societies. Debord contended that human beings are not just alienated from their labor in a capitalist economy; rather, Debord offers that advanced capitalist societies ultimately come to depend on the economy alone for survival, and, in turn, that economy relies on society to be primarily consumers of commodity spectacle. Ultimately, under such conditions, human beings become alienated from real experiences and each other. Debord writes, "In societies where modern conditions of production prevail, all of life presents itself as an immense accumulation of spectacles. Everything that was directly lived has moved away into a representation" (p. 1). For Debord, the visual spectacle is not simply a series of images, but rather, the spectacle mediates human relationships via an incessant barrage of images. In the end, real experiences, real relationships, become less valuable than the accumulation of spectacle. The spectacles become pseudoneeds; our relationships become pseudoexperiences, things that can be had, bartered, or in some way consumed. If the maintenance of our system of advanced capitalism is as Debord claims, dependent upon consumers of commodity spectacles, it is perhaps not surprising that our federal education policy embodies these ideas.

In this chapter I read our current federal education policy utilizing Debordian spectacle theory within the context of the seminal dystopian work of the 20th century, George Orwell's *1984*. In this critique, I examine federal education policy within the framework of Orwellian notions of surveillance, discipline, and control, but also within Debordian notions of spectacle. To this end, I connect the dystopian landscape Orwell imagines, with its 24 hour surveillance and thought control via propaganda, with Debord's notion of spectacle, and current federal education policy and practice. I argue that our current education policy promotes a narrowly defined idea of education—one that increasingly confines and disempowers teachers and students within a strictly controlled public education system—while simultaneously constructing a narrative that renders education a spectacle for public consumption. These current policies and initiatives undermine individual autonomy and agency through an institutionalized focus on standardization, accountability, and bureaucratic control.

George Orwell wrote *1984* in 1949 as a condemnation of totalitarian society and a warning of what such a society could become if government power was left uncontested over time. By the time he wrote *1984* Orwell had spent most of his adult life writing polemics against imperialism and fascism. His experience working as an English imperial policeman in Burma forged what would become an unending antipathy toward government-sponsored censorship, propaganda, and surveillance (Hitchens,

2002). Orwell was also a vocal critic of the fascist government he experienced first-hand in Spain, as well as the Stalinist governments of the Soviet Union throughout the first half of the twentieth century (Orwell, 1946/1981). As Hitchens asserts

> It is true on the face of it that Orwell was one of the founding fathers of anti-Communism; that he had a strong patriotic sense and a very potent instinct for what we might call elementary right and wrong; that he despised government and bureaucracy and was a stout individualist; distrusted intellectuals and academics and reposed a faith in popular wisdom. (p. 79)

Orwell was committed throughout his relatively short life of 46 years to the ideals of socialism as means by which all individuals could live meaningful lives; yet, he was also always wary of any government that wielded too much power over its citizens.

Set in Orwell's vision of a totally administered society in the late twentieth century, *1984* exemplifies modern dystopian literature in its portrayal of a future in which political terror and repression, coupled with government propaganda and indoctrination strip individuals of free thought and agency. In Orwell's futuristic Oceania, government power is enforced through modern video technologies that monitor each individual's every move for any subversive or liberating act. Violators of government rule face the threat of physical punishment such that, over time, the general population is stripped both of their ability *and* desire to be autonomous beings. The Party, led by the ubiquitous, Big Brother, maintains strict control over the population through the manipulation of thoughts, information, and behavior. Violators of Party rule are dealt with severely and promptly, often, they simply disappear. While the novel offers a prescient warning against totalitarian governments, attempts of its central character, Winston Smith, at dissent draw attention to the ongoing human need for autonomy, connectivity, and hope. Smith represents one of the last free-thinking, autonomous beings in Oceania.

Oceania is administered by four ministries under the auspices of Big Brother and The Party. The "Ministry of Truth" controls news and entertainment; "The Ministry of Love" maintains law and order; the "Ministry of Plenty," which was responsible for economic affairs, and the 'Ministry of Peace," which maintains and administers a never-ending war. While Orwell did not envision a "Ministry of Education" at the time of his writing *1984*, one does not need a robust imagination to appreciate how a "Ministry of Education" would fit seamlessly in Orwell's dystopia. While each of the ministries plays an essential role in maintaining power in Oceania, it is perhaps the "Ministry of Truth," the administrator of that which is accepted as knowledge which wields the most power. Orwell's protagonist, Winston Smith, maintains a job in Oceania as a rewriter of history, ensuring that the language of Newspeak serves the interests of the Party alone. Newspeak acts as the administrator of truth and knowledge for the people of Oceania. To this end, it can be understood as the official curriculum of Oceania. According to Orwell's lead character, Winston Smith, Newspeak has been devised to meet the needs of Big Brother and The Party. Orwell (1949/2001) writes, "The purpose of Newspeak is not only to provide a medium of expression for the world-view and mental habits proper to The Party, but to make all other methods of thought impossible" (p. 41). Newspeak narrows the discourse and range of thought so that criticality and notions of subversion are expunged from the minds of the populace. In forwarding these notions of political language, drawn from Orwell's experience as an imperial policeman in Burma, Orwell is envisioning a time where language and thoughts are not just controlled, but also used by those in power to redefine truth.

In addition to maintaining the strictly controlled standards for speech and thought via Newspeak, The Party in Oceania allows zero tolerance of deviation from its hegemonic rule. Through 24 hour surveillance via ubiquitous telescreens, each individual's every word and action is monitored. Dissenters and violators of Party rule are physically and mentally abused/tortured by Party enforcers. Consider Winston's "reeducation" at the hands of the Party, which occurs in the closing pages of the novel. O'Brien, who Winston once believed to be an ally in rebellion against the Party, turns out to be one of the Party enforcers and administers Winston's brutal brainwashing. When speaking of how The Party asserts power over its citizens, O' Brien states,

> Obedience is not enough. Unless he is suffering, how can you be sure a man is obeying your will and not his own. Power is tearing human minds to pieces and putting them back together again in new shapes of your choosing. (Orwell, 1949/2001, p. 238)

Through surveillance, the control of information, and the manipulation of minds, the Party finds its ultimate power in controlling that what is accepted as truth.

EDUCATION AS SPECTACLE

There is a rich literature regarding imagery and spectacle written over the last fifty years as communication technologies became increasingly ubiquitous features of modern life. I have chosen to highlight Debord's book cited throughout this chapter, but readers should also look to Jacques Ranciere's (2009) rebuttal in *The Emancipated Spectator*, or earlier works by

Frankfurt School scholars such as Theodore Adorno (1991/2001) and Herbert Marcuse (1964/1991), as well as Daniel Boorstin's (1961) book on imagery and spectacle, *The Image*. The idea of education as spectacle has been forwarded more recently in the work of Mary Lee Smith (2004), Kevin Vinson and E. Wayne Ross (2000) and Vinson, Ross, and Walsh (2010).

Debord's work echoes Boorstin's (1987) writings on the construction of image for public consumption in Boorstin's, *The Image: A Guide to Pseudo Events in America*. In his critique of the rise of advertising as an industry via communicative technology, Boorstin coined the term "pseudoevent" to describe the encroachment of synthetic experiences upon reality (p. 10). Boorstin argued that visual and televisual advertising were forwarding a nonreality on society that was prescripted and packaged for public consumption. He extended his concept of the pseudoevent to describe capitalist consumption with the idea of the pseudoideal. As Boorstin (1961/1987) argues, "An advertisement conjured up an image in order to persuade people that something was worth buying. It combined a pseudoevent with a pseudoideal. The pseudo-event must be vividly newsworthy; the pseudo-ideal must be vividly desirable" (p. 45).

Debord (1967/1977) extends Boorstin in offering that the spectacle, "presents itself as something enormously positive, indisputable and inaccessible. It says nothing more than 'that which appears is good, that which is good appears'" (p. 12). The appearance itself provides validation for the consumer that what is seen is good and therefore worthy of consumption. It is here where the capitalist economy thrives, in the consumption of the spectacle. Again, from Debord,

> the real consumer becomes a consumer of illusions. The commodity is the factually real illusion, and the spectacle is its general manifestation. The spectacle is the moment when the commodity has attained the total occupation of social life ... it aims at nothing more than itself. (p. 14)

Turning to the idea of education as spectacle, Vinson and Ross (2000) offer the following regarding the 21st century education spectacle, "education must be understood according to a setting in which spectacle and surveillance come together, a state of affairs in which discipline is established and maintained as individuals and groups are monitored simultaneously by both larger and smaller entities" (p. 2).

Education policy today can be understood as a convergence of Orwellian notions of control (bureaucrats rely on various forms of surveillance to monitor student and teacher performance via testing) with Debord's spectacle (the public consumes the spectacle of school efficacy via published accountability reports and test scores). In time, the public understanding of education becomes dominated by consumption of spectacle, without any understanding of the complexities of actual school life. When the education spectacle is understood as a problem, it allows for the creation of solutions that often only contribute to the problem. This can be seen in the embrace, by politicians and the public, of the "schools are failing" narrative that has dominated education discourse since at least *A Nation at Risk* (National Commission on Excellence in Education, 1983), if not earlier. When lack of school efficacy becomes understood as a widespread problem as a commodity spectacle, that spectacle can then work to reinforce the problem. Murray Edelman (1988), in *Constructing the Political Spectacle,* asserts that the construction of social or political problems often has a far-reaching effect: it helps perpetuate or intensify the conditions that are defined as the problem. Over time, the public stops asking what the real problem is and instead turns to "politicians or experts" who may have helped to construct the problem in the first place.

To tie this argument back to the genesis of this work, Orwell's *1984,* recall the landscape Orwell imagined in Oceania. Government power in Oceania is enforced through modern technologies that monitor each individual's every move for any revolutionary or subversive act. The Party, led by the ubiquitous, *Big Brother,* maintains strict control over the population through 24 surveillance via television monitors. Party power is covertly maintained via the control of what is understood as knowledge. Winston Smith maintains a job in Oceania as a rewriter of history, ensuring that the language of Newspeak serves the interests of the Party alone. In Newspeak, terms like freedom are formally defined by their dialectics. For example: "freedom is slavery:" "war is peace." This is Orwell's *doublethink*—the key to the Party's maintaining power via the control of language. Consider Orwell's explanation of this type of doublethink:

> To know and not to know, to be conscious of complete truthfulness while telling carefully constructed lies, to hold simultaneously two opinions which cancel each other out, knowing them to be contradictory and believing in both of them, to use logic against logic, to repudiate morality while laying claim to it, to believe that democracy was impossible and that the Party was the guardian of democracy, to forget, whatever it was necessary to forget, then to draw it back into memory again at the moment when it was needed, and then promptly forget it again. (Orwell, 1949/2001, p. 31)

The relationship Orwell draws between language and power can be understood within Foucauldian notions of power and knowledge. As Foucault argues in *Discipline and Punish* (1979), power produces knowledge; there is no bureaucratic or administrative power without the control of language and knowledge. James Tyner (2004) extends Foucault in an analysis of Orwell and argues:

> Orwell envisioned a totalitarian state so disciplined-spatially, temporally and socially-that all vestiges of humanity and individuality were to be subsumed under the control of the state. Consequently, Orwell suggests that the production and manipulation of knowledge are critical to the usurpation of power. (p. 145)

Orwell's *Newspeak* is a prescient example of political power being realized in overt government control of language and that which is accepted as worth knowing.

In looking at the role of language in creating the education spectacle, Mary Lee Smith (2004) extends Foucauldian notions of the language and power nexus, as well as Edelman's (1988) spectacle theory, in her assertion that the ambiguity of language is the key to the creation of political spectacle. Ambiguity creates confusion; it can, when used effectively by politicians and policymakers, keep the public engaged, enthralled, or even outraged. Smith argues,

> Such symbolic ambiguity creates a kind of fog. It holds the public in thrall. The gain in test scores may not be real, but it seems real, and the public lacks the means to see their way through. Politicians use ambiguous language to unite a public and create an impression of consensus that does not exist. (p. 13)

Over time, ambiguity perpetuates a lack of understanding to what political language, including the political language surrounding education, actually refers.

SPECTACLE AND SURVEILLANCE IN RACE TO THE TOP SCHOOLING

Current federal education policy, spurred on by Arne Duncan's Race to the Top (RTT) reform efforts over that last 3 years, have continued to centralize and standardize federal control over what teachers must teach and how students must demonstrate learning. This is accomplished via increased surveillance of teachers and students as well as the continued construction of the education spectacle. The RTT initiatives offer grants for states that make the most progress in tracking and recording student performance, boosting teacher quality (measured by published test results), improving failing schools (again measured by published test data), and embracing the idea of nationalized standards. These initiatives demonstrate the essence of using language in forging a political spectacle, or in this case, an educational spectacle. Within these federal initiatives are phrases such as "meeting benchmarks," "showing continuous improvement," and the behavioral and performance characteristics of "good" teachers versos "bad" teachers. All of these terms are laden with standardizing images of what it means to learn, to teach, to be validated within education. All of these terms are also ambiguous, and each is used to forge the education spectacle.

Now, not to be forgotten amidst our RTT is the fact the No Child Left Behind Act (NCLB) is again being bantered about for re-authorization by Congress. There are proposed changes to the original NCLB, but none of the changes aim to alter what NCLB does to teachers and students. For example, instead of requiring all students to be proficient in basic skills by 2014, NCLB will now require that schools continue to improve. As with the initial publication of NCLB, there is a reliance on one-size-fits-all education with standards for what is to be studied, and tools for measuring and tracking students and teachers. Further, the *Common Core Standards for Education*, rolling out in many states in 2012, are essentially moving public education in the United States to a day when very soon every student, in every public school, can study the same curricular material, at the same time, on the same day.

Our current national focus on standardization and accountability in public education is not a new development. However, the focus has, over the last thirty years, certainly intensified. The federal report, *A Nation at Risk* (1983), published during Ronald Reagan's first administration, signaled the dawn of the high stakes, accountability movement in education. While curriculum standards were not a new idea at the time, by the late twentieth century, standards were not only being continually refined, they were increasingly tied to high-stakes assessments. Those assessments served as a means of accountability designed to prove what students knew, and how well teachers taught. As Diane Ravitch (2010) argues:

> What once was the standards movement was replaced by the accountability movement. What once was an effort to improve the quality of education turned into an accounting strategy. Measure, then punish or reward. No education experience was needed to administer such a program. Anyone who loved data could do it. The strategy produced fear and obedience among educators; it often generated higher test scores. But it had nothing to do with education. (p. 16)

Ravitch's argument here speaks to a movement away from what education should be about, to a movement toward what education should produce. Too often, this has equated to a focus on test scores. In what could be an Orwellian plot line, the knowledge that students are required to master, that which teachers are required to teach, is strictly controlled by those relatively few people with the power and access to manipulate the spectacle that is national education policy. As countless scholars, teachers, students, and parents have argued over the past decade, federal education policies such as NCLB, and the more recent, RTT, promote a narrowly defined model for public education that relies on surveillance, standardization, and accountability.

Through the use of technologies such as standardized testing instruments and data-driven teacher assessment tools, our current education policies force teachers and students into an Orwellian educational landscape not unlike the administered environment Winston Smith rebels against throughout *1984*. The twenty-four hour surveillance via the telescreens in Oceania has been replaced in schools today by an incessant battery of data-mining instruments. Consider the following from David Granger (2003), who argues against what he calls the paraphernalia of positivism in education today:

> Today's students, too, might be described as captives of highly structured, passivity- inducing environments, environments in which they are prodded to respond individually and in a kind of profusion of scripted questions whether they find them personally engaging and relevant or not. The basic purpose of this environment is likewise to take the uncertainty out of the process, in this case the inherently uncertain process of teaching and learning, of interacting with concrete human beings. Carefully controlled artificial conditions thus become the preferred way to carry out what is a calculated process of dehumanization. (p. 14)

This reliance on data, with the ongoing battery of tests conducted in carefully controlled, highly structured environments not only removes free inquiry from education, it also maintains strict control over the relationship students and teachers have with information and each other. What is created is an environment where human interaction and growth are less important than proving one's worth via some test scores or achievement rubric.

Having laid the groundwork for RTT, the NCLB narrative is replete with similar uses of language to further the education spectacle. Statements such as "continuous improvement" and "proficiency for all" are packaged for public consumption as utopian ideals for public education. However, these statements are not unlike Orwell's critique of political language in his imagined *Newspea*k, as each is rich with ambiguous meaning. Further, recalling Debord here, the terms "proficiency," "continuous improvement," and "adequately yearly progress," have been constructed in such a way as to forward the education spectacle. Over time, these terms, often misunderstood, and perhaps purposefully misused, can be utilized to convey a lack of efficacy in schools that cannot produce expected results. In turn, a manufactured public outrage of failing schools exerts more pressure on education policymakers to enact more surveillance, more accountability, and more control over the education spectacle.

While our current national education policies do not create as dire circumstances as those present in Orwell's Oceania, the ongoing undermining of individuality and humanity in our schools via standardization and accountability creates an environment that is nearly as dangerous for American youth. Soon, no aspect of our pre-K-12 education will be without standards for achievement, nor will it be without incessant surveillance of behavior and performance as our current education leaders continue to look for increased means of control and accountability. As Henry Giroux (2009) asserts:

> Today, in the age of standardized testing...thinking and acting, reason and judgment have been thrown out the window just as teachers are increasingly being deskilled and forced to act as semi-robotic technicians good for little more than teaching to the test and serving as a reminder that we arriving at a day when the school curriculum will be teacher-proof. This loss of autonomy results in the sabotaging of critical democratic education and the rise of a culture of security that now defines schools through the narrow optics of measurement and discipline. (p. 2)

Within this system Giroux describes, students, not unlike Orwell's Winston Smith, are subject to the institutionalized power. Where schools should be, and arguably once were, sites for critical learning and engagement, they are increasingly viewed as containment centers where students either acquiesce or face increasingly strenuous consequences.

Orwell wrote *1984* when electronic information technologies were still in their nascent stages; his ideas of telescreens and 24-hour video surveillance were primarily conjecture. However, one does not need to look far today to realize that we live in an increasingly scrutinized society. With the proliferation of Internet and broadband technologies social media and the ubiquity of video technology, we are all, in fact, watching each other on a regular basis (Peek, 2009). Consequently, the desire to see, and be seen, has grown exponentially in the past 10 years alone. In many ways citizens today has embraced the power that Orwell saw in technology and turned it on ourselves in a way that Debord seemed to know we would. Modern society is moving with increasing haste toward a time when everybody can watch everybody all the time. We have, in many ways, embraced Orwell's idea of Big Brother. Perhaps, even worse, in some ways we have become him.

So what do we as teachers, scholars, and citizens today make of our dystopian public education system today where covert, institutionalized surveillance and control continues to undermine human agency? Is the situation, in keeping with a dystopian narrative, as bad as it gets? Or, do we look to dystopian literature to remind us the work that still needs to be accomplished to prevent such situations from remaining? Resisting the ongoing control over education rendered by the surveillance-spectacle presents both philosophical and pedagogical challenges. As Vinson, Ross, and Walsh (2010) point out, Debord takes a direct approach to superseding the power of the spectacle. Along with the other members of the Situationist International, Debord (1967/1977) wrote of derive and detournement, as two means of active resistance. Derive creates interactive spaces where individuals engage with their natural urban surroundings; acting without preconceived or commodified ideas of reality. Derive requires an embrace of serendipity, and appreciation for emergent circumstances not confined by ideology. Applying derive as resistance against conformist schooling requires that we think differently about schools and see them as spaces where students and teachers engage with changing spaces and circumstances without being tied to what I will call the artifacts of education. This requires a rejection of the determinism rendered from the confluence of surveillance and spectacle of education discussed earlier in this work. Further, derive requires that teachers and students work to actively and collaboratively disrupt the spectacle.

Detournement literally refers to an act of redefining that which is accepted as truth. For example, the public's understanding of the efficacy of public schools has been shaped to fit the image of what is commonly regarded as schools as working, or schools as failing, regardless of what those terms actually mean. An example of this can be seen in headlines such as schools must compete in a RTT to win federal funding. The words themselves speak of a race to the top of something, as if a competitive race is something schools *should* engage in. Yet, after further examination, one might question why schools must compete in a race for federal money that should be used to equitably fund schools in the first place. As an act of resistance, detournement requires that students and teachers actively subvert the hegemony of the spectacle found in initiatives such as RTT. In practice, refusing to participate in, or sabotaging the system by opting out of tests represents a detournement. Doing so allows for the creation of meaning, the redefining of truth claims.

In Orwell's *1984,* rebellion, such as the subversive acts forwarded by Debord and others, had long been expunged from the imagination of the population in Oceania. In education today, we see the use of the power of language as a means to redefine what it means to be educated. Increasingly, an educated person is the individual who navigates the system in such a way to not disrupt, to not challenge, to not contest that which is packaged as the official curriculum or the education spectacle. While Orwell never wrote specifically about education, one cannot help but read our current education policies as moving us toward an Orwellian future. The reading of our current education situation within the context of dystopian literature only heightens the need for ongoing resistance against the forces that move us closer each day toward a truly dystopian education.

REFERENCES

Adorno, T. (2001). *The culture industry: Selected essays on mass culture*. New York, NY: Routledge. (Original work published 1991)

Boorstin, D. (1987). *Image: A guide to pseudo-events in America*. New York, NY: Antheneum. (Original work published 1961)

Debord, G. (1983). *Society of the spectacle*. Detroit, MI: Black & Red. (Original work published 1967)

Edelman, M. (1988). *Constructing the political spectacle*. Chicago, IL: University of Chicago Press.

Foucault, M. (1979). *Discipline and punish: The birth of the prison*. New York, NY: Vintage Books.

Giroux, H. (2009, October 20). Schools and the pedagogy of punishment. *Truthout.org*. Retrieved from http://archive.truthout.org/10200910

Granger, D. (2003, Spring). Positivism, skepticism, and the attraction of paltry empiricism: A Cavellian perspective on current school reform efforts. *Educational Change*, 11-24.

Hitchens, C. (2002). *Why Orwell matters*. New York, NY: Basic Books.

Marcuse, H. (1991). *One-dimensional man: Studies in the ideology of advanced industrial society.* Boston, MA: Beacon Press. (Original work published 1964)

National Commission on Excellence in Education. (1983). *A nation at risk: The imperative for educational reform.* Washington, DC: U.S. Department of Education.

Orwell, G. (1945/2000). *Animal farm*. New York, NY: Penguin Books. (Original work published 1945)

Orwell, G. (1981). *A collection of essays*. New York, NY: Harcourt. (Original work published 1946)

Orwell, G. (2001). *Nineteen eighty-four.* New York, NY: Harcourt. (Original work published 1949)

Peek, M. (2009). The observer and the observed: Re-imagining privacy dichotomies in information privacy law. *Northwestern Journal of Technology and Intellectual Property, 8*, 51-64.

Ranciere, J. (2009). *The emancipated spectator.* London, England: Verso.

Ravitch, D. (2010). *The death and life of the great American school system*. New York, NY: Basic Books.

Smith, M. L (2004). *Political spectacle and the fate of American schools.* New York: Routledge.

Tyner, J. (2004, March 1). Self and space, resistance and discipline: a Foucauldian reading of George Orwell's *1984*. *Social and Cultural Geography 5*(1), 129-149.

Vinson, K., & Ross, E. W. (2000). Education and the new disciplinarity: Surveillance, spectacle and the case of SBER. *Cultural Logic 4*(1), 1-25.

Vinson, K., Ross, E. W., & Walsh, J. (2010). Controlling images: Surveillance, spectacle, and the power of high-stakes testing. In K. Saltzman & D. Gabbard, (Eds.), *Education as enforcement: The militarization and corporatization of schools* (pp. 274-290), New York, NY: Routledge.

CHAPTER 14

DYSTOPIA, DISCIPLINARITY, AND GOVERNMENTALITY

A Foucauldian Analysis of the Novels of Isamu Fukui

Joshua Garrison and Leslee Grey

INTRODUCTION

In 2008, then 15-year old author Isamu Fukui published *Truancy,* a dystopian novel in which children are terrorized by an educational system that demands complete obedience and seeks total control. The novel was followed by the publication of a prequel, *Truancy Origins* (Fukui, 2009) while a third volume, *Truancy City,* is slated for publication in 2012. A self-described "unhappy" student during its writing, Fukui's is a unique contribution to the rapidly expanding genre of young adult dystopian fiction (Miller, 2010). In the books, the author imagines a world in which contemporary educational policies are taken to their most horrible extremes. Both volumes chronicle the resistance of the "Truancy," an armed, violent insurrection led by students intent on destroying the power of the "Educators" and their institutions.

Dystopia and Education:
Insights Into Theory, Praxis, and Policy in an Age of Utopia-Gone-Wrong, pp. 213–228

In a 2008 interview with National Public Radio, Fukui noted that he was moved to write the book upon realizing that there was "a fundamental problem with the educational system in general" (National Public Radio, 2008). *Truancy* (Fukui, 2008) and its prequel, *Origins* (Fukui, 2009), have inspired a following among disaffected high school students. Fukui's novels offer numerous critiques of the ways in which adults treat children. In fact, the books' companion website "is dedicated to anyone who has ever suffered in the name of education" and provides young people with a forum where they can share and discuss the struggles they face at school (www.thetruancy.com, para. 1). Fukui's *Truancy* books and the online community that it has inspired constitute a unique form of educational resistance, one created for and by young people. Although *Truancy* can be categorized as science fiction, its themes resonate with current educational policies and practices, exposing the ways in which schools are increasingly adopting tactics traditionally employed by law enforcement (Giroux, 2004). As the documentary *The War on Kids* (Soling, 2009) highlights, schools seem to place more emphasis on disciplining and punishing young people than they do on actual learning.

In this essay we examine the *Truancy* novels from a Foucauldian perspective; more precisely, we are interested in just how closely these two unlikely collections of texts resemble one another. That the dystopian imaginings of an adolescent can be used to illustrate some of the central points of the philosophical project of an influential French thinker constitutes a remarkable and rare opportunity for scholars of young adult literature and critical theory alike. Indeed, with the recent explosion of young adult dystopian literature (cf. Collins, 2008), one sees Foucault's work dramatized with greater frequency. Although we argue that Foucault's analysis of modern society, with respect to notions of disciplinarity and governmentality in particular, provides an accurate and useful roadmap for constructing a critique of contemporary society, it seems as if that same analysis permeates the fears of contemporary Americans. That such a wide body of dystopian literature exists, and that much of it is written for young audiences, is curious indeed. This unlikely confluence of texts certainly provides opportunities for young readers to think critically, if not radically, about schooling and their own place in society.

CARCERAL EDUCATION

In *Discipline and Punish*, Foucault (1977/1995) examines the workings of power in such institutions as prisons and schools, specifically the workings of panoptic surveillance and the creation of delinquent identities. In Fukui's novels, the author portrays the workings of an architectural power that have "never failed to control a child" (Foucault, 1977/1995, p. 172; Fukui, 2009, p. 13). He describes the school building as "made out of reddish bricks"; with its tiny, "infrequent" windows, it seems "literally styled after a prison" (Fukui, 2009, p. 26). Ruled by a ruthless, tyrannical Mayor and his scheming policy Enforcers, the children of Education City are under constant control. For example, each student has a barcode-like identification mark tattooed on his or her arm. As Fukui (2008) puts it, "All kids are branded as a single faceless mass and herded through school like cattle" (p. 320). The "Educators," who run the city and its schools, make sure that the students are scanned whenever they enter or leave school, so that each can be monitored. Under the guise of providing safety, free period rooms enclose students between classes so that their every action is tracked. Here, as in Foucault's (1977/1995) depiction of schools, surveillance guarantees order ... students are prevented from coming into contact with one another so that "there is no copying, no noise, no chatter, no waste of time" (Foucault, 1977/1995, p. 201). Foucault (1977/1995) explains that a key element of disciplinary power is to fracture groups so that power is more easily exercised upon the individual: "The crowd, a compact mass, a locus of multiple exchanges, individualities merging together, a collective effect, is abolished and replaced by a collection of separated individualities" (p. 201).

Designed in the 18th century by the English philosopher Jeremy Bentham, the panopticon was a prison whose design allowed for the constant monitoring of inmates. Foucault (1977/1995) argued that this architectural design "swarmed" across society and was "transferred and adapted" to other institutions, including schools (p. 211). Panoptic institutions, such as prisons or schools, teach individuals that they can be subjected to surveillance, and thus punishment, at any time. Such knowledge renders the individual docile and easily controlled. It is not by accident that under this panoptic gaze—always watching, like Orwell's (1949) Big Brother—children in Education City are complicit in their own marginalization. As Foucault explains, "He who is subjected to a field of visibility, and who knows it, assumes responsibility for the constraints of power." Subsequently, "he makes them play spontaneously upon himself; he becomes the principle of his own subjection" (pp. 202-203). Fukui (2009) echoes Foucault's thesis precisely: "Your schoolwork, your grades, all your precious achievements, all it represents is complicity!" (p. 62).

In Fukui's (2008) fictional school, policies are imposed as they would be in a prison—"mandatory searches" conducted by Disciplinary Officers, locking student restrooms to establish their use as a "privilege," and causing students to be tardy to their next classes (a serious and punishable offense at the school) are among the tactics employed by school officials in an effort to render pupils powerless. Constantly subjected to this prison-like treatment, students are always and already constructed as delinquents. "Children of this City," one *Truancy* character explains,

> have no rights. They tell us that we are not equal. If we argue, we are disciplined. If we resist, we are punished.... The Educators have always patiently taught us of our own inferiority, to the point where many of us had begun to believe their words. (pp. 428-429)

In Education City, children who cannot be properly trained according to the school's standards, such as those with disabilities, are never allowed to attend school. A teacher explains that disabilities make children "unfit for education and thus unfit for normal life in this City ... students must conform to education and not the other way around ... if you're unfit for school, you're unfit for society! Children should conform to the rules," she continues, "and the rules are that a student is worth no more than their grade [sic]" (Fukui, 2009, p. 72). Fukui's fictional classroom practices align with real-life individualistic, market-driven policies that conflate self-worth with achievement and performance on standardized tests and only value students, teachers, and schools for their high rankings, obedience, and conformity. In Education City, students who learn differently are separated from the rest of society, with no choice but to languish in the Vagrant district.

That the adults in Education City are preoccupied with oppressing young people is conspicuous. Fukui depicts the Mayor and one of the policy Enforcers discussing the implementation of a new randomly administered disciplinary "tactic" used to punish students for misbehaving in class. Under this new program, if one student misbehaves, extra homework is assigned to *all* the students. Moreover, an entire class could fail a test due to one student's "misbehavior." The Enforcer tells the Mayor that consequently, "We've seen the expected loss of student morale, as well as an overall grade decrease across the board, both of which seem to be a direct result of the program" (Fukui, 2009, p. 30). The Enforcer notes that "observed physical altercations between students [have] shot up by seven percent" due to the tension among children that the tactic has created. He tells the Mayor, "Punishing entire classes for any one student's misbehavior effectively turned the rest of the class against that student. They punish their own even more effectively than we can directly" (Fukui, 2009, p. 30).

When the Mayor's tactics are employed, students assume their identities as delinquents without question. Says the Enforcer, "so far no students have yet been observed to blame the teachers or us" (Fukui, 2009, p. 30). Under constant surveillance, with their every action subjected to the gaze of authority, students are conditioned to police themselves. In Fukui's books, the effects of the tactic are seen throughout the school, as students watch and control one another's behaviors. "Even if a class is not subject to the tactic themselves, word spreads quickly," the Enforcer explains (p. 30). The panoptic model of disciplinary institutions, as Foucault (1977/1995) describes, "is a marvelous machine which, whatever use one may wish to put it to, produces homogeneous effects of power," namely, inculcation of docility and production of delinquency, both of which benefit the ruling class of adults led by the Mayor (p. 202). Foucault demonstrates that the application of labels of "abnormality," such as truancy and vagrancy, serve to construct a delinquent identity, which allows for the enforcement and maintenance of power over individuals.

USEFUL VAGRANCY

The labels of Truant or Vagrant not only characterizes the child-as-delinquent but also places her within an extralegal system in which laws emanate not only from formal legal institutions but also from social institutions that were not traditionally endowed with legal, or punishing, power. In Fukui's Education City, students who dare oppose the strict regimen of the school are expelled, while the rest are kept under control by an inflexible and uncompromising Zero Tolerance Policy. As described by the Mayor of Education City, this disciplinary policy "will provide for the interrogation and immediate expulsion of any student [who] commits any minor infraction." In fact, "*Any* rule breaking, *anything* that can be construed as a threat, will be severely punished" (Fukui, 2008, p. 124). With no options, the youngsters who are expelled are banished from the community to live as Vagrants.

The Vagrants are young pariahs who live in a postapocalyptic portion of the City where they engage in hand-to-hand combat for resources such as food and weapons. A significant portion of the *Truancy* books portrays violent videogame style combat among the marginalized teens, illustrating how the adults in power have turned the young people against each other, isolating them to fight for scraps amongst themselves instead of engaging with their true oppressor (the Mayor) for a chance at freedom. Indeed, the school and the Mayor conspire in a form of subjugation by which those in power create a marked class of illegality that "fabricates" delinquents by branding them as Other. In Fukui's fictional society, the Truant dropouts and the pushed-out (or expelled) Vagrants are contained in their own enclosed, dilapidated District. Personifying all that is hated and feared about adolescents, the delinquents in the Vagrant district are, as Foucault (1977/1995) puts it, "sufficiently marked to serve as a support for the 'great fear' of [young] people who were believed to be criminal and seditious as a whole" (p. 275). The Vagrant class represents a vilified

mis-educated the City's youth to the Educators' benefit, he laments, "here life is whatever they tell us it is. On a whim they can teach us a fabricated history, change the norms of society, whenever and however they want ... [and we] live this life in invisible chains" (Fukui, 2008, p. 79). There is no need for real chains. In the model of Foucault's (1977/1995) panopticon, education is "used as a machine to carry out [pedagogic] experiments, to alter behaviour, [and] to train or correct individuals" (pp. 203-204).

Zyid, Umasi's more radical and sinister twin, explains to Umasi that dropping out of school and becoming a Truant

> has nothing to do with intelligence.... Some people are not meant for school. Some of them may be as smart as you want, and yet still recoil at their freedom and dignity being stolen from them by the Educators. The Educators will make them beg and sweat for an abstract grade just as a dog might perform tricks for a bone.... Those of us who were never meant to be in school.... We are offered few options. For us, all we have to choose from is death or revolution. (Fukui, 2008, pp. 320-321)

Indeed, Fukui's novels are permeated by a negative critique of contemporary schooling: "What has being a good student brought us, brought anyone, but mixed blessings at best and utter misery at worst? No pillar of justice can stand upon a foundation of disparity. School has nothing good to offer us. They only teach us the bad, by their example" (Fukui, 2009, p. 351).

Fukui's fictional backdrop of Education City provides an extreme example of how school, like prison, is successful in producing children as "legally inferior" and delinquency as a "usable form of illegality" that marks Vagrants as pathologized subjects and strengthens Mayoral control (Fukui, 2009, p. 325; Foucault, 1977/1995, p. 277). Not only does truancy have nothing to do with intelligence, it is, as noted previously, a potent social construction. Delinquency is exploitable by those in power, and is thus useful. In ways that align with Foucault's elucidations of circuits of power, Fukui's books examine the processes through which schools create truancy and the ways in which authority works symbiotically with so-called delinquents, Truants, and Vagrants to produce "homogeneous effects of power," shaping actions, behaviors, and subjectivities that benefit those in charge (Foucault, 1977/1995, p. 202).

DYSTOPIAN DISCIPLINARITY

Shortly after the publication of *Discipline and Punish,* Foucault delivered a series of lectures at the Collège de France titled "Security, Territory, Population" (1977-1978). In those talks he drew distinctions between discipline and governmentality, which he considered to be "two completely different systems of power" (Foucault, 2007, p. 66). Taking into consideration Foucault's theses on governmentality, we gain a more nuanced understanding of the multiple ways in which power is deployed in modern society. Foucault did not abandon his earlier analysis of power, but he did revise it. Simply put, whereas disciplinary power functions at the level of the individual, governmentality operates upon the social whole. As Foucault writes,

> The relation between the individual and the collective, between the totality of the social body and its elementary fragments, is made to function in a completely different way; it will function differently in what we call population. The government of populations is, I think, completely different from the exercise of sovereignty over the fine grain of individual behaviors. (p. 66)

Two populations in Fukui's novels ought to be considered if we are to view them in light of Foucault's analysis: the insurrectionary Truants and the "good" students who do not deviate from the harsh educational regimen inflicted upon them by the Educators. Both groups are sums of individuals, but The Truancy is an entity separate from the Truant, just as students-as-subject must be considered as an entity that is not dependent on any given individual. Individuals and populations are managed, or governed, in different ways and for different purposes.

Traditionally, power had been exercised over individuals in a sovereign-subject relationship, with the former exerting a will over the latter, "ensuring the total and as it were passive obedience of individuals to their sovereign" (Foucault, 2007, p. 65). Later, as the exercise of power became subtler, yet more insidious, disciplinary institutions such as Bentham's panopticon—a "mechanism of power reduced to its ideal form"—allowed for an exercise of power that was not based on force or terror (Foucault, 1977/1995, p. 205). As the Benthamite model "swarmed" throughout modern society, the sway of the sovereign's whim was weakened by the expert's rational plan—educators, physicians, military officers, and industrialists alike took their cues from the carceral domain: "The frontiers between confinement, judicial punishment and institutions of discipline … tended to disappear and to constitute a great carceral continuum that diffused penitentiary techniques into the most innocent disciplines" (p. 297).

Surveillance, examinations, distributing bodies within specialized spaces, classification, the meticulous control of an individual's activities and the total management of her time, all constituted for Foucault (1977/1995) tactics for creating the perfect disciplinary society. Like "the military dream of society," disciplinarity is antithetical to the stated purposes of the Enlightenment project:

> its fundamental reference was not to the state of nature, but to the meticulously subordinated cogs of a machine, not to the primal social contract, but to permanent coercion, not to fundamental rights, but to indefinitely progressive forms of training, not to the general will but to automatic docility. (p. 169)

Disciplinary tactics reduce subjects to the smallest units possible, and fracture masses and populations. Once divided, types of individuals are *produced by,* and *controlled through,* the knowledge that is gained through rigorous and unceasing observation—panoptic institutions break down totalities by differentiating individuals: "In a disciplinary régime ... individualization is 'descending': as power becomes more anonymous and more functional, those on whom it is exercised tend to be more strongly individualized" (Foucault, 1977/1995, p. 193).

That a Foucauldian notion of panoptic disciplinarity permeates the pages of Fukui's dystopia has been established above, and it is worth noting that Huxley and Orwell—the genre's early and still most noteworthy contributors—were well aware of those anti-Enlightenment tendencies that so profoundly impacted the course of Western modernity. Both *Brave New World* (Huxley, 1932) and *1984* (Orwell, 1949) abound with those disciplinary apparatuses detailed in *Discipline and Punish* (Foucault, 1977/1995) and the *Truancy* (Fukui, 2008, 2009) novels: surveillance, timetables, examinations, spatial distribution, and hierarchical classifications included. Foucault's (1977/1995) portrayal of modern individuality, and those tactics and techniques that hold the individual in a state of subjection, share important similarities with themes commonly found in dystopian fiction. But can the same be said of his analysis of populations and their management?

THE DISCIPLINES, GOVERNMENTALITY, AND THE *COUP D'ÉTAT*

Social institutions—schools, prisons, and factories included—impose controls over individuals with the aim of extracting from them a higher degree of usefulness: "disciplinary coercion establishes in the body the connecting link between an increased aptitude and an increased domination" (Foucault, 1977/1995, p. 138). Obedience increases use, and vice versa—the more obedient a factory worker becomes, for instance, the more use he is to the foreman; conversely, as his productive powers increase, his obedience to his supervisor becomes more absolute. Likewise, the student who is subjected to a disciplinary program is constantly engaged in "useful" activity: "an attempt is also made to assure the quality of time used: constant supervision, the pressure of supervisors, the elimination of anything that might disturb or distract; it is a question of constituting a totally useful time" (p. 150).

The same might be said of populations, which appear as "an absolutely new political personage" in the 17th century (Foucault, 2007, pp. 67-68). Like the individual, the value of a population is gauged by its usefulness. But while an individual's use can be exploited by any given number of interests, a useful population benefits the state in particular. A useful population guarantees that harvests are abundant and manufactures vibrant, and sees that the state will be competitive with its neighbors (pp. 68-69). The extraction of use from the population is a complex matter requiring coordination; it cannot be accomplished through arbitrary and haphazard measures. This new "political personage," then, is attended by the development of a centralized and systematized apparatus that manages, controls, and disciplines large and even distant groups of people:

> The population can only be the basis of the state's wealth and power [if] it is framed by a regulatory apparatus ... that prevents emigration, calls for immigrants, and promotes the birth rate, a regulatory apparatus that also defines useful and exportable products, fixes the objects to be produced, the means of their production, as well as wages, which prevents idleness and vagrancy. In short, it requires an apparatus that will ensure that the population, which is seen as the source and the root, as it were, of the state's wealth, will work properly, in the right place, and on the right object. (p. 69)

This new "apparatus," which oversees the management of populations, is government, which is different from sovereign rule. "The more I have spoken about population," writes Foucault, "the more I have stopped saying 'sovereign'" (Foucault, 2007, p. 76). Whereas sovereignty is concerned with the direct rule over territories, government occupies itself with the "general management" of populations. And the management of this new entity gives rise new to forms of knowledge (statistics, political science, public opinion, etc.) and practices, which Foucault terms "governmentality." The governmentality of "Security, Territory, Population" is analogous to those disciplinary controls detailed in *Discipline and Punish*: "Can we talk of something like a 'governmentality' that would be to the state what techniques of segregation were to psychiatry, what techniques of discipline were to the penal system, and what biopolitics was to medical institutions?" (p. 120). Thus, governmentality refers to an "ensemble" of institutions and practices that exercise power over populations (p. 108). Whereas sovereignty reigns, rules, and commands its subject, governmentality *governs* a population; it is the art of governing men. In his notion of governmentality as the art of governing men, Foucault writes, "The modern state is born when governmentality became a calculated and reflected practice" (p. 165).

This art of government, which, again, must have as its end the development of a population that serves the state in useful ways, will vary according to the philosophies and goals of those who practice it. What matters is not so much the final shape of this or that state, but the commonalities shared by states in general, which is governmentality:

> What is important ... is the moment that this something, the state, began to enter into reflected practice. The problem of knowing when, under what conditions, and in what form the state began to be projected, programmed, and developed within this conscious practice, at what moment it became an object of knowledge and analysis, [and] when and how it became part of a reflected and concerted strategy. (Foucault, 2007, p. 247)

These are broad historical questions, to be sure, but what matters here is that Foucault's (2007) notion of governmentality—the knowledge and practices of population management—reveals the *raison d'état*, or reason or interests of the state. Quoting Chemnitz, Foucault defines *raison d'état* as "a certain political consideration that is necessary in all public matters, councils and plans, which must strive solely for the preservation, expansion, and felicity of the state, and for which we must employ the most ready and swift means" (p. 257). Foucault is interested in several implications that arise from conceiving the state in this way: first, the definition casts the state as necessarily protective and conservative, its primary goal being to maintain itself; second, "there is no prior, external purpose, or even a purpose subsequent to the state itself" (p. 258). Foucault continues,

> There is nothing of this here. The end of *raison d'état* is the state itself, and if there is something like perfection, happiness, or felicity, it will only ever be the perfection, happiness, of felicity of the state itself. There is no last day. There is no ultimate point. There is nothing like a uniform and final temporal organization. (p. 258)

Governmentality, then, is an endless and indefinite process, "with no foreseeable term or final aim" (Foucault, 2007, p. 260). This point is particularly important for Foucault as it serves to introduce *raison d'état's* governing partner, the *coup d'état*. Drawing from 17th-century texts, Foucault cautions his readers against an anachronistic reading of this phrase; in fact, in the context in which Foucault uses *coup d'état,* the term has nothing to do with overthrowing a state. Rather, the *coup d'état* is an action taken by the state against its *own* legal codes. As Foucault defines it, the *coup d'état* is "a suspension of, a temporary departure from, laws and legality ... it is an extraordinary action against ordinary law, an action retaining no order or form of justice" (p. 261). Recalling the Chemnitz quotation cited above, it should be clear that the *raison d'état* and *coup d'état* are by no means in opposition to one another—if the former generally employs a conservative and protectionist approach to ensure the state's preservation, the state can just as easily engage in temporary "illegalities" should the aim of self-preservation require it. While states might generally respect the laws on which they are based, this is not always the case:

> there will be times when *raison d'état* can no longer make use of these laws and due to a pressing and urgent event must of necessity free itself from them. In the name of what? In the name of the state's salvation. It is this necessity of the state with regard to itself that, at a certain moment, will push *raison d'état* to brush aside the civil, moral, and natural laws that it had previously wanted to recognize and had incorporated into its game...The *coup d'état* is the state acting of itself on itself, swiftly, immediately, without rule, with urgency and necessity, and dramatically. (p. 262)

The state's overriding interest in self-preservation trumps the obligation it has to obey its own laws. More alarming are the two primary methods by which the *coup d'état* is enacted, as both are forms of power that Foucault argued were alien to the modern disciplines: violence and spectacle. That each is necessary for the functioning and maintenance of the modern state is not a point generally assigned to Foucault, but his lectures of 1977-1978 are clear on this point. He writes, "when necessity demands it, *raison d'état* becomes *coup d'état,* and then it is violent. This means that it is obliged to sacrifice, to sever, cause harm, and it is led to be unjust and murderous" (p. 263). Further, this violence must be spectacularly staged: "It must be recognized immediately according to its real features, by extolling the necessity that justifies it" (p. 264). And, finally, Foucault concludes, there is "this theatrical and tragic harshness of the state that in the name of its always threatened and never certain salvation, requires us to accept acts of violence as the purest form of reason, and of *raison d'état*" (p. 267).

In *Discipline and Punish*, Foucault (1977/1995) went to great lengths to demonstrate that the disciplines, and the punishment of criminals in particular, "developed as a technology of subtle, effective, economic powers, in opposition to the sumptuous expenditure of the power of the sovereign" — the great penal reformers of the 18th century would replace public displays of torture with the private correctives of the prison, the vengeance of the sovereign with the calculated and curative regimens of the criminologist (pp. 102 & 174). In essence, then, disciplinarity and the *coup d'état* operate in opposite ways. Can these two strategies exist in the same governmental context? While opposed, Foucault does not see their coexistence as a contradiction. The disciplines are employed to create masses of articulated individuals, while governmentality is concerned with managing those masses/populations and extracting from them that which is most useful if the state is to be maintained in its present form. Should those populations stand in the way of the fulfillment of the *raison d'état*—whether they be dissidents or revolutionaries—then the state retains at its disposal the more traditional tools of social control: violence and spectacle, which are deployed when the state must commit illegalities in order to guarantee its indefinite perpetuity. The *coup d'état* ensures the security of the state.

TRUANCY'S EDUCATIONAL *COUP*

Highly exaggerated forms of disciplinarity and governmentality characterize dystopian states in modern fiction, and Fukui's *Truancy* novels are no exception. That Fukui's thoughts on education and his fears about the future can be read as a kind of Foucauldian horror story suggests that Foucault's analysis of modern society is in itself "dystopian." Assuming that these two bodies of work were independently conceived (and there is no evidence that Fukui is himself versed in Foucault's work), one cannot but be impressed that Foucault's work in the 1970s almost perfectly foreshadows the many themes recently dramatized in the explosion of young adult dystopian fiction. That Fukui brings to life many of the disciplinary tactics found in *Discipline and Punish* has been established above; the remaining concern is exploring the ways in which the author anticipates Foucauldian notions of governmentality, *raison d'état,* and the *coup d'état.*

Fukui's characterization of the dystopian state in which his novels unfold—known as "Education City"—is neither detailed nor complex; it does, however, illustrate *raison d'état* in fairly accurate terms: "The reason we exist," says one of the Mayor's cabinet members, "and the only objective we're to pursue is control" (Fukui, 2009, p. 58). Zyid, the more sophisticated of the novels' twin protagonists, describes The City in the same way: "It's all about control, about maintaining their supposedly perfect society" (pp. 61-62). Education was the means by which the City's citizens were controlled, and their educational tactics relied on surveillance, examinations, and the complete supervision of a student's time and space, much in the same way that Foucault characterizes schools in *Discipline and Punish.* Writes Fukui (2008),

> Slowly but surely, the Educators were taking control of every last step a student took. Every second not spent in a classroom had to be accounted for; every child walking down the street was suspect—they would stop at *nothing* to keep control of *everything*. (p. 38)

From the Educators' point of view, then, the population of young people is neatly divided into two groups: those who enhance The City's control by adhering to its strict and unforgiving regimen (the Students) and those who undermine its control by refusing it (the Vagrants) or by fighting it (the Truants). The outliers, whether active or inactive, pose a direct challenge to The City's *raison d'état* and, as the Foucauldian analysis predicts, such a challenge to the state's ability to preserve itself will be dealt with violently and theatrically.

Light on life inside of the schools, but heavy on street battles between the Truants and Educators, the bulk of Fukui's novels are dedicated to the notion of the *coup d'état.* The City's Enforcers will stop at nothing to protect the state's *raison,* and the author eagerly depicts the City's government as a champion of illegality. The Mayor's new expulsion policy is a good example of the *coup* at work:

> Firstly, make it illegal for any expelled student to return to their homes or contact their parents and guardians after being expelled... In this way we can prevent the expelled students from ever seeing their parents again. After that, we'll be free to execute them all quietly without anyone making any fuss. (Fukui, 2008, p. 102)

When one of the Mayor's subordinates begins to protest, he reminds him that "I took an oath to protect this City and its schools, and I intend to fulfill it by *any* means necessary" (Fukui, 2008, p. 102). Later, speaking to the news media, the Mayor treats his subjects to a display of political theater when he announces the enactment of "a daring new set of countermeasures" that aspire to eradicate student rebellion at its earliest stages: "We must identify the children in our schools that pose a threat to their peers, and we must do it before they strike," he says. "Only by dealing with these individuals harshly at the first sign of trouble can we ensure the continued safety of our children" (p. 133). The new policies signal *Truancy's* dystopian climax, and marks the moment when an already authoritarian regime collapses into a full-blown police state:

> Along with the Mayor's announcement came a new warning to all students as a whole.... Students are cautioned not to joke in any way about performing any act of violence, nor are they to break any rules, as leniency will not be shown. Any student suspected of having rebellious tendencies at all can be arrested, interrogated, and even expelled on the spot. (p. 133)

When the logic of policing is applied to the preservation of the *raison d'état,* Foucault (2008) notes that police serve as the instrument of the *coup d'état:* "[The police are] the permanent *coup d'état* that is exercised and functions in the name of and in terms of the principles of its own rationality, without having to mold or model itself on the otherwise given rules of justice" (p. 339). In the end, then, the dystopian state exists simply to exist and maintains its existence by any means necessary. That Fukui's adolescent imaginings and Foucault's genealogy of the modern state and its institutions share so much in common says much about the context in which these books were written.

REFERENCES

Collins, S. (2008). *The hunger games*. New York, NY: Scholastic Press.

Foucault, M. (1995). *Discipline and punish: The birth of the prison.* (A. Sheridan, Trans.). New York, NY: Vintage. (Original work published 1977)

Foucault, M. (1980). *Power/knowledge: Selected interviews and other writings: 1972-1977.* (Colin Gordon, Ed.) (C. Gordon et al. Trans.). New York, NY: Pantheon.

Foucault, M. (2007). *Security, territory, population: Lectures at the College de France, 1977-1978* (G. Burchell, Trans.). New York, NY: Palgrave Macmillan.

Fukui, I. (2008). *Truancy: A novel.* New York, NY: Tom Doherty Associates.

Fukui, I. (2009). *Truancy origins.* New York, NY: Tom Doherty Associates.

Giroux, H. A. (2004). *The terror of neoliberalism: Authoritarianism and the eclipse of democracy.* Aurora, ON: Garamond Press.

Huxley, A. (1932). *Brave new world.* London: Chatto & Windus.

Miller, L. (2010). Fresh hell: What's behind the boom in dystopian fiction for young readers? *The New Yorker.* Retrieved from http://www.newyorker.com/arts/critics/atlarge/2010/06/14/100614crat_atlarge_miller?currentPage=all

National Commission on Excellence in Education. (1983). *A nation at risk: The imperative for educational reform*. Washington, DC: U.S. Department of Education.

National Public Radio. (2008, May 18). Student chronicles high school misery in *Truancy.*" Radio broadcast. Retrieved from http://www.npr.org/templates/story/story.php?storyId=90570251

Orwell, G. (1949). *1984.* London, England: Secker & Warburg.

Soling, C. (Producer/Director). (2009). *The war on kids* [Motion picture]. United States: Spectacle Films.

CHAPTER 15

EDUCATION'S HANDMAIDS?

The Role of the Teacher in the Age of Accountability

Alison Happel and Becky Atkinson

INTRODUCTION

Under No Child Left Behind (NCLB), educators are experiencing an increasing lack of autonomy and individuality within their classrooms. Because of the quantitative push by politicians and policymakers for measurable results, markers of progress, and "accountability," teachers are increasingly being expected to use what some have called teacher-proof pedagogy and scripted curriculum rather than strategies and curriculum they select and develop themselves (Giroux, 1988; St. Pierre, 2004). Teachers are becoming functionaries of education instead of creative, autonomous professionals who shape their own pedagogy and curriculum.

In this chapter we argue that the dystopian handmaids in Margaret Atwood's (1986) *The Handmaid's Tale* can be used to understand the current and potential ramifications of the loss of teacher autonomy under NCLB through a feminist poststructural appropriation of Foucault's (1982) pastoral power. We find that Foucault's concept of pastoral power offers an analytical framework that illuminates how seemingly "caring"

Dystopia and Education:
Insights Into Theory, Praxis, and Policy in an Age of Utopia-Gone-Wrong, pp. 229–247

and benign governmental intentions bring increased surveillance, regulation, and normalization to control the "docile bodies" of those for whom they express care and concern. We will draw the parallels between how the discourses of accountability and security operate as benign and "caring" forces through which the technologies of "high standards" under NCLB, as do those of "women's safety" within *The Handmaid's Tale*, compel compliance and ultimately decrease autonomy and individuality for their respective subjects.

Using this framework, we read and examine NCLB through the dystopian lens of *The Handmaid's Tale* because of several shared resonances between the realities depicted in the novel and the realities consequential to the legislation. Both came about as responses to what were seen as uncontrollable and dangerous practices allowed by the previous liberal leadership. In the country that existed prior to Atwood's futuristic society of Gilead, women regularly faced dangers from assault; consequently, women rarely ventured out at night. Additionally, disease and pollution threatened the future viability of the species. For the United States education system, Congressional policymakers approved NCLB as a response to what was seen as the failure of schools to rectify the racial and economic inequalities reflected in the achievement gap between white and minority students, and that between poor and middle class students (Darling-Hammond, 2007; Gay, 2007; Ravitch, 2010). These purported achievement gaps were seen as a threat to the nation's future economic stability and dominance in the global markets (Ravitch, 2010).

Second, Atwood's Gilead and the U.S. Congress, both, by the way, male dominated, responded to these concerns with increased control over women, explicitly regulated control in the case of Gilead, implicitly by NCLB mandates. Women in Gilead were viewed as "defective," and thus in need of policing and "Re-Education" about their single purpose in life—that of giving birth to healthy children (Atwood, 1986 p. 204). Under NCLB, teachers, 83% of whom are women, are seen as ineffective and inadequate, and thus need to be "held accountable," and to become "highly qualified" in order to produce contributing citizens in a strong and viable economy (Planty et. al, 2008). Finally, governing bodies in both *The Handmaid's Tale* and NCLB use discourses of safety and security as rationale for their legislative mandates of regulation and control.

Dystopian literature is useful for educational policy critiques because it "exaggerates our modern context so that we can challenge it" (Wilkinson, 2010, p. 22). Atwood usefully delineates the genealogy of dystopias, and she suggests that science fiction writing can do specific things that other genres cannot. She asserts that science fiction has the potential to "explore the consequences of new and proposed technologies in graphic ways, by showing them fully up and running" and it can also "explore proposed changes in social organization in graphic ways, by showing what they might be like for those living under them" (Atwood, 2004, p. 515). Feminist dystopian literature is especially poignant on this count because it often highlights structural issues of racism, classism, and sexism that other dystopian literature either ignores or marginalizes (Ketterer, 1989).

Specifically, feminist dystopian literature is particularly useful in relation to educational policy because it can be used to explore the structural and individual ways in which gender regimes are potentially oppressive and often unjust. Historically, the majority of novels within dystopian literature have been written by men, and they highlight the point of view of men (Atwood, 2004). As Booker (1994) elaborates,

> Some prejudices and conventions are more difficult to overcome than others, and the lack of genuine attention to gender issues in so many utopian and dystopian works right up to the present day suggests that patriarchal habits are among the most ingrained of all of the characteristics of Western civilization. (p. 338)

Often, women in these dystopian novels are portrayed as "either sexless automatons or rebels who've defied the sex rules of the regime" (Atwood, 2004, p. 516). *The Handmaid's Tale* defied that historical trend, and it has consequently been widely classified as a feminist dystopia (Booker, 1994; Ketterer, 1989; Tolan, 2005). Although Margaret Atwood is known for writing biting and intricate feminist critiques of culture through both her fiction and nonfiction, she challenged the automatic categorization of *The Handmaid's Tale* as feminist by explaining her intention in writing the novel:

> I wanted to try a dystopia from the female point of view—the world according to Julia [from *Brave new world*], as it were. However, this does not make *The Handmaid's Tale* a "feminist dystopia," except insofar as giving a woman a voice and an inner life will always be considered "feminist" by those who think women ought not to have these things. (Atwood, 2004, p. 516)

Regardless of her intentions, we suggest the novel functions in feminist ways by pointing to potential logical trajectories of patriarchal institutions, ideals, and practices enacted under the modern welfare state's increasing engagement in "caring" for the physical and emotional well-being of its population.

Atwood's Gilead exercises its power over its population through its "caring" concern for the continuation of the species and women's safety. In framing the future of Gilead's society as dependent on the safe and secure functioning of women's reproductive capabilities, Atwood's feminist dystopia highlights plausible futures by taking seriously structural and individual issues related to gender and sexuality. Feminist dystopias are especially productive to utilize when engaging in educational critiques because of the highly gendered history of teaching and education.

BRIEF PLOT SUMMARY OF *THE HANDMAID'S TALE*

The novel takes place in the near future in what used to be Cambridge, Massachusetts. The Republic of Gilead was established after a staged Islamic terrorist attack by members of a movement calling themselves the Sons of Jacob. The movement killed the president and most of the members of Congress, and immediately took control of governmental properties and duties. Gilead is based in right-wing, Christian fundamentalist values and practices, and the government used fear and propaganda in order to make a seemingly smooth transition into power. After consolidating its power, the new government immediately began to curtail certain citizens' rights through their control and manipulation of electronic banking. Women and other "undesirables" were stripped of their rights slowly, which culminated in the circumstances in which the main story takes places.

The story centers around the experiences of a 33-year-old woman called Offred; her birth name is never revealed, and Offred (a patronymic name meaning Of Fred) was the name given to her by the new regime. The narrative is made up of Offred's taped accounts and recollections, so readers are able to juxtapose Offred's life before the military coup to her current circumstances. This also allows the reader to understand how her life and circumstances shifted so dramatically in a relatively short amount of time. Through Offred's story, the reader learns that Gilead passed a number of laws that denied women jobs, property, money, and access to printed material of any kind. After these laws were passed, all of the women who were not put into the categories of Wives, Widows or Econo-wives were distributed into four groups: (1) women with viable ovaries were called Handmaids and were assigned to a Commander and his sterile wife; (2) women who were post-menopausal or unmarried and sterile were called Aunts and their job was to indoctrinate and police the Handmaids; (3) women who were deemed part of the underclass (readers are led to assume that these were mostly women of color and other women not deemed suitable to reproduce) were called Marthas, and they served the Handmaids and Commander; (4) women who did not fit any of the above categories who were not put to death were called Unwomen, and they were usually given the job of cleaning up toxic waste which was considered a death sentence.

Offred served as a Handmaid to a high-ranking Commander who presumably had a significant amount of influence in the creation and maintenance of Gilead after the military coup. Offred, like all other women in Gilead, has no autonomy. She is strictly monitored, and every activity that she is allowed to participate in is heavily surveilled, and all activities are usually centered on the protection and/or utilization of fertility. Although it is strictly forbidden for Offred to have any kind of relationship with the Commander outside of The Ceremony, the Commander begins to bring her to his office to play Scrabble. Here, he allows her to read, now an illegal activity for women.

Towards the middle of the novel, Offred's walking partner, Ofglen (another Handmaid), takes an enormous risk and tells Offred about a secret resistance movement called Mayday. Weeks later, Ofglen is dead, and suicide is suspected. At the end of the novel, the Commander's wife finds out that Offred had been meeting secretly with the Commander, and the novel ends with Offred being taken away by the secret police, called the Eyes. The reader is left uncertain as to whether Offred is being liberated by members of the resistance movement, or if she is being taken away by the government in order to be executed for her illegal activities and relationships. Thus Atwood closes the novel in uncertainty as to Offred's fate, but she clearly illustrates the power of unseen forces to surveil and discipline unruly bodies such as Offred's and Ofglen's in order to maintain the security of Gilead. Similarly, Foucault engages this notion of unseen power as pastoral power and its effects on those in its purview in the name of responsibility and security.

CONCEPTUAL FRAMEWORK: FEMINIST POSTSTRUCTURALISM AND PASTORAL POWER

Foucault (1972/1980) theorized that contemporary modern day power is decentered and amorphous. It does not act as a one-way force exerted from an originary source; it is enacted through networks of power relations in and through modern social and cultural institutions to shape and construct "docile" bodies and individuals, and "inserts itself into their actions and attitudes, their discourses, learning processes and everyday lives" (p. 39). Pastoral power figures in Foucault's (2004/2007) work as a specific form of power descriptive of the paternal and hierarchical relationships extended through governments' various institutions charged with governance and regulatory responsibilities in ensuring the security of their population.

According to Foucault, pastoral power traces its genealogy to the Christian church's development of the pastorate and provides a uniquely Western precursor to the "government mentality," or "governmentality" of the modern welfare state (Graham & Neu, 2004; Foucault, 2004/2007). Modern progressive government welfare states, rather than wielding sovereign power directly over bodies of their populations, use pastoral power's technologies of salvation, self-sacrifice, individualization, and surveillance with confession in order to manage and control populations. These technologies construct procedures and practices to shape individuals into a "new form ... submitted to a set of very specific patterns" whereby they can be integrated into a totalized collective manageable by the state (Foucault, 1982, p. 783). This renders the population accountable to and controllable by governmental or institutional agencies. The exercise of these technologies is carried out as an extension of the government's care and concern that individuals be integrated into and subjected to the collective population, and moves it in the direction of progress—economic, social, cultural, scientific, technical, political—deemed appropriate by governmental leadership in order to maintain order and security.

Many feminist poststructuralist scholars, despite some feminist critiques of Foucault's work, find Foucault's theorization of a decentered power useful and productive for describing how power works in feminist critiques (Diamond & Quimby, 1988; McLaren, 2002; Ramazanoglu, 1993). Foucault's conceptualization of decentered power as sets of relations working among and through individuals and institutions, as well as through entanglements with governments, makes possible a critique of gender as constitutive of and constituted through those sets of political relations. It is the relations themselves that are gendered and that produce and articulate gender. Thinking of power as sets of relations recognizes and gives support for feminist poststructuralism's concern with critiquing and destabilizing gendered relations of power that sustain women's oppression and marginalization. Further, feminist scholars point out that, as subjects can be differentiated by their potential for actions, even power that is conceptualized as decentered can be leveraged differentially and unequally (MacLeod & Durrheim, 2002; McLaren, 2002). This observation makes possible the appropriation and articulation of Foucault's (2002) theories of power for feminist critical goals. MacLeod and Durrheim (2002) conclude,

> Thus the fact that power is not held by any person or group and does not operate from a centre does not mean that people and groups are positioned equally within it or that global forms of domination cannot be spoken about. For feminism this means that enmeshment in patriarchal culture can be acknowledged. (p. 44)

Finally, Foucault's (1982) specifying that power requires "acting subject/s" whose potential for action is precisely the reason they are subject to the power relations, supports our paralleling NCLB and *The Handmaid's Tale*, as suppression and regulation of teachers and women rely on their capabilities to carry out their potential for action. To meet NCLB requirements, teachers must "give birth" to successful citizens who can contribute to U.S. society and economy; for Gilead to ensure its future, women must safeguard their fertility and health and "give birth" to healthy and fertile future citizens.

PASTORAL POWER IN EDUCATION AND *THE HANDMAID'S TALE*

The concept of pastoral power has been used to characterize similar governing, regulatory, and seemingly unassailably benevolent processes and discourses in education (Baker & Heyning, 2004; Foucault, 2004/2007; Graham & Neu, 2004; Popkewitz, 1998). Pastoral power's processes of managing populations through overseeing the inculcation of proper habits, knowledge, and dispositions do not "just look after the whole community (nation), but each individual in particular," with the assumption that what is good for the collective is good for the individual (Toll & Crumpler, 2004, p. 386). Thus, the four technologies—salvation, self-sacrfice, individualization, and surveillance with confession—enable the structuring of procedures and practices that both individualize and totalize in the service of the state.

In what follows, we explore how we see these four technologies operating in both the novel and in NCLB. We separate the four technologies in order to analyze how they exist within the novel and in NCLB. Although we see them as mutually supportive and interrelated, we tease the concepts apart for clarity within the discussion. We conclude the chapter by considering how this analysis of *The Handmaiden's Tale* can be used by teachers and educators to work within and/or resist the externally mandated parameters of NCLB.

Salvation

According to Foucault (1982), individual salvation originally implied the church's investment in leading people to salvation in the "next world" (p. 783). He illustrates how the modern state appropriated this idea and used it in different contexts. Here Foucault discusses the new form of pastoral power utilized by the modern state:

> It was a question no longer of leading people to their salvation in the next world but, rather, ensuring it in this world. And in this context, the word "salvation" takes on different meanings: health, well-being (that is, sufficient wealth, standard of living), security, protection against accidents. (p. 784)

This technology of pastoral power is seen in *The Handmaid's Tale* in a number of ways. The government was heavily invested in maintaining the health and reproductive viability of fertile women because of how thoroughly disease and pollution had decimated the population. They claimed that their policies and practices regulating fertility and reproduction were for the good of both society and women in general, and they did this by suggesting that women were not safe under the government that was overthrown. The government successfully substantially curtailed women's rights in order to control and regulate their fertility by claiming that they were interested and invested in "women's safety." When Offred reminisces about the organization of society before the regime change, she echoes the government's investment in salvation by stating, "Women were not protected then" (Atwood, (1986, p. 24). The government was heavily involved in the salvation of both women and society by regulating procreation through their control of women's bodies, and they did this through heightened security and surveillance of the population. For example, because the government purportedly believed that the survival of the population was at stake, women were not allowed to control when or where they engaged in sexual activity. Instead, the handmaids were expected to regularly report the details of their menstrual cycle, and when they were fertile, they had sexual intercourse with the commander in a public ritual that was heavily surveilled, managed, and controlled.

Similarly, themes of salvation thread throughout the NCLB policy. The policy points its rhetoric towards the salvation of both teachers and students, although these relationships are conceptualized in different ways. As Cochran-Smith and Lytle (2006) suggest, NCLB implies a number of troubling conceptualizations/images of teachers that accuses teachers of inadequate content area knowledge, ignorance of "scientifically based" research practices, and inadequate training. With the implementation of NCLB, the increasing influence of the push for standards and accountability from governmental agencies, policymakers, and professional organizations as well as the momentum from current public discontent about "teacher quality," increased public scrutiny of teachers, and neoliberal threats to university based teacher education programs all point to the lack of trust in teachers and public education and their need to be "saved."

This confluence of factors emphasizes the teachers' integral role in student learning, and directs attention to improving "teachers' dispositions or abilities, so they can better intervene in students' learning processes—think of the standards and rubrics for the obligatory critical self-reflection in teacher education programs" (Taubman, 2009, p. 146). Taubman points out that these political, academic, and societal interests, with the cooperation of professional organizations such as NCATE (National

Council for Accreditation of Teacher Education), place the blame for student failure on "bad teaching," and offer the tonic of "disciplinary technologies and audit practices" to make things right (p. 144). NCLB, with its emphasis on standardized testing and "highly qualified teachers," invests in the idea that teachers are in need of saving via federal and state regulatory regimes.

Similarly, students are conceptualized as being in need of salvation throughout the policy, as exemplified by the name of the policy. The name itself, No Child Left Behind, suggests that children have been, and continue to be, left behind by public education. It then follows that these children are in need of saving, and citizens are left to assume that this is what the policy will attempt to do through mandated standardized testing and public reporting of testing outcomes. By pointing to the failure to close the achievement gap, and the inadequacy of teacher preparation programs, NCLB and related policies suggest that students need to be saved from mediocre, unproductive, "barren" teachers, and the bureaucracy of the public school system.

It is assumed by policymakers, politicians, and citizens, that if we can save teachers and students, we can then save the nation. Bush's first Secretary of Education, Rodney Paige, in response to an Organization for Economic Co-operation and Development report, stated:

> This report documents how little we receive in return for our national investment. This report also reminds us that we are battling two achievement gaps. One is between those being served well by our system and those being left behind. The other is between the U.S. and many of our higher achieving friends around the world. By closing the first gap, we will close the second. (U.S. Department of Education, 2003)

As Paige's comments demonstrate, since the publishing of the report, *A Nation at Risk* (National Commission on Excellence in Education, 1983), many national leaders believe that our nation's international competitiveness and economic security are directly linked to public education. This linkage heightens the pressures on educational policy to show merit for the "national investment," and suggests that teachers have ultimate responsibility for closing both achievement gaps

Self-Sacrifice and Individualization

Self-sacrifice as a technology of pastoral power refers to power that "must also be prepared to sacrifice itself for the life and salvation of the flock" (Foucault 1982, p. 783). Processes of individualization separate, identify, and evaluate individuals for the purposes of integrating them into a totalized collective. Contradictorily, one of the conditions by which individuals subject themselves to the collective is by taking "a new form and ... a set of very specific patterns" determined by the state (p. 783). In *The Handmaid's Tale* and NCLB, personal security as well as the preservation of the collective expect and demand individuals' relinquishment of self, desire, and "the freedom to choose." Since the notion of self-sacrifice works particularly closely, and in tension, with the processes of individualization, both technologies will be discussed in this section.

Atwood uses Offred's name to depict not only her assignment to Fred, but to mark her sacrifice of individuality by evoking the words "offered" or "offering." The individualizing tactics of the close personal monitoring of Offred's menstrual cycles, diet, exercise, behavior, and monthly doctor visits subject her to the collective as an offering or sacrifice for the good of all. In fact, such self-sacrifice—giving up of self, desire, and the "freedom to choose" for the good of others—runs as a theme in the Aunts' re-education of the handmaids at Gilead's Red Center. The Aunts alternately praise and coerce (wearing cattle prods on their belts) the women into accepting their moral "duty" and obeying the strict rules for handmaids' dress and deportment. Self-sacrifice for Gilead's handmaids centers on their lives, desires, and identities being reduced to their reproductive capabilities. Offred observes that handmaids are desexualized and expected to have no desire: "We are for breeding purposes ... no room is to be permitted for the flowering of secret lusts...there are no toeholds for love.... We are two-legged wombs, that's all: sacred vessels, ambulatory chalices" (Atwood, 1986, p. 136).

In prior times, "the days of anarchy," according to Aunt Lydia, women had "freedom to"—as in freedom to choose (Atwood, 1986, p. 24). The consequences of "too much freedom" left them vulnerable to immorality, physical assault and violence, allowed for civic instability, and feminist protests. Gilead ensures "women's safety" in compelling (coercing) them to give up their freedom to choose in favor of their freedom from violence and death, and consent to accept the restraints of "freedom from." This "freedom from" was the focus of women's "re-education" or as Offred says later, indoctrination. The handmaids' moral and self-sacrificing service to Gilead is contrasted with the Unwomen—feminists who in the previous government exercised their freedom to choose birth control, sexual partners, political affiliations, or abortions. In these earlier days, they marched for women's rights, publicly protested male violence against women, and loudly challenged the prevalence of pornography. Aunt Lydia condemned such behavior as immoral and irresponsible, "Jezebels! Scorning God's gifts ... such wickedness. They were lazy women.... They were sluts" (p. 113). She pointed out that just as the assaults and violence towards women emerged as a consequence of the freedom to choose, the immorality of birth control and abortions were reprehensible consequences of the freedom to choose. Aunt Lydia summarizes, "There is more than one kind of freedom ... freedom to and freedom from. In the days of anarchy, it was freedom to. Now you are being given freedom from. Don't underrate it" (p. 24).

Teachers face their own loss of autonomy and individuality through individualizing processes of accountability's "audit culture" (Taubman, 2009) that demand forms of self-sacrifice. Teachers successes or failures are singled out through regularly scheduled progress monitoring of their students' formative assessments, grade level data meetings in which individual teacher's students' progress is discussed, and, for some, frequent reports to principals on student progress and teachers' records of intervention. These individualizing tactics open up teachers' practice to the school community for collective scrutiny so that a public gaze is directed to each teacher's instructional practice and learner "outcomes." These feed into the collective of their schools as the schools take actions to maintain or meet average yearly progress (AYP) (state determined performance standards), or avoid state intervention or takeover, and hold the potential for increased job security. As a result, numerous studies have documented some egregious practices such as districts directing teachers to target the average or just below average performing students for increased instructional time and attention in order to raise their test scores and to "do what they can" for the lowest performing students put in place to reach these state determined performance standards. Researchers have identified such practices as "educational triage," or "target practice," and the "collateral damage" they bring about as consequences of district-led strategies enacted at all levels to "meet AYP" (Atkinson, 2012; Booher-Jennings, 2006; Gillborn & Youdell, 2000; Haladyna, 2008; Lipman, 2004; Madaus & Russell, 2010; Nichols & Berliner, 2007).

Under NCLB, teachers find themselves sacrificing desire for autonomy as professionals and freedom to select, design and evaluate pedagogy and curriculum ostensibly for the sake of their schools, and for the sake of their students' performance on standardized tests. Many districts have adopted what has been called "scripted curriculum" in math and reading that require strict adherence to the script provided each lesson (Achinstein & Ogawa, 2006; Beatty, 2011, Shulman, 2004). Struggling schools, especially those in low socioeconomic areas, are required to adopt these "scientifically-based" programs approved by the U.S. Department of Education for purchase by Title I funds (Beatty, 2011). These programs literally put words in teachers' mouths; teachers' own elaborations based on experience and the wisdom of practice or illustrative examples are strongly discouraged.

Furthermore, many districts require that teachers follow a "pacing guide" to ensure that all content assessed in the state tests has been presented in the classroom. In a recently published qualitative study, "Target practice: Reader response theory and teachers' interpretations of students' SAT 10 scores in data based professional development," four of nine teachers interviewed about how test scores affect their teaching identified district mandated, and for some, state mandated practice that precluded their own participation in curriculum making (Atkinson, 2012). Several stated that teachers were not allowed to "bring anything inside the program." A third grade teacher in the study expressed frustration at being directed to change his teaching but "(they're) not giving me room to change because I have to follow a program." Even data meetings, intended to be collaborations among professionals sharing data, are scripted, and silence teachers' voices, as noted by another teacher: "Most of the time they (data meetings) were scripted—she (Reading Coach) knew what she wanted to say" (p. 208). It is not too much of a stretch to think of this dehumanized and standardized approach to be a form of teaching by remote control. Despite the presence of the teacher's body and mind in the classroom, and all the experience, knowledge, and wisdom of practice s/he embodies, the publishers and state departments of education actually determine instruction and content. It parallels a similar surrogacy central to Gilead's repopulation strategy.

The moral implications of these practices surface in the language used to describe teachers' compliance with scripted curriculum in terms of "fidelity." Teachers' fidelity to the scripted curriculum is monitored closely by representatives from the curriculum publishers, and by computer delivered and administered formative assessments that report student performance to the publisher and the principal. The lack of student progress is blamed on the students or the teacher's lack of fidelity, or "unfaithfulness" to the pacing and content of the curriculum script (Achinstein & Ogawa, 2006). So, teachers who deviate from the script commit adultery? The irony of this does not escape many teachers, an observation offered anecdotally. In one of the classes taught by the author (Atkinson), a teacher was heard to say that she and her colleague refer to themselves as the "Scarlet A's" when they get off track. A comment such as this brings into relief the startling resonance between the positioning of the handmaids in the novel and teachers in the educational policy, and their exploitation enacted in a morally bankrupt climate of self-interest and self-protection maintained by policymakers and many educational leaders at the expense of the most vulnerable, the "docile bodies" of the students, and, to some extent, the teachers.

Surveillance With Confession

According to Foucault (1982), the final technology of pastoral power concerns particular conceptualizations and regulations of the individual, or the subject, and the need for the individual to engage in acts of confession in order for his/her thoughts and intentions to be known. We understand the fourth form of pastoral power as one that necessitates surveillance and regulation. Foucault states that pastoral power "is a form of power that looks after not just the whole community but each individual in particular, during his entire life" (p. 784). This implies the state's investment in surveillance of the individualized subjects in order to monitor and regulate thoughts and actions. Foucault suggests that pastoral power "cannot be exercised without knowing the inside of people's minds, without exploring their souls, without making them reveal their innermost secrets. It implies a knowledge of the conscience and an ability to direct it" (p. 784).

This last form of pastoral power is easily identified within *The Handmaid's Tale*. As has been illustrated throughout this chapter, the men in power, those in charge of creating and maintaining the new laws and rules for social behavior, were overtly invested in regulating and surveilling women's bodies and minds. The men of Gilead created the society so that they could always watch and monitor women's movements and bodies. The republic of Gilead was more than a physical space—it was a way of life that was designed around the control of women and reproduction. "'The Republic of Gilead,' said Aunt Lydia, 'knows no bounds. Gilead is within you'" (Atwood, 1986, p. 23).

The government went to great lengths to re-educate women so that they internalized their new form of subjectification. For example, as mentioned earlier, the handmaids were not allowed to see or talk to anyone they knew from their lives before the military coup. Offred had a daughter before the instatement of Gilead; she was not able to see her daughter, nor did she know anything about what happened to her daughter after the military coup. Similarly, she was not allowed to make friends or have any free time during which to socialize. Additionally, the men in charge of the regime believed that reading was a temptation that would make the handmaids unhappy with their lives, and so they were not allowed to read books or magazines or any kind of printed material. The regime went so far as to physically restrain the handmaid's field of vision when they went on walks to organized and tightly controlled events. Offred is required to wear wings on her head: "The white wings too are prescribed issue; they are to keep us from seeing, but also from being seen" (Atwood, 1986, p. 8). The handmaids, and all people within Gilead, were expected to report (read: confess) any inappropriate conversations or actions of anyone with whom they came into contact.

Under NCLB, teachers and students are constantly under surveillance so as to monitor student "progress" and achievement/merit. NCLB claims to create high standards for all students through its use of standardized testing and its insistence that all teachers conform to its definition of "highly qualified." Standardized test scores are used to measure and evaluate teachers, administrators, schools, and states. Test scores are conceptualized as being a direct reflection of the quality of instruction in which teachers are engaging. The numbers, or data, are a form of surveillance in that they are used by policymakers, politicians, and parents to monitor, judge, and regulate teachers. Similarly, test scores allow politicians and administrators to argue for merit pay. Merit pay codifies the methods of surveillance used by the government. Merit pay bases teachers' pay on test scores, and it further institutionalizes the strict surveillance via test scores that so many teachers find unfair and simplistic (Giroux, 2011; Larsen, 2005).

Further, in 2009, the policy of NCLB began to morph into various iterations, all with similar practices related to surveillance and covert control of teachers and schools. The newest national educational policy/plan, Race to the Top, was a purported improvement to NCLB put forth by President Obama and his secretary of education, Arne Duncan (U.S. Department of Education, 2009). It was a $4.35 billion dollar contest that rewarded states that complied with the policy's aims and goals, which included improving teacher performance, increasing test scores, increasing the number of charter schools in the state, and complying with standardized curriculum. States found themselves into forced competition in order to vie for money and grants. Money would only be rewarded to states if they could lay out an improvement plan for their educational system, and improvement was defined and predetermined by the creators of Race to the Top. States were required to illustrate how they would successfully surveil their school districts in order to regulate their practices and policies all in the name of increasing test scores. Although policymakers boasted about reforming NCLB in order to respond to the complaints about the policy from teachers, administrators, and parents, Race to the Top employs almost identical tactics, namely the threat/promise of money for schools and a reliance on test scores, in order to ensure compliance from teachers and administrators (Carr & Porfilio, 2011).

CONCLUSION

We conclude by pointing to the ways that Atwood's heroine, Offred, found ways to do as Foucault (1982) suggested: "Maybe the target nowadays is not to discover what we are but to refuse what we are" (p. 785), despite governmental wielding of the four technologies that would remove desire, self, and autonomy from her. We find that her covert refusal to believe the Gilead rhetoric while obeying its dictates and taking advantage of the disruptive gaps available to her suggests ways that teachers can refuse the reductive subjectivity shaped for them by NCLB policy and practices, and move into openings through which they can form new subjectivities.

Throughout the story, Offred repeatedly refused what she was being shaped to be by cultivating subjectivities that allowed her to subvert and resist the codified renderings placed on her by Gilead's patriarchal regime. Offred formed multiple relationships with others in Gilead, both romantic and platonic, and in these relations she found ways to rupture the preformed identities created for her by the men of Gilead. She was able to form an alliance with her walking partner, Ofglen, from whom she learned about the resistance movement. Ofglen and Offred worked together to create space and time during which they could relate to one another as subjects; they defied Gilead's insistence on being objectified bodies that existed only for procreation purposes, and instead they created a relationship through which they could pass along critical information and ask forbidden questions about the regime.

Similarly, rather than acquiescing to being a body preserved exclusively for procreative purposes for her "owner," Offred flagrantly slept with a body guard, and during these times shared memories that would have been deemed dangerous and inappropriate by the regime. She also formed a more intimate, but forbidden, relationship with her owner, the Commander. By so doing, Offred was able to read and have relatively provocative and stimulating conversations which were expressly forbidden by the regime. Because the Commander had the freedom to exercise certain of his wants and desires for Offred to fulfill, she finds opportunities to exercise a freedom of choice, small though they are. Offred recognized the restraints for what they were, but worked within them to form relationships and gain information that led to her escape plan. Offred ultimately does *get away* in some sense of the word. Even though the ending to her story is ambiguous, the account of what she called her "reconstruction," survived to tell the story.

Finally, even though she was to have no desires other than to have a child for Gilead, she repeatedly expressed desires for her lost daughter, her exiled mother, her disappeared husband. We suggest that even as Offred seemed to be agreeing with Gilead's mandates throughout the novel, the stories she tells and her cynical reflections help the reader see that she does not buy it all, that she is able to critically analyze her situation and resist in contextually useful and productive ways.

Just as Offred found and created space within which to resist surveillance and regulation, teachers can refuse to be the technicians they are being pushed to be by seeking out critical and creative ways to resist the regulatory mandates placed on them by policies such as NCLB and Race to the Top. Teachers can recognize that their potential for action is what they have some control over to the extent that they can speak up and suggest changes to some of the egregious practices in which they are compelled to participate. For example, as some have already done, teachers can learn how to read accountability data analytically and critically, and then talk with colleagues about its political implications instead of blindly and uncritically following district directions. Further, teachers can resist the individualizing features of accountability policies that separate and put them in competition with each other by allying with colleagues to research and use available resources found in critical teaching networks, professional organizations, and teachers' accounts of their grappling with NCLB mandates. Educators can become informed collectively about the contending views of the nature and value of the evidence-based research used by various "experts" to legitimate their curriculum programs and delegitimize teachers' knowledge of their students and wisdom of practice.

Colleges of education should move towards working to provide space for these kinds of critical conversations, and undergraduate and graduate classes should push preservice and practicing teachers to engage in thoughtful and deliberate acts of resistance that benefit the teachers and students. For example, colleges of education can help teachers simultaneously negotiate the politics of their schools and states while encouraging fellow teachers and their students to critically analyze the assumptions inherent in common school policies, such as reliance on standardized test scores. These kinds of acts of resistance cannot be determined outside of the cultural and political context of a teacher's specific school; rather, colleges of education must be prepared to respond to each individual teacher's context, while encouraging teachers to share their experiences of their localized responses to NCLB.

By situating the plight of women within Gilead next to the plight of teachers under NCLB, we have sought to contribute to the ongoing scholarly critique of NCLB. We suggest that this feminist Foucauldian critique through feminist dystopian literature offers new ways to raise questions not only about NCLB, but about the workings of various power relations in the ongoing gendering of teaching. This feminist appropriation of pastoral power highlights the ways in which decentralized power relations inform and influence teachers and students, and in so doing, also point to how they can therefore be destabilized. This work reminds us that our own potential for action is what these various technologies depend on in order to activate and sustain the power relations in which we are all entangled. But, it is the same potential for action that can redirect, refocus, deviate, transgress, even promiscuously deviate, that offers opportunities for new subjectivities through which changed action and hope emerge.

REFERENCES

Achinstein, B., & Ogawa, R.T. (2006). (In)fidelity: What the resistance of new teachers reveals about professional principles and prescriptive educational policies. *Harvard Educational Review, 76*(1), 30-63.

Atkinson, B. (2012). Target practice: Reader Response theory and teachers' interpretations of students' SAT 10 scores in data based professional development. *Journal of Teacher Education, 63*(3), 201-213.

Atwood, M. (1986). *The handmaid's tale.* Toronto, Canada: O. W. Toad.

Atwood, M. (2004). The handmaid's tale and Oryx and crake "in context." *PMLA, 19*(3), 513-517.

Baker, B., & Heyning, K. (Eds.). (2004). *Dangerous coagulations?: The uses of Foucault in the study of education.* New York, NY: Peter Lang.

Beatty, B. (2011). The dilemma of scripted instruction—Comparing teacher autonomy, fidelity, and resistance in the Froebelian kindergarten, Montessori, Direct Instruction, and Success for All. *Teachers College Record, 113*(3), 395-430.

Booher-Jennings, D. (2006, June). Rationing education in an era of accountability. *Phi Delta Kappan,* 756-761.

Booker, M. K. (1994). Woman on the edge of a genre: The feminist dystopias of Marge Piercy. *Science Fiction Studies, 21*(3), 337-350.

Carr, P. R., & Porfilio, B. J. (Eds.). (2011). *The phenomenon of Obama and the agenda for education: Can hope audaciously trump neoliberalism?* Charlotte, NC: Information Age Publishing.

Cochran-Smith, M., & Lytle, S. L. (2006). Troubling images of teaching in No Child Left Behind. *Harvard Educational Review, 76*(4), 668-697.

Darling-Hammond, L. (2007). Race, inequality, and educational accountability: The irony of "No Child Left Behind." *Race, Ethnicity, and Education, 10*(3), 245-260.

Diamond, I., & Quimby, L. (Eds.). (1988). *Feminism and Foucault: Reflections on resistance.* Boston, MA: Northeastern University Press.

Foucault, M. (1982). The subject and power. *Critical Inquiry, 8*(4), 777-795.

Foucault, M. (1980). *Power/knowledge: Selected interviews and other writings 1972-1977.* New York, NY: Pantheon Books. (Original work published 1972)

Foucault, M. (2007). *Security, territory, population: Lectures at the College de France 1977-1978.* (G. Burchell, Trans.). New York, NY: Picador. (Original work published 2004)

Gay, G. (2007). The rhetoric and reality of NCLB. *Race, Ethnicity, and Education, 10*(3), 279-293.

Gillborn, G., & Youdell, D. (2000). *Rationing education: Policy, practice, reform, and equity.* Buckingham, England: Open University Press.

Giroux, H. (1988). *Teachers as intellectuals: Toward a critical pedagogy of learning.* Westport, CT: Bergin & Garvey .

Giroux, G. (2011). *Education and the crisis of public values.* New York, NY: Peter Lang Publishing, Inc.

Graham, C., & Neu, D. (2004). Standardized testing and the construction of governable persons. *Journal of Curriculum Studies, 36*(3), 295-319.

Haladyna, T. (2006). The perils of standardized achievement testing. *Educational Horizons 85*(1), 30-43.

Ketterer, D. (1989). "*The Handmaid's Tale*": A contextual dystopia. *Science Fiction Studies, 16*(2), 209-217.

Larsen, M. (2005). A critical analysis of teacher evaluation policy trends. *Australian Journal of Education, 49*(3), 292-305.

Lipman, P. (2004). *High stakes education: Inequality, globalization, and urban school reform.* New York, NY: Routledge.

Macleod, C., & Durrheim, K. (2002). Foucauldian feminism: The implications of governmentality. *Journal for the Theory of Social Behavior, 32*(1), 41-60.

Madaus, G., & Russell, M. (2010). Paradoxes of high-stakes testing. *Journal of Education, 190*(1/2), 21-20.

McLaren, M. (2002. *Feminism, Foucault and Embodied Subjectivity.* Buffalo, NY: State University of New York Press.

National Commission on Excellence in Education. (1983). *A nation at risk: The imperative for educational reform.* Washington, DC: U.S. Government Printing Office.

Nichols, S., & Berliner, D. (2007). *Collateral damage: How high stakes testing corrupts America's schools.* Boston, MA: Harvard Education Press.

Planty, M., Hussar, W., Snyder, T., Provasnik, S., Kena, G., Dinkes, R., et al. (2008). *The condition of education 2008* (NCES 2008-031). Washington, DC: National Center for Educational Statistics.

Popkewitz, T. (1998). *Struggling for the soul: The politics of schooling and the construction of the teacher.* New York, NY: Teachers College Press.

Ramazanoglu, C. (Ed.). (1993). *Up against Foucault: Explorations of some tensions between Foucault and feminism.* London, England: Routledge.

Ravitch, D. (2010). *The death and life of the great American school system: How testing and choice are undermining education.* New York, NY: Basic Books.

St. Pierre, E. A. (2004). Refusing alternatives: A science of contestation. *Qualitative Inquiry, 10*(1), 130-139.

Shulman, L. S. (2004). Autonomy and obligation: The remote control of teaching. In L Shulman (Ed.), *The wisdom of* practice (pp. 133-164). San Francisco, CA: Jossey-Bass.

Taubman, P. M. (2009). *Teaching by numbers: Deconstructing the discourse of standards and accountability in education.* London, England: Routledge.

Tolan, F. (2005). Feminist utopias and questions of liberty: Margaret Atwood's *The handmaid's tale* as critique of second wave feminism. *Women: A Cultural Review, 16*(1), 18-32.

Toll, C. and Crumpler, T. (2004) Everything is dangerous: Pastoral power and university researchers conducting interviews. In B. Baker & K. Heyning (Eds.), *Dangerous coagulations? The uses of Foucault in the study of education.* New York, NY: Peter Lang.

U.S. Department of Education. (2002). *No Child Left Behind PUBLIC LAW* 107–110. Retrieved from http://www2.ed.gov/policy/elsec/leg/esea02/107-110.pdf

U.S. Department of Education. (2003). Education review international report. Retrieved from: http://www.ed.gov/nclb

U.S. Department of Education. (2009). *Race to the Top: Program executive summary.* Retrieved from http://www2.ed.gov/programs/racetothetop/executive-summary.pdf

Wilkinson, R. (2010). Teaching dystopian literature to a consumer class. *English Journal, 99*(3), 22-26.

CHAPTER 16

ALL I REALLY NEEDED TO KNOW ABOUT TOLERANCE I LEARNED FROM ZOMBIES

Nick McDonald and Rick McDonald

INTRODUCTION

We should begin with a brief explanation of how zombie movies—and the wide-scale fascination with all things zombie—constitute one variety of dystopian fiction. If "Utopias" are perfect, fictional, good places and "Dystopias" are fictional worlds of deprivation, evil, and terror, then zombie movies are one of the most prolific contemporary sources of dystopian fiction. The dystopian usually relies on the disruption of a utopian society; in a zombie apocalypse, this disruption occurs in our real world. The numerous oppressive forces present in zombie literature and other dystopian literature demonstrate that utopia is rarely a desirable thing. The zombie apocalypse might appear as not dystopian, but by turning the real world into chaos the zombies create for themselves a new utopian society: the zombies have no strife, no prejudices, and no social problems. Their utopian existence creates a dystopia for the humans who remain.

Dystopian fiction typically reveals the partially repressed political and cultural fears about our world in a manner consonant with the current

Dystopia and Education:
Insights Into Theory, Praxis, and Policy in an Age of Utopia-Gone-Wrong, pp. 249–264

reception of horror stories in general and the zombie genre in particular. Beyond the gore and splatter of the typical zombie movie lie specific insights into how our contemporary world has strayed into the dystopian. Furthermore, the survivalist fantasies engaged by most zombie movies strongly resonates with contemporary groups that believe a biblical or political catastrophe will devastate society within our lifetime and plan to survive the ensuing chaos. Zombies represent the hidden fears of our eventual societal collapse brought to fruition by practices such as the tolerance for unworthy others—others whose alterity we assume radically threatens our own existence.

We never intended to write an essay on tolerance or the state of tolerance education in popular culture; we sort of fell into it, barely noticing we were flailing around in the waters of popular arguments about tolerance, like so many zombies in Ridley's swimming pool during *Dairy of the Dead* (Romero, Grunwald, Engelbardt, Spiegel, Fireman, Harrison, & Katz, 2007). Being father and son, we love to argue, and zombies are our meat and potatoes, so we decided to debate the changing attitudes towards zombies as part of a presentation at the 2010 Popular Culture Association. Eventually, we realized that the zombie-movie pandemic sweeping our culture over the last 10 (at least, but possibly 40) years had itself been infected by a broad spectrum of disease about otherness within popular culture.

Because zombie movies are fodder for the masses, and because the creative intellects behind them wanted to do more than merely scare us, by necessity storylines developed that commented upon issues which circulate freely in popular culture. As a result, the tie between zombies and notions of respect for the "other" has always had some part in the zombie genre. The movie which, for most, started it all, *Night of the Living Dead* (Hardman & Streiner, 1968), clearly carried tolerance as one of its initial messages, and although its racial tolerance differs significantly from the "racial" tolerance suggested by *Fido*, the social commentary is generally agreed to be similar (Carlson, 2007).

The United Nations Educational, Scientific, and Cultural Organization's (UNESCO) numerous statements on the importance of tolerance and teaching tolerance to promote peace in our world substantiate that this issue is an international concern, and the considerable attention paid to tolerance education in U.S. educational journals over the last 20 years reveals its particular importance to educators within this country. Although the debates about what constitutes tolerance and how to teach it still can be found within the pages of such academic journals as *Teaching Tolerance, Educational Philosophy, The Review of Education/Pedagogy/Cultural Studies,* and *Multicultural Education*, what we have found in our research on the changing perspective on zombies in popular culture may provide valuable new insight into American society's reception of ideas concerning tolerance.

Additionally, since education level often shows little correspondence to the desire for, or popularity of, zombie movies, it may be that the debate on tolerance reflected in zombie movies escapes the causal link between years of schooling and the level of an individual's expressed tolerance (Vogt, 1994, p. 274). With that in mind we present for you an expansion of our original debate on "Zombie Alterity," with appropriate references to pedagogical theories concerning the teaching of tolerance. Possibly, George Romero and his progeny have stumbled upon successful techniques for the exploration of tolerance of alterity which education theorists have overlooked.

THE ZOMBIE CRAZE

With the number of professional and amateur zombie movies growing at a rapid pace, zombie popularity on screen, in games and in books has shed light on some interesting new tensions not readily apparent in the earliest installments of Romero-style classic zombie movies. (Kyle Bishop's, 2009, *Dead Men Still Walking*, documents the steady rise in the making of zombie movies in the first decade of the 21st century.) Films like *Land of the Dead* (Canton, Goldman, & Grunwald, 2005), *Shaun of the Dead* (Park, 2004), *Fido* (Carlson, 2007), *Diary of the Dead* (Romero et al. 2007), *Otto* (LaBruce, Bruning, & Hartman, 2008), the video game *Fallout 3* (Pagliarulo, 2008), *Survival of the Dead* (Devonshire, 2009), and even some elements of the television series *The Walking Dead* (Darabont et al., 2010-2011), present zombies from a perspective wherein some tolerance of their otherness seems to be foregrounded. Contemporary media may be fostering tolerance by presenting complex zombie situations which encourage viewers to reexamine the role of zombies in popular culture.

Today's media seems to recognize the complexity of even our own individual identity; it may not be such a surprise that we accept that zombie identity is similarly multifaceted. The disparate attitudes perceivable in the popular-culture depictions of zombies contain and reflect some of the similarly disparate attitudes about the benefits and detriments of teaching tolerance in our world. Although Fernando Reimers (2006) is a strong advocate for tolerance education, he recognizes that tolerance can be perceived negatively. For those attempting to establish a strong national identity, the "local and national pressures to educate for community, national identity and work compete with the pressure to educate for global civility within the normative framework common to all nations" (p. 290). Tolerance can be perceived as detrimental to individuals and the in-groups to which they belong. With that said let us begin our debate between Father and Son on the nature of alterity and tolerance within the zombie-movie genre.

Son

In many recent films and video games, at least one of the functions that zombies have is to serve as metaphors for disenfranchised minorities. In *Raising the Dead,* Kyle Bishop (2006) calls zombies "the ultimate foreign other" (p. 201). Their possible representation of "marginalized others" quite rightly calls into question whether or not people should go out of their way to kill them. Zombies signify much more than simply walking, reanimated corpses. In many cases they represent people—types of people that we may not like, or may not understand.

With an increasing emphasis on diversity in our modern world there are many formerly disenfranchised groups of people that have recently begun to gain acceptance. For some people this means recognition of groups they might be uncomfortable around, and as much as we like to wish that we would not have to deal with people we don't like and don't understand, there is no way of completely avoiding them. Symbolically killing these people is not the worst thing a person can do, but symbolic action can, in time, have real effects. As H. C. Werner Weidenfield (2002) explains concerning tolerance education in Europe:

> profound political cultural and social changes are leading to a pluralization of lifestyles, the disappearance of traditional environments and social groups as well as the emergence of new multiethnic and multicultural societies. As a result, people with often fundamentally different value systems and life styles live together and next to each other.... Against this backdrop educators and education policy makers are faced with the crucial task of creating concepts and learning environments that foster the skills and abilities indispensable for a peaceful life in a world of diversity. (p. 95)

Oddly enough, I believe the zombie genre has taken up this consideration of difference and offered some possibilities for how to treat the radically other with tolerance. Don't misunderstand me, if people are being attacked by zombies, then they should defend themselves; but this begs the question of whether characters kill zombies because the zombies put them in danger or because of the alterity of the zombies.

In some of the most recent films and games, "the living" are murderous aggressors who could just as easily accomplish their goals by leaving the zombies alone. Let me explain: in George Romero's fourth "Living Dead" movie—*Land of the Dead*—the zombie called "Big Daddy" seems like he would have been content to walk back and forth between his office in the gas station and the gas pump all day long (Canton, Goldman, & Grunwald, 2005). The zombies in his town—who later seem to look to him for governance—appear to be enjoying a lovely day; they are happily walking the human-free streets of their town, and a zombie band is playing at the town's bandstand. Into this utopian setting comes a brutal group of killers—the humans.

The violence begins just so the humans can loot the shops in the town. The brutal human gang rolls into town guns blazing. The humans know they did not need to drive through the town and kill zombies; they have clearly had past success distracting the zombies using fireworks. They stood to gain nothing by killing the zombies and ultimately doing this causes the zombies to retaliate out of vengeance. Had they left the zombies alone then, their own city would have never been attacked. (Clearly, different possible interpretations of this scene exist, most notably in Meghan Sutherland's (2007) "Rigor/Mortis: The Industrial Life of Style in American Zombie Cinema" where she reads the scene as a recognition of the stagnation inherent in zombie existence.) Regardless of whether the zombies represent stagnation or if they are content with their "unlives," it is the zombies, and not the humans, who act in self-defense. The humans in this scene act out of a hatred of the zombie's otherness; the zombies are merely reacting to the violent provocation of the humans.

Father

I agree that zombie movies comment on issues important to our actual world. Most critics believe that Romero is commenting on "Race" in *Night of the Living Dead (*Hardman & Streiner, 1968), "Consumerism" in *Dawn of the Dead (*Rubinstein, Argento, & Cuomo, 1978), and "the Military Industrial Complex" in *Day of the Dead* (Rubenstein, 1985), but casting the zombies in a sympathetic role goes far beyond using the destruction and chaos they cause to comment on the misplaced priorities within human society.

Even something as acceptable as teaching people to respect the differences of others who live in their world can be utterly problematic; Reimers (2006) points out in "Citizenship, Identity and Education" that tolerance education often butts up against the governmental forces which serve as its benefactors, explaining "national identity is often constructed by opposition to 'others'"(p. 289). The result being that at least some facets of the government that support tolerance education must struggle with whether their desire for a peaceful, tolerant world can coexist with a desire to further a society's national interests at the expense of other nations.

Many zombie movies deal with people from different backgrounds being given the common identity of survivor, but if we look through the lens of "zombie as other," we change the dystopian nature of the horror from a fear of our inevitable annihilation (whether individual or societal) to a fear of our inherent potential inhumanity. Since the human survivors must show tolerance to other survivors from dissimilar backgrounds and work together with them to rebuild their lives, the story depicts disenfranchised human groups being given the chance to take a place in society which they are normally denied. If we consider the zombies as the excluded minority, this denies the tolerance-affirming action of different human social groups working together toward a common goal.

Accepting the zombies as the group worthy of tolerance could lead to the debilitating realization that as we recognize the inherent value of "the other" we ultimately worsen our individual chances for survival. I prefer a more traditionalist view where zombies are an external threat that fills us with dread. Their desire to destroy us is what makes this variety of horror horrible. For the zombie to be a marginalized other we would need to have denied them some rightful place within human society—we would be oppressing them (whether unwittingly or maliciously). I have a difficult time accepting that you can oppress a creature whose primary goal is to devour you.

Don't get me wrong, I can agree theoretically with the idea that all creatures deserve tolerance. I might even go as far as Elisabet Langmann (2010) and argue that "others" deserve our hospitality in a Derridian/Levinasian sense. Langmann finds that Jacques Derrida and Emmanuel Levinas share similar attitudes about one's ethical responsibility to respond positively the alterity of the other. I agree that hospitality (and/or tolerance) is an ethical responsibility that we should direct toward others, regardless of whether we find their person or behavior, acceptable. As Langmann writes, "Hospitality can be seen as a response to radical difference, that 'troubles identity' and puts the very boundary between host and guest, inside and outside in question" (p. 339).

Nevertheless, I do not believe that zombies can be misunderstood "others" and remain zombies. I guess it becomes a matter of definition. When I say zombies (especially in the context of a discussion of horror movies), I mean reanimated corpses who have an insatiable desire to consume human flesh. If anyone is being oppressed in this scenario, it is us humans, not the zombies. The only potential moments for exposure to tolerance seem for me to be the interactions with other humans and possibly a vicarious awareness of humanity as a threatened minority. Although I can conceive of the rights of the radical other, theoretically, actually welcoming the zombie as other, in some Levinasian sense, seems out of the question in any practical/literal context.

Son

Okay, but you're leaving something out. One of the most important things about zombies is that they ARE us, and so fear of our own inhumanity is always an issue with zombies. Because humans can become zombies, the fear that I could lose my humanity by becoming a zombie is present throughout the genre, as well as my fear of others who have lost their humanity by becoming zombies. One reason people are afraid of zombies is because becoming a zombie is an inevitability in a zombie movie. R. H. W. Dillard (1987) discusses this in his essay on *Night of the Living Dead*. And, to my way of thinking, this makes zombies the natural progression of humanity within the dystopian constructs of the movie.

Zombies represent a loss of humanity that cannot be prevented without killing the zombie. As a result, the desire for zombies to be just misunderstood people is a very human response to them. Zombies are often our neighbors, family, and friends—and are almost inevitably what we will become—Dillard (1987) calls them, "kindred dead" (p. 15). It's the inability to see loved-ones as zombies that does in Barbara from *Night of the Living Dead* when she sees her recently-zombified brother Johnny appear towards the end of the movie (Hardman & Streiner, 1968). Similarly, in *Shaun of the Dead*, Shaun's best friend, Ed, becomes a zombie (Park, 2004). After all the madness of the zombie apocalypse stops, and the people in the world of *Shaun of the Dead* start to put zombies to work, Shaun sets up Ed in the backyard shed so they can continue to play video games: the "otherness" of the zombie is overridden by Shaun's friendship (Park, 2004). People don't like to see their friends and family die, and their friends and family becoming monsters that wish to kill them only makes these deaths harder to deal with. Although our loved-ones may fall victim to the otherness of zombiedom, we don't necessarily change our relation to them as a result.

In our current culture, there are many groups that are slowly achieving greater acceptance and tolerance. These victories have given some people the idea that tolerance has been achieved in every reasonable way—that the next "other" is too strange to ever be accepted. Tolerance, however, is not something which people should be able to decide has been finally achieved; tolerance is an ongoing process. Elisabet Langmann (2010) uses Derrida's concept of hospitality as a substitute for tolerance, arguing: "if we are truly hospitable, Derrida wonders, should we not also welcome the uninvited visitor and not merely the invited guest" (p. 340)? Hospitality, or tolerance, is not a particularly meaningful thing if it only extends to the "invited guest" (a group that has already received tolerance). Extending hospitality to the "uninvited visitor" (a group that has yet to receive tolerance) carries greater weight. For Langmann:

> This experience of not-knowing who, when, or even if the other will arrive is an openness that answers to an ethical demand in the Levinasian sense of infinite responsibility, to welcome and make room for anyone who might stand on the thresholds of our home. Whereas hospitality as a right of invitation is always offered by a sovereign figure of power to an identified and particular someone, hospitality as an ethical response is offered unconditionally to any anonymous stranger, before the other has even been identified as either guest or parasite, either friend or enemy. (p. 341)

When tolerance can be withheld it means that the person giving the tolerance is the one who has the power, and giving up that power is a difficult thing. To do so is to leave oneself vulnerable to whatever the benefactor of the hospitality would do, but often there are times where denying the chance visitor could be just as detrimental as letting them in.

Father

Maybe we've now transitioned into an argument that is more about theory versus practice. I like the concept of hospitality or tolerance, and I accept that they require doing more than just what is convenient. A definition Paul Vogt uses for his 1994 special issue of *The Review of Education Pedagogy/Cultural Studies* runs: "tolerance involves support for the rights and liberties of others, others that one dislikes, disapproves of, disagrees with, finds threatening, or towards whom one otherwise has a negative attitude" (p. 273). We only show tolerance when we accept and welcome people we previously found unacceptable; but, there are practical realities necessary to survival within the fiction of zombie movies.

Romero attempts to have some traditionally authoritative voices direct some of the response toward the living dead within *Night of the Living Dead* and *Dawn of the Dead* (Hardman & Streiner, 1968; Rubinstein, Argento, & Cuomo, 1978). Newscasters repeatedly direct the living to burn the bodies of the newly dead, making clear that the "reality" of the zombie apocalypse does not leave time for the niceties a family might desire for the deceased. Individuals must kill and burn the bodies of the dead as quickly as possible. It does not matter who that zombie was to you, he or she is now just one of the many mortal threats in a dystopian world where the dead come to life.

Although we love our family, friends, and selves, often self-aware human characters in these movies (after they have been bitten) at least consider shooting themselves in the head to ensure that they do not naturally (or un-naturally) make the progression to zombiedom. These suicides deny that zombies are us, that becoming a zombie is inevitable. It is here in this struggle against the near impossibility of continued humanity that the human race makes its finest stand. In a moment of defiance, we spit in the eye of death and zombification. And THIS is why people go to zombie movies.

Against unimaginable odds, and horrifying dangers, humanity wants to believe that if we dig deep, if we try our best we can defeat the forces of evil. It's an emotional catharsis—one that accompanies the cathartic feeling of vicarious action stemming from brutally destroying the brains of our mindless, slow-moving, relentless attackers. In distinguishing between "natural horror" (real horror in our world) and "art horror" (the horror we experience in horror movies), Noel Carroll (1987) explains that it is the thought of the monstrous, not its actual existence, that elicits the emotional response that attracts viewers to horror movies (p. 56). Although he denies horror is legitimately cathartic, he recognizes the mass aesthetic stimulation which art horror arouses (p. 57).

If horror is about facing our fears, zombie horror is about facing and beating back the things that represent those fears. The thrill of vicariously vanquishing evil is one of the addictive properties of horror and is the mainstay of zombie films. This vicarious reveling in the violence of zombie films may be the most difficult element of the zombie-film experience to understand in relation to tolerance, but from one perspective there may be some redeeming qualities. The threat to our existence from some source outside established/living humanity allows us to put aside our differences in order to unite as humans with a common purpose; that is if you see attacking hoards of flesh-eating former humans as something external to humanity.

Son

Okay, but I have to return to this point: one of the main fears in zombie movies is ourselves. The old Locke versus Hobbes question of whether you can trust people when there's no society between you and everyone else. When people are completely free of social rules what will they do? Locke thinks that the reason that humans create society is to make interactions easier, not because they need it to protect them from one another. Hobbes, on the other hand, believes that society is necessary because people must be compelled to get along, and that people would not be able to interact without social barriers protecting them from each other.

Most zombie movies dramatize the position that if societal norms become especially stressed, eventually people will turn on each other. An example from gaming would be in *Fallout 3* where Allistair Tenpenny offers the player significant compensation (500 bottle caps) to destroy a town full of uninfected people because he claims it spoils his view from his upscale apartment complex (Pagliarulo, 2008). Mr. Tenpenny also refuses to allow ghouls (zombies that can still think and do not desire flesh) to enter his tower and occasionally shoots at them with his rifle from his balcony. We see similar irrationally violent behavior in the movie *Dawn of the Dead* when a group of marauders attacks the mall that the heroes have made into their home (Rubinstein, Argento, & Cuomo, 1978). Up until this point the characters had been relatively safe; the zombies were no problem for them; it is other humans who cause them to be destroyed. These examples exemplify humanity's inhumanity and both occur without the zombies being expressively key to the event.

While vanquishing evil is an important part of horror, zombies are rarely evil. To be evil, beings must have knowledge of what they are doing. A shark that eats a person is not evil; it's just hungry. Often the evil in a zombie film is within the people or human society, not the zombies; the zombies are more of an environmental condition. The villain of *Fido* is Mr. Bottoms, the chief of security for Zomcon, and while the zombies factored into the setting of the film, they are not the villains (Carlson, 2006). This is true in many of the traditional zombie movies; in *28 Days Later,* the British soldiers capture several human characters and attempt to force themselves on the women (MacDonald, 2002). In *Day of the Dead*, the main villain is Captain Rhodes and his struggle with the scientists who want to understand the zombies is the main conflict of the film (Rubenstein, 1985). The characters spend most of the movie preparing for their eventual conflict with Captain Rhodes and not really worrying about the zombies except as the plot device that forces them to have to deal with him.

Even in the movies where we don't immediately think about zombie rights, the zombies are not really the "bad guys." The zombies spark the conflict, but they are not usually a direct part of the conflict. In most zombie media, the goal of the humans is not to rebuild society, but to survive. In some ways this is affirming that a space needs to be established for the zombie/other which the previous society did not have. In the essay "Constructive Conflicts," H. C. Weidenfeld (2002) explains:

> The phenomena of intolerance that we are increasingly witnessing today (be it in the form of disinclination to listen to others, growing aggressiveness against socially disadvantaged, old and handicapped people, discrimination of minorities or lack of respect in dealing with foreign nationals) are thus not so much direct consequences of social change caused by modernization. Much more often they are a reaction to the subjectively perceived uncertainty, inadequacy, insecurity and diffuse fear about the future created by that social change. (p. 96)

Individuals need to be forced to interact with people that make them uncomfortable, and their response to that cannot be to shoot the "other" in the head. Our methods of dealing with alterity need to change, because people can no longer isolate themselves from the rest of the world; they must learn to be more comfortable with "the other" and treat them with tolerance.

Father

I can see how a person might argue that characters like Captain Rhodes could use a dose or two of tolerance education; so maybe I can concede that point, but I want to return to your analogy about zombies as just another dangerous species, like sharks. If zombies are like sharks; they're like people-eating sharks that have established their primary feeding area at a popular public beach. Even the most shark-loving of us would demand those sharks be removed somehow, but better yet if we have to give them the status of living organisms, Zombies are like cancer or flesh-eating bacteria. We recognize them as living organisms, and maybe it's okay to study them in a lab, but we don't welcome them into our lives or attempt to introduce them to the general public.

Moreover, I do not agree that zombies are not the focal point of most zombie movies. The movies may be about humans, and specifically about the viewer's reaction to the scene, but I think that reaction is one of fear—and not fear of how inhuman humans can be, but fear of being eaten by a slow-moving army of inevitable, devouring monsters. Maybe I'm repeating myself here, but viewers are facing their fear of death and vicariously choosing to act in self-defense when faced with that death. This fantasy is made probable by the relative slowness and vulnerability of zombies. Viewers could in actuality reasonably defeat a zombie, and believing that they could defeat zombie after zombie in a potentially unending chain is potentially life affirming and a good sign of mental health.

As Simon Pegg (2009) points out in his afterword to the graphic novel *The Walking Dead: Miles Behind Us*, the protagonists in zombie movies are not super heroes; they are average people. In the face of unfathomable danger, viewers choose to believe in their capableness; they don't know what's coming next in life, but as long as the individual challenges are surmountable and they just keep going (or slaying to maintain the metaphor) they are going to be just fine. I can see how recent movies, especially like *Otto* (where the clearly zombiod character is possibly only working through his acceptance of his homosexuality) or *Fido* (where characters live in a 1950s-esque world with technologically-tamed zombie slaves), could lead one to believe that zombies ought to be given rights as individuals, but in a dystopian world where the dead rise and intend to eat the living, "zombie as homosexual" or "zombie as slave" is not really the point (LaBruce, Bruning, & Hartman, 2007; Carlson, 2008).

For me, at the base level, zombies represent threats to our very lives, not just potential threats to our way of life or our standard of living. Richard Pratte (1985) in "Tolerance, Permissiveness, and Education" points out that for some people expressions of tolerance can be interpreted as nothing more than a weakness of will, an inability to stand up for strongly held beliefs that might seem offensive to the "other" (p. 107). In such a situation, tolerance could constitute a denial of our own ethical beliefs.

Son

The ever-present difficulty of our ethical beliefs as Americans is that to affirm people's freedom there are some times when we have to accept things that seem strange to us. If the other threatens us, perhaps we should not tolerate them, but opposing them merely to avoid looking weak, seems like weakness itself. If we look back at your alteration of my analogy of "zombie as shark" to "zombie as bacteria," the metaphor works just as well. A person who rarely is exposed to bacteria does not gain the resistance to them needed if they come in contact with stronger bacteria. There is no way for a person to completely insulate themselves in our modern world, and people need to gain the ability to deal with "the other," because there will always be an "other."

If a person has no experience dealing with people who make them uncomfortable they will eventually run into problems, and as far as being a dangerous "other" goes, zombies are slow and one live person should be able to fight off one or two of them. I don't deny that there are actually times when, if the other is a danger to a person, they should not have to tolerate them. People should defend themselves from zombies but, what you seem to be advocating is killing them for the fun of it. While some people may hunt animals for fun, killing zombies means killing someone who was once human. Killing humans for the fun of it seems like a bad precedent to set. Movie zombies are clearly metaphoric representations and as such can represent our fear of people we do not identify with, people whose motivations we do not share and whose actions we do not understand. You're advocating taking pleasure in this killing, and that seems like madness.

Let me explain: People have many points of view others have trouble understanding, but just because I think that people who watch Fox news are mindless zombies, and just because they probably feel the same about me because I listen to NPR (National Public Radio), we should not kill each other. If a person is harassing someone over their beliefs then the harassed individual is within their rights to defend themselves. People should not, however, go out of their way to pick fights with people just because they hold opposing viewpoints. The humans in horror movies must defend themselves, but taking pleasure from killing zombies seems unhealthy.

Father

Okay, I guess it comes down to what zombies represent, and because of our particular situation as Father and Son I'm tempted to think this could be a generational thing. Are zombies so clearly a metaphor for actual living beings that they have ceased to be pure evil? Of course there's not just one way to look at a zombie, but let me make my last pitch in direct defiance of your closing argument.

I don't advocate violence in our everyday world, but I have a fondness for movie violence. And for me the most-acceptable, the most-defensible movie violence is the killing of the horror monster. Zombies, for me, are an enemy it's okay to hate. They were created for us to fear and hate. Maybe I'm admitting to some dangerous levels of insecurity, but I like the idea of destroying the forces that seek to devour me. (And, with statements like that I may be actually ceding the debate to you.) I would argue that killing zombies can be cathartic, but the word is so often disputed, so I'll say it may be therapeutic to envision facing and defeating our fears.

I feel pretty good about killing zombies. I'm sure some of those good feelings come from indulging my "survivalist fantasies" as Bishop (2006) argues in "Dead Men Still Walking," but it feels healthy to imagine a world where one could muster the ingenuity and courage to survive the chaos of a post-apocalyptic, dystopian world (p. 21). I get that zombies can be (and possibly always are) metaphors, but I can't resist the idea offered by Tallahassee in *Zombieland* that destroying Zombies IS fun and "Sometimes you have to enjoy the little things" (Polone & Fleischer, 2009).

I hope we don't eventually come to the point where killing movie zombies is wrong, but I understand how metaphors can be used to alienate and oppress groups of people, and I have to agree with my Son that if zombies represent anything in our real world, then dealing with them violently ought to be our last resort.

Ever since George Romero allowed Riley to assert that the zombie leader "Big Daddy" and his horde deserved to live since they were "just looking for a place to go, same as us" at the end of *Land of the Dead*, zombies have come to represent more than just "pure evil"—or possibly we no longer accept such simplistic concepts as "pure evil" (Canton, Goldman, & Grunwald, 2005). How one interprets zombies, like so many other symbols in our world, will necessarily need to change with each context and circumstance.

As H. C. Weidenfeld (2002) argues concerning teaching tolerance on a world-wide scale: "Teaching constructive ways of dealing with uncertainty must become a pillar of educational theory" (p. 101). He further asserts:

> Only if individuals accept that every person has the same right to develop his abilities to the full will they be able to either accept diversity and opposing views out of the insight into their necessity, or jointly look for solutions to conflict. (p. 99)

If I'm not careful, I'll end up arguing that black and white categories like "pure evil" and "pure goodness" are useful to our society, and I do not believe that such oversimplifications of the incredible complexity and diversity of opinions and people in our world are at all beneficial or productive. Nevertheless, I'm possibly nostalgic for a world where I can guiltlessly project my discontent with the human condition onto imaginary, evil characters to achieve some catharsis. I'm not sure art will give up this practice, but possibly such pleasure can no longer remain guiltless. So, I guess, this is me losing the debate. We should conclude, then.

CONCLUSION

Arguing about zombies and the importance of tolerance within the same essay, may seem demeaning to the importance of tolerance education. Nevertheless the difficulties of teaching tolerance forces us to seek whatever means we have to analyze situations in which tolerance is taught as a byproduct. What should be the limits of tolerance? We must tolerate the radically other—that seems clear—but what about dangerous stupidity? Are there "thoughts" that cannot be tolerated? Or should we only suspend tolerance in instances of dangerous and harmful actions? What we have learned from zombies is that one must err on the side of risk. One must be willing to consider the radical alterity of others and accept it in all forms which do not promise significant, real harm to us or others. Our debate proves, we think, that trends within the zombie genre reflect an acceptance that humans must think more deeply about radical otherness.

If audiences can be made to wonder about the extent of their relation to so traditionally dangerous a fictional figure as the flesh eating zombie, can we also accept our relation to other actual humans whom we have similarly demonized? The compassion that we can express for a zombie like the title character from the movie *Fido*, and our ability to accept that his zombie–inclinations can be tamed by love, must represent an untapped depth to our ability to rethink traditional expectations (Carlson, 2007). If we can question the evilness of fictionally-created representations of evil, doesn't that imply we have the capacity to reconsider other situations similarly presented as black and white? Possibly, like the zombies in *Day of the Dead* (Rubenstein, 1985) or *Survival of the Dead* (Devonshire, 2009), WE can be conditioned to give up our violent hatred of "the other" and curb OUR desire to destroy each other, particularly in our schools.

REFERENCES

Bishop, K. (2006). Raising the dead. *Journal of Popular Film & Television, 33*(4), 196-205.

Bishop, K. (2009). Dead man still walking. *Journal of Popular Film & Television, 37*(1), 16-25.

Canton, M., Goldman, B., & Grunwald, P. (Producer), & Romero, G. (Director). (2005). *Land of the dead* [Motion picture]. United States: Universal Pictures.

Carlson, T. (Producer), & Currie, A. (Director). (2007). *Fido* [Motion picture]. Canada: Lion Gate Films

Carroll, N. (1987). The nature of horror. *The Journal of Aesthetics and Art Criticism, 46*(1), 51-59.

Darabont, F., Hurd, G. A., Alpert, D., Kirkman, R., Eglee, C., & Mazzara, G. (Producer). (2010-2011). *The walking dead* [Television series]. Atlanta, GA: AMC Studios.

Devonshire, P. (Producer), & Romero, G. (Director). (2009). *Survival of the dead* [Motion picture]. United States: Magnet Releasing.

Dillard, R. H. W. (1987). Night of the living dead: It's not like just a wind that's passing through. In G. A. Walker (Ed.), *American horrors* (pp. 14-29). Chicago, IL: University of Illinois Press.

Hardman, K., & Streiner, R. (Producer), & Romero, G. (Director). (1968). *Night of the living dead* [Motion picture]. United States: Market Square Productions.

LaBruce, B. Bruning, J., & Hartman, J. (Producer), & LaBruce, B (Director). (2008). *Otto; Or up with dead people* [Motion picture]. Germany & Canada: New Real Films.

Langmann, E. (2010). Welcoming difference at the limit of tolerance education. In G. Biesta (Ed.), *Philosophy of Education Yearbook* (pp. 337-345). Retrieved from http://ojs.ed.uiuc.edu/index.php/pes

MacDonald, A. (Producer), & Boyle, D. (Director). (2002). *28 days later* [Motion picture]. United Kingdom: 20th Century Fox.

Pagliarulo, E. (Designer), & Howard, T. (Producer), & Pely, I. (Lead Artist), (2008). *Fall out 3* [Videogame]. Rockville, MD: Bethesda Softworks.

Park, N. (Producer), & Wright, E. (Director). (2004). *Shaun of the dead* [Motion picture]. United Kingdom: Universal Pictures.

Pegg, S. (2009). Afterword. In R. Kirkman (Ed.), *The walking dead: Miles behind us* (Vol. 2). Berkely, CA: Image Comics.

Polone, G. (Producer), & Fleischer, R. (Director). (2009). *Zombieland* [Motion picture]. United States: Columbia Pictures.

Pratte, R. (1985). Tolerance, permissiveness, and education. *Teachers College Record, 87*(1), 103-117.

Reimers, F. (2006). Citizenship, identity and education: Examining the public purposes of schools in an age of globalization. *Prospects, 36*(3), 275-294.

Romero, G., Grunwald, P., Engelbardt, S., Spiegel, A., Fireman, D., Harrison, J., & Katz, A. (Producer), & Romero, G. (Director). (2007). *Diary of the dead* [Motion picture]. United States: Artfire Films.

Rubinstein, R. P., Argento, C., & Cuomo, A. (Producer), & Romero, G. (Director). (1978). *Dawn of the dead* [Motion picture]. United States: Laurel Group Inc.

Rubenstein, R. (Producer), & Romero, G. (Director). (1985). *Day of the dead* [Motion picture]. United States: Laurel Entertainment.

Sutherland, M. (2007). Rigor/Mortis: The industrial life of style in American zombie cinema. *Framework, 48*(1), 64-78.

Vogt, W. P. (1994). What is tolerance and why should we teach it? *Review of Education/Pedagogy/Cultural Studies, 16*(3-4), 277-296.

Weidenfeld, H. C. (2002). Constructive conflicts: Tolerance learning as the basis for democracy. *Prospects, 32*(1), 95-102.

ABOUT THE CONTRIBUTORS

Becky Atkinson is an assistant professor of social and cultural foundations at The University of Alabama. Her research interests include pragmatic semiotics in social foundations and qualitative research, teacher knowledge research, critical theory, feminism and material feminisms, and reader response theory and methodology. Most recent research concerns how teachers make meaning of test data within the context of accountability.

Dennis Attick is currently an assistant professor in the Department of Teacher Education at Clayton State University in Morrow, GA. Prior to working in higher education Attick worked for 12 years at an alternative school for adolescents in Atlanta. His research interests include philosophy of education, as well as the intersection of technology, culture, and education.

William Ayers, formerly distinguished professor of education and senior university scholar at the University of Illinois at Chicago, has written extensively about social justice, democracy and education, the cultural contexts of schooling, and teaching as an essentially intellectual, ethical, and political enterprise. His books include *Teaching Toward Freedom*; *A Kind and Just Parent*; *Fugitive Days*; *To Teach*; and (with Bernardine Dohrn) *Race Course*.

Benjamin Baez is associate professor of higher education in the Department of Leadership and Professional Studies at Florida International University. He received his law degree in 1988 and his doctorate in higher education in 1997, both from Syracuse University. He recently published three books: *The Politics of Inquiry: Education Research and the "Culture of Science"* (with Deron Boyles); *Understanding Minority-Serving Institutions: Interdisciplinary Perspectives* (coedited with Marybeth Gasman and Caroline Turner); and *Intellectual Property in the Information Age* (with Jeffrey C. Sun). He has also published, *Affirmative Action, Hate Speech, and Tenure: Narratives About Race, Law, and the Academy.* His teaching and research interests include economic policies on education, knowledge and its production, faculty-employment issues, diversity in higher education, and the law of education.

F. Tony Carusi is an adjunct assistant professor of education at the University of Southern California. His background in philosophy and rhetoric informs his interests in education theory and policy analysis. His work looks at the commonsensical, unquestioned routines and practices within the field of education, from pedagogy to policymaking, and the historically-situated, discursive processes whereby these routines and practices persist, particularly involving those processes that appear natural in spite of critical resistance efforts.

Kerry Freedman is professor and head of art and design education at Northern Illinois University. Professor Freedman's research focuses on questions concerning the relationship of curriculum to art, culture, and technology. Recently, she has particularly focused on questions concerning student engagement with visual culture and issues surrounding curriculum change in light of postmodern educational conditions. Professor Freedman is author of the book *Teaching Visual Culture*. She coauthored the books *Postmodern Art Education: An Approach to Curriculum and Transforming Computer Technology*. She was elected to a lifetime position on the U.S. Council for Policy Studies in Art Education, is a past National Higher Art Educator of the Year, and won the Australian Leon Jackman Award for distinguished research in art education. Dr. Freedman is also a Distinguished Fellow of the National Art Education Association, and in 2012, won the Manual Barkan Memorial Award given for best article publication in the previous year.

Joshua Garrison is associate professor of educational foundations at the University of Wisconsin Oshkosh. Educated at the Evergreen State College (B.A) and Indiana University (MS., PhD), Garrison holds a doctorate in the history of education. His primary research agenda is the history of childhood, and his work in that field earned him the "Article of the Year" award from the Organization of Educational Historians in 2009. He also publishes work on childhood media studies, educational history, and educational policy.

Leslee Grey is an assistant professor of educational foundations at Queens College, City University of New York. She holds a doctorate in social foundations of education from Georgia State University. Her research focuses on the corporatization of public schooling, youth culture, and LGBTQ issues in education. Her most recent project explores parental involvement in school reform in New York City.

Alison Happel is an assistant professor of counseling, educational psychology and research with a specialization in educational research at the University of Memphis. She teaches qualitative research methods courses, and she specializes in feminist research methods. Her current research focuses on ecojustice education and public schools.

Jessica A. Heybach is an assistant professor of education at Aurora University. She has published and presented on issues at the intersection of curriculum theory, visual culture, and philosophy of education. She recently defended her dissertation at Northern Illinois University that explored how horrific and tragic images of war and artwork impact controversial classroom discussions regarding human rights, justice, and democracy.

Taylor Lacy Klassman is a class of 2013 undergraduate student at Denison University. She spends almost all of her time reading and writing papers as a student of religion and English literature. Taylor is also a manager at Denison's student-run coffee shop and loves talking to strangers. She is honored to have her first publication in this very anthology.

Kip Kline has published and presented work in the area of philosophy of youth and adolescence, including youth culture and aesthetics and adolescent identity. In 2010 he gave invited lectures at the department of aesthetics at Aarhus University in Denmark. Also, he was the president of the Ohio Valley Philosophy of Education Society in 2010. He is currently working on projects that examine media representation and discourses of youth. Kip Kline received his PhD in philosophy of education from Indiana University, Bloomington in 2007.

Steven P. Jones is professor in the department of Reading, Foundations, and Technology at Missouri State University, and Director of the Academy for Educational Studies. His academic and research interests include philosophy of education, teacher education, and the reform of public education.

Philip E. Kovacs is an associate professor in the Department of Education at University of Alabama—Huntsville. He recently edited the book: *The Gates Foundation and the Future of US "Public" Schools*. His research interests include the role of think tanks, institutes, and foundations on U.S. "public" schools; democratic pedagogies, and a new interest in deschooling.

Rick McDonald is a professor of English literature at Utah Valley University. He specializes in Medieval literature, critical theory, and Renaissance and Classical literature. Rick is an active member of the Popular Culture Association's Horror in Text Media and Culture group and is vigilant in preparing for the zombie apocalypse.

Nick McDonald is a student in the Secondary English Education program at Utah Valley University. He has been an active participant of the Popular Culture Association in the areas of horror, geek studies, and queer theory.

Andrew N. McKnight is associate professor of educational foundations at the University of Alabama at Birmingham. He is interested in the application of philosophical and qualitative research methods to contemporary educational and cultural issues. His work has been mostly concerned with the intersections of social theory, ethics, current educational policy, and the emotional contexts of schooling.

John E. Petrovic is professor of educational philosophy and policy studies at The University of Alabama. His research focuses on the way liberal political theory informs educational policy and practice. He serves on the editorial board of the *American Educational Research Journal* and has published in a wide variety of journals including *Journal of Moral Education, Educational Studies, Language Policy,* and *Journal of Language and Politics*. He is currently working on a second book on language policy.

Bradley D. Rowe received his doctorate in philosophy of education from The Ohio State University. He is currently a lecturer at Ontario Institute for Studies in Education, University of Toronto. His scholarly and teaching interests are in educational philosophy, ecological education, deschooling, and food studies.

Eric C. Sheffield is associate professor, foundations of education, at Missouri State University. He is assistant director of the Academy for Educational Studies and serves as the editor for the academy's national peer reviewed online journal, *Critical Questions in Education.* Before coming to Missouri State University, he taught high school English for 14 years. Eric's most recent books include *The Role of Religion in 21st Century Public*

CPSIA information can be obtained at www.ICGtesting.com
Printed in the USA
BVOW001111210413

318638BV00001B/9/P

9 781623 962838

Schools (2009), coedited with Steven P. Jones and *"Strong" Community Service Learning: Philosophical Perspectives* (2011).

Stefan Sheffield was born in 1990 in Gainesville Florida; he was raised in Florida until he moved to Springfield Missouri in 2004. He graduated from Republic high school in 2008 and is studying electronic media production at Ozarks Technical Community College. Stefan has been working for GameStop for the past 4 years and is a videogame enthusiast and would love to see videogames recognized as an art form with as much artistic merit as any other medium.

Becky L. Noel Smith is a former K-12 educator, currently working on a master's degree at University of Central Florida, whose frustrations with institutional oppression have driven her to seek the type of solace and therapy that only come from the soul-searching work of inquiry. She is tremendously grateful to her mentor and the few dear friends who have helped her work through this process.

Eric D. Smith is associate professor of English at the University of Alabama in Huntsville. He is the author of *Globalization, Utopia, and Postcolonial Science Fiction: New Maps of Hope* and numerous articles on modern and contemporary British and postcolonial literatures.